MW00774496

SHAY ELLIOTT

SHAY ELLIOTT

The life and death of Ireland's
first yellow jersey

Graham Healy

with Richard Allchin

SHAY ELLIOTT
The life and death of Ireland's first yellow jersey

Copyright © Graham Healy and Richard Allchin, 2011

All rights reserved. No part of this publication may be reproduced, stored in
a retrieval system or transmitted, in any form or by any means, electronic,
mechanical, photocopying, recording, or otherwise, without the prior consent of
the publishers.

First published in 2011 by

Sport and Publicity   Mousehold Press
75 Fitzjohns Avenue   and   Victoria Cottage
Hampstead   Constitution Opening
London, NW3 6PD   Norwich, NR3 4BD

ISBN 978-1-874739-59-3

Printed by CLE Print, St Ives, Cambridgeshire

CONTENTS

Author's acknowledgements:

I would like to thank the following for the help that they have given me: Peter and Mary Crinnion, David Gill, Gerry Duffin, Brian Robinson, Donal O'Connell, Billy Long, Pat Norton, Barry Hoban, Ken Duff, Mick Byrne, Pat McQuaid, Tony Hoar, Vin Denson, Phil O'Brien, Brendan Lynch and Liam McKenna.

I also received considerable assistance from Martin Dwan, producer of the excellent documentary on Shay's life, 'Cycle of Betrayal', who also helped with the interviews of Jean Bobet, André Darrigade, Raymond Poulidor and Rudi Altig.

My thanks also go to Richard Allchin and Adrian Bell for their input, and also their help with the photographs.

I would also like to extend my gratitude to John Marron and my brother David for their valuable feedback, to my parents, and finally, thanks to my wife Nina for her patience and support over the past number of years.

Graham Healy

Publisher's Introduction and Acknowledgements:

We have long wanted to publish a biography of Shay Elliott, the first Irish International road racing star, which would give due recognition to his unique achievements. An exceptional amateur, Shay carried his success into the professional ranks; he and Brian Robinson were the great pioneers of Irish and British cycle racing in the mid-1950s. Shay's story is one of success, heartbreak, joy and eventual tragedy. His *palmarès* reveals more historic 'firsts' than any other English-speaking rider who travelled to the continent. Just to mention a few achievements: he was the first to win stages of all three Grand Tours and the first to reach the podium in the final classification in one of these great events; he was the first to win a major single-day race and the first to secure a medal in the professional World Road Race Championship.

There are a number of people we need to thank for enabling us to fulfill our wish to publish an Elliott biography. First and foremost, of course, we must express our gratitude to Graham Healy for all his research and hard work which allowed this book to be produced in the first place. Martin Dwan's original and wonderful film on Shay, "Cycle of Betrayal", was of great help to us all in our work. Thank you, Martin.

Many others have helped us and we owe our gratitude to Roger St Pierre, David Reed, Graeme Fife, Brian Robinson, Barry Hoban, Vin Denson, Brian Tadman, Phil Liggett, Citroen Tony, Keith Bingham and others at *Cycling Weekly*. We must also thank Pat McQuaid for kindly providing us with a foreword to this book about his countryman and Jeff Platten for generously giving us permission to use his excellent painting of Shay Elliott.

On a more personal note I would like to express my heartfelt thanks to Sean Kelly, Frank Quinn and David Harmon for always being the first to help and for being such good friends over the years. It is their kind of support that has kept us trying to publish quality books about cycle sport.

Lastly I would like to thank my good friends Steve Cummings, Dan Lloyd and Sean Yates whose love for the sport keeps me interested and directly connected with the changing times.

Finally, thanks are again due to Adrian Bell and Micky Clark who have always given so much to make our publications possible.

Richard Allchin

FOREWORD
by Sean Kelly

When I started out cycling I was naturally competitive and was more interested in my next race. Of course, I had heard the name Shay Elliott and I knew a little about him, but I wasn't aware of the considerable historic milestones he had laid in European and Irish cycle racing. Even after I finished racing I still hadn't realized his palmarès was quite so remarkable, and that, along with Britain's Brian Robinson, he was responsible for turning a huge page in the development of international cycling. Now, part of my life is taken up as a commentator for Eurosport television, and on many occasions I have been reminded of Shay's exploits. By the time I came to be interviewed for the fine film biography of Shay's life, 'Cycle of Betrayal', I was very conscious of how many 'firsts' he had achieved – not just in terms of his numerous victories, including his stage wins in all three Grand tours, but also his leader's jerseys and a podium in those events. There was also a silver medal in the World Road Race Championship, which I never bettered – not for lack of trying!

Shay left behind him a great legacy for Irish Cycling which, to be honest, I had not fully appreciated when I started racing, but there is no denying that Shay was the first Irishman to make a big impact on European cycling, and I am proud to have followed in his glorious wheel-tracks. Now I am the first to acknowledge his substantial historic impact, which maybe helped me and others from Ireland to reach the heights of our sport.

Sean Kelly

FOREWORD

by Pat McQuaid

Cycling had traditionally been a small sport in Ireland, but road racing started to flourish after the second World War. My father Jim was one of the strongest cyclists in the country in the early 50s. However, in 1952 along came an eighteen-year-old kid, who was more than a match for my father and his contemporaries.

I was too young to remember Shay racing in Ireland before his move to the continent, but growing up in a cycling crazy family, his exploits were often the main topic of conversation around our dinner table. His successes, alongside those of the other English-speaking pioneers, Brian Robinson and Tom Simpson, showed us that there was no reason why we couldn't compete with continentals. When I started cycling in the early 60s, Shay was the inspiration to my friends and me.

I still remember my excitement as a fourteen year old when Shay won a stage and took the yellow jersey in the 1963 Tour de France. Indeed, I well remember that winter, one Saturday evening when I was called from my bed to come down and meet Shay and his wife, who passed by to see my parents. I stood nervously looking at my idol! Shay helped to open the door to Kelly, Millar, Anderson, Lemond and Roche amongst many others. Upon his return from the continent Shay volunteered his knowledge and experience to help the 1972 Irish Olympics team, of which my brother Kieron was a member. Unfortunately, tragedy struck the year before, and he died when still a young man. His loss to Irish cycling was immeasurable.

This book serves as a fine tribute to Shay. The extent of his *palmarés* was remarkable: he established World records on the track as an amateur, and as a professional he was the first rider from the English-speaking countries to stand on the podium of a Grand Tour. He won stages in all three and wore the leader's jerseys in two of them. On more than one occasion he came so close to winning one of the classic monuments, his success denied him by extreme bad fortune.

Shay's performances are historically woven into Irish and World cycling, as he was one of the very first pioneers to cross the cultural barrier and extend the sport of cycle road racing beyond its traditional foundations. This has been one of my primary aims as President of the UCI, and I would like to think of Shay smiling down on us and recognising how far we have all come in the fifty-five years since he made his continental debut as a professional cyclist in France. His legacy is fundamental to all our hopes for cycling to develop into a world wide sport which anybody, from any background, anywhere in the world can take part in and enjoy. Thanks Shay.

Pat McQuaid,
President of UCI

Shay in Yellow
by
Jeff Platten

Prologue

In July of 1998 the Tour de France began in Dublin. It was the first time that the race would start outside the European mainland. Unfortunately for those involved, the stages in Ireland were somewhat overshadowed by an emerging scandal that would become one of the darkest episodes in the history of a race that had seen many troubles before. As the Tour entourage were assembling prior to the start, a soigneur for the Festina team was caught with a car full of performance enhancing drugs at the French-Belgian border. It resulted in the team being expelled from the race, and the entire event very nearly being abandoned. Other riders were arrested, team hotels were raided by the police, and there were strikes by the riders on two of the days. There were no Irishmen in the race, as it had come a decade too late to involve the two top Irish cyclists, Stephen Roche and Sean Kelly. The race did honour the pair though, as the route passed through their home towns of Dundrum and Carrick-On-Suir. The race also paid homage to a lesser known Irish cyclist, Shay Elliott.

In the week preceding the start, an exhibition to honour the exploits of Shay was organised by the Bray Wheelers in the Town Hall. The items on display included one of his yellow jerseys from the 1963 Tour de France. Shay's eldest brother, Eddie, also helped the organisers with the exhibition, which was opened by double Tour winner Laurent Fignon. There was also a moving homage to Shay at his graveside in his adopted village of Kilmacanogue. After his untimely death he had been buried in the shadow of the Sugarloaf mountain in North Wicklow, and it would be difficult to find a more picturesque setting anywhere in the country.

The director of the Tour de France and former professional rider, Jean-Marie LeBlanc, laid a wreath at the grave of Shay, and the ceremony was also attended by multiple Tour winner Bernard Hinault, Sean Kelly and Stephen Roche, amongst others. As part of his homage Leblanc recalled how, as a teenager, he had asked Shay for his autograph when he was racing in Valenciennes. The Société du Tour de France may have its weaknesses, but it could never be faulted for the manner in which it honours its heroes.

One man who was conspicuous by his absence was Jean Stablinski. Many former professional cyclists are part of the Tour entourage, chauffeuring journalists, mingling in publicity marquees on behalf of sponsors, or providing opinions on television. Stablinski or 'Stab' as he was often known was amongst the ex-pros who was in Dublin for the start of the Tour.

Stablinski had been invited to Kilmacanogue but made his excuses, and declined to attend. It seems that he did not know what reception he could expect. As I delved more into Shay's story, I came to understand why Stab, who had been Shay's best man at his wedding and godfather to his son, Pascal, might be reluctant to attend the commemoration. The Frenchman had played a fundamental role in his career, helping the Dubliner to gain the yellow jersey, but he had also been involved in his downfall. Unfortunately, Stablinski like so many of the protagonists in Shay's story is no longer with us, as he died after a long illness in the Spring of 2008. I was unable, therefore, to speak to him to try and get his side of the story. I have tried, as best as possible, to piece together the facts impartially, as to what happened in the main incidents that would cause the two former friends to fall out and no longer speak to each other. In an ideal world I would have liked to asked Stab as to whether he felt he had done anything wrong, had he any regrets, and did he feel that he was unfairly judged.

I feel it also needs to be remembered that the story of Shay is not just about the story of his downfall. This is also the story of one of the English-speaking pioneers, who, alongside Brian Robinson and Tom Simpson especially, paved the way for other Irish, British, Americans and Australians to compete on level terms with their continental counterparts. Shay had managed to win some great races. In fact, he was the first English-speaker to win stages in the three big tours, those of France, Italy and Spain. He was also the first English-speaker to win a one-day classic when he won Het Volk, over the cobbled roads of Belgium. The difficulty of this breakthrough should not be underestimated, as there were many obstacles to overcome, such as language, culture and by times, xenophobic behaviour of those who did not want outsiders involved in their sport.

Undoubtedly, globalization of the sport was inevitable, but I don't think it would have been rapid or smooth for those who came after, if it had not been for the likes of Shay. This is the story of how a young

Dubliner managed to rise to the top of a brutal sport, and how, like so many others before and after him, he would finally be rejected from the sport to which he had given so much.

1

The family Elliott

Shay entered the world on 4 June 1934, the second of three boys born to James and Ellen Elliott. His older brother Eddie had arrived a few years beforehand with a larger gap to the youngest, Paul. He was named after his father, but the family called him Séamus – the Irish version of his name – to avoid confusion.

According to Gerry Duffin, who was to become Shay's coach and who knew the family well, his parents had met a decade previously at the outbreak of the Irish Civil War, waged between two opposing groups of Nationalists. On the one hand were those who supported the Anglo-Irish Treaty, under which the 26-county Irish Free State had been established; on the other, were those for whom the Treaty, which had allowed the six counties of Northern Ireland to remain under British rule, represented a betrayal of Irish Republican aspirations. The skirmishing between the two groups of Nationalists that had been taking place since the signing of the Treaty in January 1922 flared up into what was effectively the start of the Civil War in April, when the anti-Treaty Republicans seized the Four Courts, on the banks of the Liffey, and several other important buildings in the centre of Dublin.

James Elliott was one of the 120 members of the Dublin Brigade under the command of Liam Mellowes, who were stationed in the Four Courts. After a tense, two-month stand-off, they came under fire as the Irish government forces (using artillery borrowed from the British garrison) bombarded the Four Courts. Ellen Farrell, or 'Nell' as she was known to her friends and family, was also involved in the siege of the Four Courts; although only a young girl at the time, she was already a member of Cumann na mBán, an Irish republican women's paramilitary organisation that had been formed in 1914 as an auxiliary of the Irish Volunteers. Throughout the siege she risked her life as a courier for Mellowes' forces, carrying messages to and from the building. Two days after the bombardment started, with the building in flames, the men of the Dublin Brigade surrendered. James had come through uninjured, but he, along with the others, was incarcerated for some time in Mountjoy Prison, while Mellowes was executed by firing squad later in the year.

The Civil War continued for another twelve months. It claimed more Irish lives than the War of Independence against Britain that preceded it, and left Irish society divided and embittered for decades afterwards. To this day, the two main political parties in the Republic of Ireland, Fianna Fáil and Fine Gael, are the direct descendants of the opposing sides in the War.

As the country moved towards a more peaceful time after 1923 James and Nell's friendship grew. Nell started to accompany Jim on his many fishing and hunting trips. She would later say that she seemed to spend her whole life with Jim plucking feathers. Jim would often take her out to Kildare 'lamping' for rabbits. She would sit on the roof of the car with a big torch to light up the fields where Jim was hunting. It was no surprise that eventually they married. The first family home was in Rathfarnham, at the foot of the Dublin mountains. Despite the war that was later to rage across Europe, the Elliott boys enjoyed a happy childhood, as Ireland was neutral. However, in 1941, the Germans bombed Rathfarnham, close to where they lived. The reason offered by Hitler's government was that German aircraft had mistaken the Irish east coast for the west coast of Britain, although the view most commonly held in Ireland was that they were simply off-loading their bombs to ensure a safe return to base. The Elliotts would later move to a two-bedroom house in Crumlin. Jim was a mechanic by trade and had established a business on the South Circular Road, a petrol station and garage. It made life easier for him to live nearer the business. Business had been slow in the first few years of his venture, but through hard work, he managed to turn it around.

James (or Jim as he was generally known) Elliott was a tall, quiet man and a very keen motorcyclist. One of his ambitions had been to compete in the famous TT races on the Isle of Man. He never realised that, although he was a quite successful rider in Ireland, winning races on the open road all around the country. Nell was quite different in character from Jim. She was the life and soul of the household, small in stature, and an excellent cook. She adored her three sons.

In addition to motorsports, Jim had also always loved hunting and fishing, and he taught Shay to shoot when he was young. Jim would take him down to Longford early on a Saturday morning, where, after a day spent hunting, they would stay overnight with cousins. Shay followed his older brother Eddie into the local Christian Brothers school, where he showed great interest in sport. He played both hurling and Gaelic football, but cycling would be the sport that would really appeal to him.

Cycling had been quite popular in Ireland in the latter half of the nineteenth century. R.J. Mecredy of Trinity College Cycling Club was particularly successful, winning numerous titles in both Ireland and England. He was one of the first cyclists to use the pneumatic tyre (which was first manufactured in Dublin by Dunlop in 1888).

During the following decade Harry Reynolds was the country's most successful rider. He raced with distinction on the track and became Ireland's first world cycling champion, winning the sprint title at the World Championships in Copenhagen in 1896. The inhabitants of his home town of Balbriggan in County Dublin had raised the funds necessary to send Harry to Denmark. Once there, he progressed through the earlier rounds with ease, and faced a German and Frenchman in the final. It was a very close race, but Harry got the better of them. As he was being led towards the podium to be presented with his gold medal by the King of Denmark, the band started to strike up 'God Save the Queen'. Harry refused to take another step, and he pointed out that he was Irish. His victory had been for Ireland, and they should lower the Union Jack if they wanted the prize-giving ceremony to go ahead. The band were instructed to play an Irish piece of music, and only then did Harry receive his medal from the King. Reynolds might have gone on to become Ireland's first and only Olympic cycling champion at the 1896 games in Athens, had not both the ICA (Irish Cycling Association) and GAA declined to take part in the first modern Olympic Games.

After the turn of the century, however, the popularity of cycling as a sport declined, particularly as a result of the formation of the Gaelic Athletic Association (GAA). Michael Cusack, the founder of the GAA, was a staunch nationalist, and disliked any sports that seemed to have an association with Britain, such as cycling, which he deemed to be an English import because of its association with Trinity College, which in turn was intrinsically linked to the Protestant establishment. The early years of the GAA coincided with the revival of Irish nationalism, and the greatly increased participation in Gaelic sports resulted in a decline in the popularity of what were now regarded as 'foreign sports'. Eventually, even the smallest villages in the country would usually have their own

GAA club, and often the social life of the locality would revolve around the club, with its emphasis on Gaelic football and hurling. The sport of cycling was not really revived until after World War II, and only in the late 1940s were there the first massed-start road races.

Shay started cycling when he was thirteen, and one of his first trips was to Naas, some thirty kilometres from Dublin. At the time, he was playing Gaelic football at school, but he had really enjoyed some of the cycling trips he had gone on. One of his school friends, Noel O'Brien, was a member of the St. Brendan's cycling club and asked Shay if he would be interested in joining. He decided to try it: what appealed to him about cycling was the fact that he wasn't reliant on others and he found he could push himself further than he could with other sports.

St. Brendan's used to organise round-the-houses races over about 30 kilometres. It was in one of these races that Shay had his first competitive outing. It was a five-lap race in the village of Tallaght in south-west Dublin. The lap started in the village, went up around Old Bawn at the foot of the Dublin Mountains and finished back in the village. The bike he used had been made up from various bits and pieces that he had bought or borrowed from a local bike shop. Despite having a fixed gear, and touching the road with his pedal at every corner, he managed to finish second.

Although Jim and Nell were delighted that their son had come home with a prize, they were somewhat concerned that he was too young to be racing bicycles. They wanted him to leave it for another year or so, but Shay was already hooked. His father would soon change his opinion and started to encourage his interest, if only because it might prevent Shay from following him into the much more dangerous sport of motorcycle racing. Not long after Shay had started to develop this new interest, Jim enlisted the support of a friend of his, Gerry Duffin, who owned two bicycle shops in Dublin. During World War II Gerry had served as an aircraft engineer in North Africa, where he organized a cycling club which arranged races even during the hostilities. In the 1950s he had the franchise for Bianchi bikes in Ireland, although he was later driven into bankruptcy by the introduction of import duties designed to protect local manufacturers, which made the foreign bikes and equipment too expensive. He encouraged Shay in his early cycling career, and continued to provide him with equipment from his stock, which included some of the best then available in Ireland.

That was not all he provided Shay with. John Cleary recalls Gerry Duffin taking him and Shay to the Great Southern for a steak after Shay had won the Coast to Coast Classic. They were refused admission because they were wearing tracksuits. Gerry argued with the manager who finally relented, on the condition that they wore ties! Gerry bought a couple of ties in the hotel shop, and wearing them over their tracksuits, the boys sat down to their steaks.

As his interest in the sport grew, Shay managed to get his hands on old copies of French cycling magazines, which were very difficult to find in Ireland. These magazines would fascinate him with their photographs of the great champions – Fausto Coppi, Hugo Koblet and Louison Bobet – although he didn't understand a word of the language. Shay enjoyed physical education classes in school, but had little aptitude for formal education. He left school in his mid-teens and, through a contact of Jim's, started his panel-beating apprenticeship at the age of 16. He served his time with Autocars on Fenian Street, only a few hundred metres from where he would set up his own business when he returned to Ireland many years later. As part of his apprenticeship, Shay had to attend classes in Bolton Street college, however he would only make sporadic appearances in college. He and John Cleary spent most of their time either on the bike or visiting the local cinema in Mary Street.

After his encouraging beginning Shay competed well in a number of races in his first season in 1950. His last race was a time trial that started in Donnybrook and went in a circuitous route through Bray and Enniskerry. His father, still somewhat concerned about his young son, asked Noel O'Brien if he thought Shay would be able to get over the hill at Enniskerry riding a fixed wheel. Noel wasn't entirely sure, but re-assured Jim anyway, saying that he thought the boy should manage it. In the end it wasn't a problem for Shay; he finished in a time good enough to claim second place behind Noel. Shay had shown great promise during the year, and was convinced that he could only get better.

St. Brendan's Cycling Club had given Shay his opportunity to begin racing, but it was predominantly a touring club, and a bit too sedate for Shay. On top of that, for whatever reason, one of the older members of the club had taken against him. One evening in the billiard room of the sports club he came up to Shay, who was there playing billiards, and told him he should leave. Shay placed the cue back in the rack and quietly walked out. He decided that he would look for another club.

The next season, by which time he had managed to get his hands on a good lightweight bike, he joined the Southern Road Club, a club more geared towards racing. He achieved his first big win this season in the 50-kilometre Grand Prix of Ireland. Going into the last lap of Phoenix Park two English riders, Alan Buttler and Bill Henshaw, were clear of the bunch, with an unknown young Irish lad on their wheels. Buttler turned to his team-mate and suggested they make him do some of the work. 'He's no good. He's had it,' was Bill's confident reply. Shay dropped the two of them on the last climb of the Khyber Pass to go on to win.

One of the more established cyclists of the time, Mick Byrne, would later recall his first encounter with Shay. There had been talk among some of the other cyclists he raced with about a new kid who had started recently, and was really strong. During one race, that started and finished on the Navan Road and consisted of a big loop through Meath, Mick saw that strength for himself. An early breakaway group had gone clear, and after the race went through Navan in the direction of Trim, Byrne set off in pursuit. He was gradually making inroads into the lead when he heard a sound coming up from behind. He turned around and recognised young Elliott on his wheel. Byrne asked Shay to come up and do a turn at the front, but this offer was turned down.

'I can't Mick, I've got a team-mate up the road,' Shay replied.

Byrne tried a different approach, as he tried to entice the youngster to the front to block the wind for him. 'Sure, if you go to the front, Shay,' he said, 'I'll be happy enough with one of the minor placings.'

For all his youth Shay was no soft touch, and wasn't going to buy this line from the more experienced Byrne. Eventually, however, Shay did go to the front. He attacked, dropped Byrne, and got up to the leading group by himself. Despite not having been able to stay with Shay, Byrne did, after a long chase, bridge the gap. However, when he finally got up to the break Shay had long since disappeared up the road for a fine solo victory.

That kind of precocious talent didn't go down well with some of the older riders, who would try to intimidate him or rough him up. On one occasion he was pushed into a ditch, but that only happened once. Jim, who was always looking out for his son, took the law into his own hands and threatened the perpetrator with serious repercussions if it were to happen again.

By the end of the season, particularly with his victory in the Grand Prix of Ireland, Shay was being regarded as one of the country's best prospects. He had improved significantly during the year, but once again, he felt he had outgrown his club; the Southern Road Club was not big enough to help him fulfil his ambitions, and at the end of 1951 he decided to move again to a more established club.

2

Early days

The most successful club in the city at the start of the 1950s was the Dublin Wheelers, which had been formed twenty years previously and had grown into one of the biggest clubs in the city. Riding for the Wheelers meant Shay could get support in races and he felt sure that they could help him fulfil his potential. But there was another reason which could have drawn Shay towards the Dublin Wheelers: they were members of the Cumann Rothaíochta na hÉireann.

At that time competitive cycling in Ireland was deeply divided between three organisations: the long-established National Cycling Association (NCA); the Northern Ireland Cycling Federation (NICF) which was linked to the British NCU; and the recently formed Cumann Rothaíochta na hÉireann (CRE). There was considerable hostility between the NCA and CRE, and what divided them and fuelled their disagreement was the same issue of nationalism that had provoked the Civil War 30 years earlier. The NCA refused to acknowledge the partition of the island and claimed jurisdiction over cycling throughout the 32 counties. Its membership was predominantly rural, with close links to the Gaelic Athletic Association.*

In 1947 a motion put to the Union Cycliste International by the NCU (the British representatives on the international body) requiring the NCA to limit its area of jurisdiction to the 26 counties of the Republic of Ireland was approved. The NCA refused to accept this; in the eyes of such staunch Republicans this was tantamount to endorsing the partition of the island. The result was the NCA was now disbarred from international races, while any team affiliated to the UCI was prohibited from taking part in races organised by them. Two years later, many of the Dublin-based clubs broke away from the NCA to form the CRE, which

---

* The NCA were the original organisers of the *Rás*. When it was first run in 1953 it was known as the *Rás Tailteann*, thereby associating it with the *Tailteann* Games, an ancient Celtic sporting event.

accepted the political division of Ireland and limited its overview to the 26-county Republic. The CRE then sought and was granted recognition from the UCI.

Feuding between the NCA and CRE continued for years. There are stories of NCA members laying tacks on the road during CRE races and on one occasion a number of them were arrested in Kerry for attempting to dislodge a boulder which they intended to crash down on top of passing CRE riders during the Tour of Ireland. It wasn't until the late 1960s that talks began between the two bodies which would result in their amalgamation in 1987. But back in 1952 it is easy to see why a young Irish rider, full of ambition and with the potential to make his mark as an international rider, would be drawn to a club affiliated to the internationally recognised CRE. Shay's application to join the Dublin Wheelers was accepted, but only after lengthy deliberations, as it was not their policy to accept members from other clubs.

Another advantage of joining the Wheelers was that they had a very active social scene. For some club runs up to one hundred members would meet outside the Irish Press Offices on Burgh Quay. The groups would head off into the Wicklow mountains or north along the coast, the day often finishing with tea and a dance. As for the competitive side, Shay showed he would be a great asset to the club when he won his first race for them, a 50-kilometre time trial where he finished over a minute ahead of the second placed rider.

Shortly after the start of the season, the club announced that they would be sending a team to the Isle of Man later in the year. Every year a week of prestigious races took place on the island. A selection race was to be held in the Phoenix Park, which took in the climb of the Khyber Pass, and the race would also double as the club's championship. Shay was determined to make the team that would go to the Manx week, not only to race at a higher level, but also because he had never been abroad before. Of the twenty starters, there were only six left in a group to fight it out at the finish on the Main Road. Noel Tully won, finishing a couple of lengths clear of Shay. Shay was selected for the team, to the disappointment of some of those who had been with the club a lot longer. It didn't help that Shay sometimes demonstrated certain immature traits, which could upset some of the older riders. For instance, when other riders offered their congratulations to him after another win, Shay would place his little finger in their outstretched hand in a disparaging gesture. Jim would tell him off for this habit, and it soon stopped. But all things considered, the move to Dublin Wheelers was already paying dividends for Shay.

His next big test of the year was the 50-kilometre Grand Prix of Ireland, which he had won the previous year. Once again, at the finish in Phoenix Park, he emerged best from the field of 100 riders (including a number who had come over from Britain) who had taken the start line. Shay won by three lengths from Jim McQuaid, patriarch of the famous cycling family and father to Pat McQuaid, who would go on to become head of the UCI. That race in the Phoenix Park showed Shay's tactical nous which Mick Byrne had witnessed the previous year.

Jim McQuaid was renowned for his phenomenal sprint and was considered nearly unbeatable in any finish that came down to a bunch gallop. Coming to the end of the race, Shay reasoned that McQuaid knew exactly how long he could sustain his sprint and for that purpose used a particular marker along the finishing straight to judge where he would start his effort. Shay decided he would need to go from further out to beat McQuaid, and the tactic worked perfectly. This win helped to convince Shay that he could take on and beat the best who would be entered in his race during the forthcoming Manx week.

A few days later Shay, with his bike and a suitcase, turned up at Dublin Port to meet his team-mates and catch the ferry to the Isle of Man. It was his first time outside the country, and it was to be a successful journey. Shay took part in the Mannin Veg race over one lap of the famous TT circuit. After crashing half-way through the race, which left him with cuts to his hand and knee and damaged brakes, he chased and caught the leaders. Throughout the race Shay had decided not to contest any of the primes, so as to make his breakaway companions think he was weak. The ploy worked; at the finish he easily out-sprinted two riders from Liverpool. On the same day Shay's club mate Noel Tully won the two-lap Viking Trophy on the same course, so making it a great day for the Irish.

After winning the first two of the three big races, speculation started to grow that Dublin Wheelers could complete the hat trick through Donal O'Connell, who was competing in the most important of the week's events, the Manx International over three laps. O'Connell, who was on the Irish team, did go clear in a very dangerous break, but they were pulled back by the bunch, so it was not to be a glorious Irish treble.

On his return home Shay triumphed in the two-day Dublin–Galway–Dublin, also known as the 'Coast-to-Coast Classic'. He finished in the bunch on the first stage, but won the return leg back to Dublin, to be presented with the Silver Knight trophy. His team-mates, Noel Tully and Donal O'Connell were second and third respectively. It concluded a wonderful weekend for Shay and his team.

O'Connell had been selected to represent Ireland in the forthcoming World Championships in Luxembourg, along with Jim McQuaid, Jack Ryan and Joe McCormack, These three, however, had all ridden the two-day race and finished well down the field. Their current poor form caused the team selectors to consider replacing them, and Shay would obviously be one of the favourites as a substitute. In the end this didn't come to fruition and he would have to wait another season to make his debut at the Worlds.

It had been a thoroughly impressive season, all the same. Once again he'd set himself new goals, and once again he'd realised them. He had every reason to feel satisfied and entitled to enjoy some rest at the end of the year.

The off season gave Shay more of an opportunity to attend some of the social functions organized by the club. Often on a Friday or Saturday evening he'd meet up with fellow club members to cycle to various dance halls around the city. The young women in the club certainly appreciated this new addition, and he was never short of attention at these dances, as fellow team member Billy Long would later recall. 'Shay was very popular with the female members of the club. He was really outgoing and confident chatting to the girls. However, he was very single-minded and was only really interested in racing and training.'

Shay's normal routine was to start his serious training in the last week of the year, taking advantage of time off from work over the holiday period. After an early Christmas Day lunch with the family, he would set off with his coach, Gerry Duffin, to cover eight or nine hundred kilometres, before arriving back in the city for New Year's Eve. The pair would cycle around the country, normally with Shay setting the pace and an eager Gerry sitting on his wheel, and stay in youth hostels at night.

So it was that Shay went into 1953, his second season with Dublin Wheelers, in an optimistic mood. He had been in good form in his last races of the previous season, and had put in a good winter's training. His main ambition for the year was selection for the World Championships later in the season, in which he was confident he could produce a good performance. He started off well, coming third in his first road race in Wicklow behind Joe McCormack and the established sprinter Jim McQuaid. To underly his good form he won the King of the Mountains competition. It was a good start to the year and a good omen for his first major race of the season, which he was looking forward to – the Tour of Ireland.

This was the inaugural year of the Tour of Ireland, and it was planned to be part of the national *An Tóstal* celebrations. *An Tóstal* was an idea dreamed up by the Irish Tourist Board in an effort to bring more tourists to the country, although exactly what it was supposed to celebrate nobody seemed to know. Nevertheless, the total prize money for the Tour amounted to £198, which made it the richest race in the country. The race would also serve as the CRE's rival to the *Rás Tailteann*, which was organised by the NCA and was also being run for the first time that year.

The opposition from across the Irish Sea (whose cars had to be sprayed with anti-foot and mouth detergent upon arrival in Dun Laoghaire, because of the recent outbreak in England) was very strong, with Brian Robinson, who would go on to become the first successful British road-race professional on the continent, and Dick Bowes representing England. Shay's team-mates in the Dublin Regional team were Joe McCormack and Jim McQuaid.

After being waved off by the Lord Mayor of Dublin at Merrion Square on a Thursday morning, the 90 riders set out on the road to Wexford, with the start proper being at Bray. Any chance Shay had of winning the race overall, or even of finishing high up on general classification, were ruled out on that very first stage: he had trouble with his gear mechanism, which cost him fully fifteen minutes. What this misfortune did mean, however, was that there was now no pressure on him as far as overall classification was concerned, and he would be able to concentrate on stage wins.

The second stage to Waterford proved to be a disaster for a number of riders caught up in a serious accident, when a donkey cart ran into the peloton. Many of them were hurt and had to abandon the race. Amongst those involved in the crash was David Duffield (later to become the voice of cycling on *Eurosport*). Shay, fortunately, managed to avoid the crash and was able to continue.

On the mountainous third stage to Limerick, Shay's ability started to be revealed. He chased after Brian Robinson, caught him on the climb outside Macroom, and dropped him soon after. He was then joined by his Dublin Wheelers team-mate, Billy Long, and Addie, a member of the Scotland team. But they couldn't maintain the pace, and once more Shay was alone in front. Eventually, though, he was caught, just 20 kilometres from Limerick, and it was an Englishman, Paddy Boyd from Birkenhead, who took the stage win, while another Englishman, Brian Haskell of NCU London, took the overall lead.

The final stage from Limerick back to Dublin finished outside the Guinness brewery, beside the River Liffey, and was won by the Australian Nevin. Some estimates put the crowds watching the final stage at over two hundred thousand, with every vantage point along the river taken. Brian Haskell won the race overall, while Shay (after his disastrous start) had climbed up to finish tenth on General Classification – a remarkable achievement after his loss of 15 minutes on the first stage. Again he found himself presented with the King of the Mountains award at the prize giving ceremony in the heart of Dublin.

In May came the news that Shay had been selected for the Ireland "B" team for the forthcoming Manx International over 180 kilometres. The race would be three times longer than the Mannin Veg race which he had won the previous year, but this did not faze him, as there were some hard races coming up at home, which would serve as very good preparation.

The first of these was the Grand Prix of Ireland. Shay was hoping to retain the title he had won the previous two years, but this time he was dogged by misfortune. As the field of 100 riders were about to start in the Phoenix Park, the heavens opened, and as the race progressed the rain got steadily heavier. One of the first casualties was Shay, who punctured. He borrowed a bike from a team-mate, and set off in pursuit, but with its many bends the circuit had become treacherous. No sooner had he regained contact with the bunch, when he came down on a corner and was forced to retire. For all Shay's disappointment, it was a reflection on the growing popularity of cycle racing in Ireland at the time, that despite the poor weather, thousands of spectators walked, cycled or bused from all over the city to see the race.

Shortly afterwards, Shay travelled to Northern Ireland to compete in the Lurgan Grand Prix, the first of the four races which would be used to select the Irish team to compete in the World Championships in Lugano, Switzerland. He finished only fifth, while Jim McQuaid won. It was not the result he had been looking for. He would have to improve in the remaining three races if he was going to make it into the Irish team for the Worlds.

Despite being fierce competitors in races, some of the top cyclists from Dublin, including Jim McQuaid and Donal O'Connell, used to meet on a Wednesday afternoon for training spins. If Shay's work schedule allowed him, he would also join up with this group. However, much of the time,

Shay would train on his own. The emphasis at that time was on quantity rather than quality and he'd often spend up to twenty hours a week on the bike, which required a lot of dedication from somebody holding down a full-time job. It was around this time that Donal O'Connell started to notice a difference in Shay's outlook: 'I noticed a distinct change in Shay's attitude around this time. Whilst the rest of us were happy to try and be the best that we could in Ireland, he was starting to enquire about what the normal route for a cyclist to becoming a professional.'

Not content with wanting to be just the best road racing cyclist in the country, Shay was looking beyond Ireland. Although at that time the sport was viewed as essentially a continentals-only affair, he didn't see why he couldn't compete in France. More and more he was showing that hunger. Despite confiding in Donal about his intentions, Shay generally sought to keep his ambitions to himself: he didn't want to leave himself open to ridicule by those who felt that he was getting ideas above his station. After all, Ireland had never had a road racing cyclist of any significance.

Following that first, not very convincing, selection race, Shay again made the trip across the Irish Sea with a large contingent of Irish cyclists to compete in the various events of the Manx cycling week. Shay's father had always dreamed of riding his motorbike in the TT races, but had never made it, so he was especially proud to see Shay managing to get there once more.

In the major event of the week, the Manx International, Brian Robinson had led an early breakaway at the start of the second lap, but had been caught, and this effort seemed to take enough out of him to rule him out of contention. As for the Irish representatives, most of them were still in the peloton at this stage. Shay then went clear in a group of a dozen riders, which included his team-mate, Paddy Nolan. Just after Ramsay, at the start of the last climb, England's Les Wilmott attacked and built up a lead over the chasers which, at one point, stretched to over a minute. However, with only five kilometres left, the pursuers had sliced this down to a bare 150 metres. Shay then made his attack. Initially, the two experienced English riders, Arthur Ilsley and Harold King, were able to stay with him, but eventually they were dropped and Shay looked set to overcome Wilmott. Then, with less than a kilometre to the finish, he took the narrow and dangerous Governor's Bridge too fast, and came down. His bike was badly damaged, and he had to borrow a spectator's to reach the finish line – in fourth place, but still two minutes ahead of his team-mate, Paddy Nolan. For Shay the result was very disappointing: he was feeling really strong and was sure that, with a shade more caution, he could have won.

He returned home to compete in the second of the selection races for the World Championships team – a race of over 100 kilometres in the Phoenix Park organised by his own club, but it was Donal O'Connell who won, while Shay finished sixth. Another disappointment. With only a fifth and a sixth in the qualifying races he had little confidence that he would make the squad.

His situation did not improve with the third race in the selection series, and Shay was under considerable pressure going into the final race to decide the team for Switzerland. If he didn't make the team, he would have considered the season to have been disastrous. The 200-kilometre selection race in Dundalk also happened to be the National Championships.

On the morning of the race the bicycle belonging to one of the favourites, Kit O'Rourke, was stolen from outside his house in Dublin, and he was unable to compete. So, one rival was eliminated. A field of 55 riders faced torrential rain as they started from outside Oriel Park, the local football stadium, in a very testing race which only eighteen would finish. Shay, to his enormous relief, outsprinted Jim McQuaid, who was hampered with a slow puncture, by half a length to take the win. That evening, the team that would travel to Lugano was announced, and Shay's name was among them. His performance that day had been enough to convince the selectors to include him.

With his selection assured, Shay's results seemed to improve. He missed the winning break on the first day of the Coast-to-Coast, but on the return leg he led out the sprint and would surely have won if he hadn't mistaken the finishing line in the Phoenix Park and sat up 100 metres too soon, which allowed Joe McCormack to overtake him for the stage win.

A week later, Shay travelled up North to compete on the track at Portadown. Racing on a hard track for only the second time, he put in a great performance. In the 5-mile scratch race he won the prize for the fastest lap. He won the one-mile and the three-mile handicap races and in the five-mile scratch race took the prize for the fastest lap. His performance in the one-mile was particularly impressive: on the back straight of the final lap he was shut in on the inside in sixth place, but he had the strength to come round on the outside in the last few metres for a brilliant win.

In his final race before the World Championships, Shay missed out on the winning break on the first day of the Dublin–Waterford–Dublin two-day race. He made up for it on the return stage to Dublin, however, with a solo attack that at one stage saw him two minutes clear on his own. Although he was eventually recaptured, he still finished second on the stage. His recent performances left him confident in advance of the Worlds.

The following Wednesday, the Irish team departed from Dublin for Switzerland. It was Shay's first venture to the continent, and he relished the opportunity of racing against the best amateurs in the world. He rode strongly in the race and was still with the leading group when, once again, he suffered from mechanical trouble, and was forced to retire. Misfortune of this sort was also to afflict him in future world championships. Amongst the medalists in the amateur race were two cyclists who would go on to have great professional careers: Gastone Nencini would win both the Giro d'Italia and Tour de France, and Rik Van Looy would become a multiple world champion and the first rider to win every big one-day classic.

The following day, Shay and the rest of the team witnessed one of his heroes, and one of the greatest cyclists ever, Fausto Coppi, win the professional race on his own, five minutes clear of the field. It was the first time Shay had seen the likes of Charly Gaul, Ferdi Kubler and Louison Bobet racing, and it further strengthened his ambition to make it to that level.

All in all it had been a good year and Shay was understandably content with how his season had gone. He was stronger than he had been a year earlier, and he could certainly consider himself amongst the best three or four cyclists in the country. He'd achieved the aim he'd set himself at the start of the year and made it to the World Championships, even though he'd been disappointed with how that race had turned out. Once again, he rested for a few weeks, before starting his preparation again for the next season.

3

A champion in the making

Despite having had few early-season races, Shay was named on the Ireland "A" team to take part in the *An Tóstal* Tour of Ireland. His 1954 season could hardly have started better. The Tour would be starting at the end of April, and he would be riding alongside Karl McCarthy, John Lackey, Kit O'Rourke and Joe McCormack. The prize money had been increased, with £400 on offer this year.

There was a considerably increased interest in the race, with over three hundred riders sending entries in, which the organisers had to whittle down to a little over one hundred to comply with *Gardaí* regulations. Shay's mother, despite her earlier concerns with her son racing, had grown interested in Shay's career by now, and would end up following this race in a small car, borrowed from Jim. Although he didn't win, this second edition of the Tour of Ireland was to prove a major turning point in Shay's career.

After being greeted by the Lord Mayor at the Mansion House, the peloton set off from Merrion Square on the first stage of 220 kilometres to Athlone. On that first stage, shortly after the flag was dropped, Bernard Pusey of the England "A" team broke away with three others, including Lackey. Pusey got rid of the others and stayed away to the finish, despite all the efforts from his pursuers, including Shay, to close the gap. He finished five minutes clear of his nearest challenger – an advantage which was to prove too much for Shay to overcome.

The leading positions remained unchanged after the next stage. Shay had attacked outside Sligo, with 35 kilometres to go, accompanied by one of the best English riders, Stan Brittain. Within sight of the finish, the two were overtaken by Boyd of the English team, and Shay's team-mate, Kit O'Rourke. Boyd switched right across the road in the sprint finish causing Shay and Brittain to crash almost on the finishing line. However, both riders escaped relatively unscathed.

Ireland's A team had to wait until the fourth stage before getting its first success. The pace was very fast from the start of this mountainous stage through County Kerry (despite members of the NCA attempting to sabotage the race by spreading tacks on the road near Farranfore), and Shay scored highly on a number of the King of the Mountains primes. Shortly after Bantry, he and Pusey escaped, and, by the time they reached Bandon, their lead over the peloton had stretched to nearly five minutes.

Approaching the finish in Cork with their lead still intact, the two of them reached an agreement: they would sprint side by side for the win. However, when Shay saw the Englishman reach down to change gears, he jumped and gained enough of a gap to hold on for the win. At dinner that evening, Joe McCormack joked that Shay would chase his own grandmother around the parlour for a medal.

However, Shay's victory was overshadowed by a fatal accident during the stage. As the peloton was descending the steep hill into Glengarriff, a horse which had been tied to the railings of the parish hall, was startled by the music blaring from the loudspeakers of the lead vehicles, and bolted up the hill towards the oncoming riders. Most of them managed to avoid the galloping animal, but the English rider Denis Weston was struck on the chest by the shaft of a cart it was pulling. He was then dragged up the hill for a further thirty metres until the horse crashed through a wooden gate into a field. Weston died instantly, although none of the riders were told this until after the stage. The following day, all the riders wore black armbands in memory of the English rider, and a memorial service was held in the stage finish city of Waterford.

As if in keeping with the sombre mood of the peloton, the weather on the way to Waterford was truly terrible, and as the stage progressed more and more of the cyclists retired. However, one small group including Shay, Pusey and Tony Hoar broke away, with Shay taking the prime at Clonmel, but he was subsequently dropped, and Hoar took the sprint in Waterford. Only sixteen of the cyclists survived the Arctic conditions that day.

The appalling weather continued the next day for the final stage to Dublin. Tony Hoar can still recall the stage: 'I remember seeing one of the Irish riders swigging from a flask of cherry brandy in an effort to keep warm, prior to the start.' Then, as the flag was dropped, that same rider took off like the clappers, and the disintegration of the field started. Tony Hoar again: 'I saw their manager feeding from the pillion seat of a motorbike, with a vast supply of tomato soup laced with rum.'

Alan Butler remembers that they were so cold, they had to stop at Kilkenny for a drink to warm up: 'At the bar stood a farmer and before we could get to the counter he had bought us two double rums. He refused all payment, saying he had never seen anyone so blue in all his born days. We each had two more rums before their chase began.'

As Pusey had an unassailable lead, the bunch were planning on riding at a steady pace on the road to Dublin, and only race for the bonuses along the way (Shay taking the first prime of the day in Gorey). However, their plans to make life as easy as possible for themselves in the miserable conditions were scuppered when those riders who had already abandoned the race complained. They were travelling towards Dublin in open pick-up trucks, probably suffering more from the freezing cold than those who were still in the race, and in a hurry for the whole thing to finish. So the remaining riders were warned by the officials to make a proper race of it, or the stage would be cancelled.

As the pace picked up, Shay was suffering badly from the conditions and receiving pushes from team-mates, in an effort to keep up. In spite of that he was finally dropped close to the finish, but he was by no means in the worst state. One of his Dublin Wheelers team-mates, Derek Quinn, fell into a ditch during the stage, and was found by a farmer. Quinn was in such a terrible condition that the farmer took him to his house, ran a hot bath for him, and put the frozen cyclist into it. And even after the end of the stage, organisers and team managers were still receiving phone calls notifying them of the locations of riders who had abandoned the race.

The final stage, finishing in Dublin's St Stephen's Green, was won by Tony Hoar, ahead of Karl McCarthy. The race overall went to Bernard Pusey, who had more than six minutes to spare over Shay, who in turn finished ahead of Hoar. The Ireland "A" team of Shay, John Lackey, and Kit McCarthy won the team award (they were, in fact, the only complete team left) and, as a mark of respect, they carried Bernard Pusey to the stage for his prize giving – a grand affair in the Gresham Hotel on O'Connell Street.*

---

* On the strength of their performances in the Tour of Ireland Bernard Pusey and Tony Hoar were selected for the new Hercules team, which would take part in the Tour de France the following year. Tony Hoar finished in last place, but as *Lanterne Rouge* he was in great demand for post-Tour criteriums. He and Brian Robinson were the first British riders ever to finish the Tour.

Shay, as well as finishing second on general classification, won the King of the Mountains competition. It was this that would turn out to be so pivotal to his future career – more significant than his second overall – because the prize for winning the mountains competition was a free trip to the Simplex training camp at Monte Carlo the following season.

There was another Irishman whose life was to be changed by the events of that day: a young Peter Crinnion had stood by the roadside and been enthralled by the spectacle of the diminished group passing through Bray. He remembers being so impressed by the resilience of these men who were able to endure such conditions. It was this sight that made him decide that this was the sport for him. For the next few years Shay was his hero and he would follow his results avidly, as he strove to become Ireland's second professional cyclist.

Apart from the tragic event on the road to Cork, the first seven-day *An Tóstal* Tour of Ireland had been a great success. Most schools that the race passed by suspended lessons to allow the children to watch the spectacle. The crowds in the towns filled the streets, and in the country, bonfires were lit to greet the riders.

Shortly after the end of the Tour of Ireland, the CRE received, for the first time, an invitation to send an Irish team to compete in the prestigious amateur race, the Route de France. This was a 10-stage race, for teams of six, confined to amateur riders under the age of 25. The Irish team would include three from the Dublin Wheelers, Shay being one of them. Shortly afterwards there was more recognition for his burgeoning talent when he learnt that he'd been selected for the Ireland "A" team to take part in the Manx International, which would come hard on the heels of the French race.

In early June, the Irish team assembled to take the ferry to France. The team consisted of Shay, John Lackey, John Flanagan, Karl McCarthy, Tony Duggan and Derek Quinn. Paddy McQuaid was team manager, Sean Byrne the team mechanic, and Joe Loughman its Press officer. Gerry Duffin would also travel as Shay's personal trainer, while Tex Nolan was the final member of the party.

The team travelled over in Paddy McQuaid's massive 6-litre Studebaker to Brittany. After the start in Dinard, the race would go further west into Brittany, before turning south and on into the Pyrenees, finally finishing in Agen, near Bordeaux. A good ride in this race would go a long way towards helping any ambitious young rider gain a professional contract.

The speed of the race came as a considerable shock to the Irish riders, but despite this, Shay achieved some good stage placings in the opening days. Looming over the team, however, was the dread of the fearful Pyrenees. This apprehension was due, in no small part, to the race director, Jean Leulliot. The Frenchman was circulating stories about the massive climb of the 2,115 metre Col du Tourmalet. Just as in the years after 1910, when the Tourmalet made its first appearance on the Tour de France route, the tales doing the rounds were that the summit was so high that only eagles could reach it, and that any stragglers would be in danger of being eaten by ravenous bears on the snow covered slopes. Octave Lapize, the first winner of the Pyrenean stage, had made a name for himself by spitting out 'murderers' to the tour officials as they gathered anxiously wondering if anybody would actually make it to the top of the cols.

Shay was clearly undeterred by all Leulliot's scaremongering, for he went clear on his own on the stage, which had started in Lourdes. He crossed the summit of the Tourmalet alone, with a two minute lead over the next man, Frenchman Robert Cazala. On the descent, Duffin, who was noted as a wily tactician, told Shay to wait for Cazala. There were still forty kilometres to the finish, and he'd need the Frenchman's help. The tactic worked out well: the two stayed away, and Shay easily outsprinted Cazala at the finish in Montrejeau, to win what the French Press called the *Etape Reine* (the 'Queen Stage', the name given to the hardest stage in any stage race).

Meanwhile, Paddy McQuaid's Studebaker wasn't faring quite as well. It overheated on the 30-kilometre climb of the Tourmalet, and the Irish team had to pack snow into the radiator to cool it down.

That evening the team celebrated Shay's win in the hotel in Montrejeau, with John Lackey (a Protestant) tucking into a massive steak, while the rest of the team, following the traditional Catholic practice of abstaining from meat on a Friday, looked on enviously. They weren't doing as well as Shay, but they were all still in the race, and certainly not out of their depth. Eventually, the Ireland team finished third in the team classification, helped by Shay's fifth place on the last stage, from Montrejeau to Agen. Shay, himself, finished the race fourth overall, and amongst the prizes that he took home from the Route de France was a moped. The race had been won by the French rider Nicolas Barone, who would go on to wear the yellow jersey for one day in the 1957 Tour de France and enjoyed several other notable successes in France.

Shay travelled directly to the Isle of Man from France, and after his showing there, he started the Manx International as favourite. However, he could only finish in seventh position, three minutes behind the winner, the English legend, Ray Booty, on a day of strong wind and rain.

Back home, Shay's next race was the two-day Dublin–Waterford–Dublin. On the first day, after regaining contact with the leading group near Kilkenny, he broke clear with two others. Then his familiar bad luck struck: five kilometres out from Waterford, he punctured. He managed to hang on to the wheels of the others until he was finally dropped in the last kilometre, and finished the day ten seconds down on John Lackey.

The next day on the road back to Dublin, Shay was determined to claw back that ten-second deficit. He went clear from the peloton with John Lackey and Joe McCormack. Then, on the hill out of Lucan, he attacked again. At first Lackey stayed pegged to Shay's wheel, but after a few hundred metres, he could hang on no longer, and Shay drew inexorably away to finish over a minute ahead to win the stage and take overall victory. Shortly after this two-day race, the Irish team for the World Championships in Germany in late August was announced and, predictably enough, Shay was selected.

The following week Shay was in the North, successfully retaining his National Championship title. In a gruelling race over fifteen laps of a 12-kilometre circuit in Dundrod, near Belfast, he just managed to hold off Joe McCormack, who had won the event in 1952 over the same course. The two had broken away on the twelfth lap with two others, and they stayed away to the finish. Only thirteen of the starters finished the race. Shay also ended up joint first in the King of the Hills competition.

The rest of August Shay spent putting in some serious miles, as he intended to put up a good showing in his second chance at the amateur World Championships, where he was due to compete in the road-race and also the individual pursuit. He failed to qualify for the quarter finals of the pursuit – his time of 5'–35" was well outside the top eight – but despite that, took to the start line of the road race in Solingen in confident mood. He had good reason: his performances throughout the year had been impressive. Yet, once again bad luck would strike, when the newspaper he had wrapped around his spare tyre fell into his back wheel and jammed his gears, which forced him to retire.

One of Shay's team-mates had a very lucky escape during the race. Joe McCormack had taken a corner too fast and went over the top of a barrier. He fell fifteen metres down a ravine, and might have been killed but for landing in a bush growing on the side of the steep valley. He was hauled back up with ropes, immediately got back on his bike, and went on to finish in 56th position.

The rain was so intense during these championships that a grandstand had collapsed into the sodden ground. Amongst the spectators for the professional road-race, won by Louison Bobet, were the Irish team and once again, watching the professionals compete made Shay even more determined that he would one day reach that level.

Shortly afterwards, back in Ireland, Shay rode in the Circuit of Bray. It would turn out to be his last big race with the Dublin Wheelers. He broke away from the field, accompanied by two English riders, Dick Bowes and Harry Reynolds, but punctured with several laps still to go. Shay was able to borrow a bike from a local rider, Mick Byrne, who was also riding the event. Mick, however, was on a fixed wheel – in those days in Ireland not all riders could afford good quality derailleurs. Despite this, Shay regained contact with the two English riders, and next time around jumped back on his own bike, which by now had been repaired. Once again, he had to chase hard to catch up with his breakaway companions.

When he finally made contact with the duo, he dropped both of them on the hill on Putland Road. In front of a massive crowd on the seafront, Shay finished alone, eight seconds ahead of Bowes, to win for the second year in a row. His gratitude for Mike Byrne's sacrifice was evident when he invited him on to the top step of the podium to share the accolades.

At the end of the season the Dublin Wheelers held a dinner party to celebrate the 21st anniversary of the founding of the club. There, Shay was presented with a special gold medal by the President of the CRE, Bill Sleith, in recognition of his various accomplishments at home and abroad during the season. Perhaps there were some that evening who harboured ambivalent feelings about that medal. Winning had come all too easily to Shay, and despite his normally easy-going nature, he sometimes upset other members of the Irish cycling fraternity. Some of his Dublin Wheelers team-mates considered him selfish, and not much of a team player, only interested in getting first place himself. On one occasion after a race, Donal O'Connell had argued furiously with Shay for chasing him down. 'I hope to do even better for the honour of Irish cycling next year,' said Shay when he received the medal. There was very little doubt amongst those present that he would accomplish that.

Shay was now in the position where he had achieved more or less all he could in Ireland. If he was ever going to realise his dream he had no option but to join the hundreds of thousands of young people who, since the 1930s, had been leaving the country in search of work and a better life abroad. Most of them were destined for Britain, whose relatively early recovery from the depression and its enormous need for labour during the war and in the postwar reconstruction persuaded them that their future lay there. But Shay wanted to be a professional cyclist, and that meant going further afield – to the continent, or more specifically, France.

Another Irish sportsman from Shay's era, the athlete Ronnie Delany, would also leave the country in 1954 with the aim of furthering his sporting ambitions. Delany explained his decision to leave Dublin after winning a scholarship to Villanova University in the United States: 'It was a huge decision to go to Villanova. In the fifties life was very depressed in Dublin and Irish people didn't have goals and objectives like I had. Here, suddenly, was this nineteen-year-old who had set himself goals and who had to go to America to achieve these goals. I couldn't have achieved them in Ireland. There weren't the tracks, there wasn't the environment in which to train, there wasn't the competition. So, I simply had to go to America.'

Those reasons which Delany had shared with his fans precisely echoed Shay's need to go to France. Not that he wasn't understandably apprehensive about moving to France. On the bus home from college one night he asked Billy Long if he was interested in moving to France with him the following season. However, at this stage, Billy had given up racing and earning money had taken precedence.

Towards the end of the season there had been a family meeting in the Elliott home in Crumlin, where they discussed Shay's future. He had just finished his apprenticeship as a panel beater, but his real dream was simply to become a professional cyclist. It was decided that he would try his hand at cycle racing and stay on after the Simplex camp in Monaco to see if he could make the grade on the continent. If he failed, he would return to Ireland and resume his job panel beating. Undoubtedly, Jim Elliott thought back to his own ambitions of competing among the best at motorcycling, and could truly empathise with his son.

4

The best amateur in France

In January of 1955 Shay left his family home to catch the ferry from Dublin Port to Holyhead, and from there by train to London. At Victoria Station he met up with the two English riders, Mike Chambers and Alan Bladon, the Australian, Keith McCarney, and the legendary English cycling journalist, Jock Wadley, who had been asked to escort the four of them to Monte Carlo and the Simplex training camp – his prize for winning the King of the Mountains in the Irish Tour. Thirty of the best amateurs in Europe had been invited to the camp, and for Shay it was vital that he use the opportunity as a springboard for gaining a place with one of the top amateur clubs, which he hoped would lead ultimately to a professional contract

The Simplex training camp was run by Charles Pélissier, the youngest of three brothers who enraptured French cycling fans in the 1920s and 30s. They were the first to train for speed rather than mere endurance, to diet intelligently, and to forsake the alcohol which, up until then, riders had drunk during races to numb their pain. The two older brothers, argumentative men both, frequently clashed with Tour organiser, Henri Desgrange over the inhuman conditions he imposed upon the riders, and withdrew during the course of the 1924 Tour in an episode which led to the coining of the famous phrase *les forcats de la route* (convicts of the road). Charles was an altogether more amenable character, although, in keeping with the training policy he and his brothers had devised 30 years earlier, the first thing he said to Shay was that he needed to lose weight.

Pélissier had also had the good sense to invite Jock Wadley to the training camp to translate for the English-speaking contingent. At that time he was the only British cycling journalist regularly to be found on the Continent, and was immensely popular with riders and race organisers alike.

The training rides would only last two or three hours, but under the direction of Pélissier, Shay learnt a lot about racing. He found he frequently needed Wadley's help with the language, but he was also working hard on his own French. His enthusiasm to learn and train was obvious, and he also got the opportunity to train with Jean Robic, who was also staying at the hotel. Jean Robic had won the 1947 Tour de France on the last day of the race, thereby becoming the first Tour winner never to have worn the yellow jersey till the end of the final stage, since the distinctive race leader's jersey was introduced in 1919. On another ride they were joined by Louison Bobet, who would win the Tour again that summer to become the first rider to win three consecutive editions of the race.

One particular day, Bobet's renowned *soigneur*, Raymond le Bert, gave a lecture on diet, anatomy and various aspects of training. Le Bert afterwards asked for volunteers to be tested for fitness. Compared to the other slim volunteers, Shay looked positively unathletic. Le Bert was surprised by the results, and although he acknowledged that Shay was overweight, he also said that he was as solid as a rock, describing him as a *Flahute*, the word used by the French to signify a typical tough Flemish cyclist. Le Bert advised Shay that he should cut down on his liquid intake in order to lose some weight. Had he known that Shay had brought with him a tin of chocolate biscuits given to him by his aunt, who worked in a biscuit factory in Dublin, his recommendation might have been a good deal sterner.

But probably the best advice Shay was to receive came by chance, from the French journalist and race organiser, Jean Leulliot, who happened to be staying on the Cote d'Azur. He was finalising details for Paris–Nice, which he organised, and called in on the Simplex training camp, looking for a story. Leulliot took a particular interest in Shay, as he had been one of the better performers in the previous year's Route de France, another race he organised. There he learned that Shay was intending to base his season in Ghent, Belgium, and was planning to move up there in March after the training camp.

'Nonsense,' he told him. 'In Belgium you will burn yourself out. You must join a club in Paris and learn how to become a real roadman. Leave it to me. I'll find you a club.'

The following week a notice appeared in Leulliot's cycling newspaper *Route et Piste*, stating that the Irish amateur, Séamus Elliott, wanted to remain in France after the Simplex camp, and he would like to find a club in the Paris area. It also reported that Shay had class in abundance and predicted he would have a great future.

The notice did the trick: shortly afterwards a letter arrived for Shay from Paul 'Mickey' Weigant, *directeur sportif* of the prestigious Athletic Club Boulogne-Billancourt (ACBB), saying that he had been interested in what he'd read in *Route et Piste*. He asked Shay to send him details of his full *palmarés*, as the committee would need to review it before they could consider him for entry to the club. Shay eagerly wrote out his full record and sent it back to Weigant by return of post.*

Two days later Weigant replied, saying that the club's committee had been impressed by his *palmarés*, and that they would like to offer him a one-month trial with the club, which would include accommodation and free board for that first month. They also asked for his frame measurements so that a Helyett bicycle could be made up for him. Together with the mechanic based at the Simplex camp, Shay measured his frame size and sent his details to Weigant. He stated that he stood at 5'6", and would require a 22" frame.

For Shay, things could not have worked out better. The ACBB, founded in 1924 and based in Paris, was one of the most, if not the most, prestigious cycling club in France. Known as the *Petit Gris*, because of their grey and orange jerseys, they had a fine record in developing champion riders: Jean Stablinski and Jacques Anquetil, who in forthcoming years were to play important parts in Shay's career, had both been members of ACBB. The club was to be nursery to a galaxy of other great cyclists – Bernard Thevenet, Phil Anderson, Robert Millar, Sean Yates and Jaan Kirsipuu among them. It was also the club Stephen Roche was to join when he started his continental career.

Shay stayed on in Nice after the camp had disbanded, while he waited for his trial to start in Paris. He spent his time doing long training rides, as there were not many amateur races in that part of the country in which he could take part, although he did come eighth in one 80-kilometre race in Nice. He also found time to watch various professional races in the locality, such as the season-opening Mont Agel hill-climb, Genoa–Nice, the closing stages of Paris–Nice, won that year by Jean, the younger of the Bobet brothers. He even cycled across the Italian border to see the end of Milan–San Remo.

---

* Paul Weigant was more commonly known as 'Mickey' due to his penchant for wearing a Mickey Mouse badge on his jersey, during his racing days.

Shay spent much of his time training with the current French professional champion, Jacques Dupont, and the Australian cyclist, Russell Mockridge, who had befriended him at the Simplex camp. In his autobiography, published after his tragic death just four years later, Mockridge wrote of those days with the young man he identified as 'the first Irishman to become a world class cyclist…and now one of Europe's leading professional roadmen'.

Shay also used to meet up with a young Parisian, who was doing some pre-season training while staying with relations at Menton, near to the Italian border. For a number of weeks Shay did not realise that his new training partner would be a team-mate in the forthcoming season. Jean Tchamassanian had won a number of quite important races for ACBB the previous year. Despite their difficulty in conversing – Jean spoke only a few words of English, and Shay's French at that stage could hardly be considered fluent – they quickly became good friends.

The week following Milan–San Remo, Shay travelled to Paris in the company of Jock Wadley to start his trial with ACBB. He had sent a telegram to Weigant telling him when he expected to arrive in Paris. Wadley would have recognised Weigant, but this proved unnecessary. At the Gare de Lyon there stood Weigant (together with the club president, Monsieur Potin – the owner of the Félix Potin grocery chain) holding aloft a photograph of Shay.

After the warmth and sunshine of the training camp in Monte Carlo, Shay had some difficulty acclimatising to the cold of Northern France. His first race, Paris–Ezy, took place in especially foul weather and Shay rode particularly badly. So badly, in fact, that he was considering returning home: 'It was cold and wet during Paris–Ezy, and I was hopeless, my legs and feet were completely numb. I was very miserable at the end and was sure Monsieur Weigant would be angry with me. He had told me during the week that the club would be giving me a month's trial and if I did not meet with any success during that time, they would not be able to pay my expenses any more. I thought that after Paris–Ezy that I should have to go back to Ireland.'

However, the following week there was a vast improvement. In the hilly French classic, Paris–Evreux, the first major event of the French amateur calendar, he won, finishing five seconds ahead of Robert Andry and Roger Darrigade (the brother of André, although he was never to reach his World Championship heights). Perhaps driven by fear of an ignominious return home he had prepared hard all that week – 100 kilometres on the Tuesday,

50 on Wednesday, 100 on Thursday – and in a field of 185 riders over a 180-kilometre route he had beaten the cream of the French amateurs. 'All this last week I trained hard,' he said, 'but I never expected to win a great classic like Paris–Evreux.' There was now no doubt that his month-long trial with the club would be successful, and he would hold on to his place with ACBB for the remainder of the season. Furthermore, the winner of this race usually went on to gain a professional contract for the following season.

After moving to Paris Shay stayed in a number of different hotels until July, when he moved in with a family in Passy, a part of the 15th Arrondissement on the right bank of the Seine. It was the family of Jean Tchamassanian, who he had befriended on the Côte d'Azur before the start of the season. He would go on to stay with the family for the rest of the season, and also for his first few seasons as a professional. The family were very passionate about bicycle racing, with Jean's mother and grandmother being particularly knowledgeable, and they worked hard to try and ensure their son achieved his aim of turning professional.

Madame Tchamassanian explained how it was that Shay ended up living with them: 'It was in July that Jean came home and told us that the young Irish boy in the club was ill with bronchitis. He was living in a hotel at the time, and was not really being looked after properly. Jean had just joined the army, and suggested Shay had his room. I agreed. When he was better we had become so fond of him that we asked him to stay on. He's now like another son to us.'

Shay's diet, as well as his health, improved while he lived with the Tchamassanians, as Jean's mother was fully aware of what foods were detrimental to a cyclist. During meals Shay would be limited to one glass of red wine, and Madame Tchamassanian would not allow him to have any of her sauces or bread. Shay did not mind though, as he could feel the benefits of this regime.

His knowledge of French also improved even further during his stay with the family. Jean would say that Parisians would think that Shay was from some distant region of France, rather than a foreigner from Ireland. The races around Paris would start early, at 7 or 8 o'clock, so this would mean that Shay would have his pre-race meal at around 5 o'clock in the morning, often a steak cooked by Madame Tchamassanian. Everybody in the house would get up to see him off and wish him luck. Madame Tchamassanian would often then travel to wherever the race was taking place to see the finish.

Due to French legislation, Shay was not allowed to work without a permit, which removed the temptation to take a part-time job to supplement his meagre income from racing, and helped him to focus just on training and racing. His daily schedule would typically consist of a training spin in the morning, and then rest in the afternoon. Occasionally, he might go to the cinema, but his social life was generally very limited. ACBB supplied his bicycle, courtesy of Helyett, and all of his equipment and gear. The rules of amateur racing in France at the time prevented riders from displaying any advertising on their jerseys during a race, but this wouldn't prevent them donning jerseys with logos on a lap of honour, or during the podium presentations. Helyett would receive plenty of publicity in the 1955 season thanks to Shay. Despite the level of publicity that he provided to ACBB and the club's sponsors, his bonuses were quite modest – a mere £50 by the end of the season.

After his successful month's trial, ACBB agreed to pay half the cost of his board and lodging for the remainder of the season, confident that he could pay the remainder through his prize winnings. The average prize money for a win in the Parisian area was about £10, and Shay won about £100 that season, on top of his bonuses. He could have earned more prize money by racing in regional France, where the prize money was more substantial. However, if he wanted to gain a professional contract, it was better to race around Paris: scouts for the professional teams were more likely to attend these races, and there was considerably more publicity to be gained from them.

The club scene was a lot more serious in France than anything Shay had known back in Dublin. ACBB was purely a racing club whose 40 or so members were divided between first, second and third categories. On a Monday night there would be a 'post-mortem': the members of ACBB would meet to discuss the previous weekend's races, and riders would be assessed on their performances. The club would then select their teams for the following weekend's races. At the end of each season, those who had not impressed were let go and replaced. In Ireland, any cyclist who wanted to join a club would be more than welcome, and there would be no obligation to race, let alone get good results. They were essentially social cycling clubs.

At this time, the rules in French amateur racing forbade team-mates from helping each other in races. They could not exchange wheels in the event of a puncture or help pace a team-mate back to the peloton. They weren't even allowed to give food or drink to one another (not that this necessarily stopped them from doing so, of course). Shay would generally take all his food and drink with him at the start of the race. During a 200-kilometre race, this would usually consist of three bidons, one with black coffee, one with plain water, and one with rice and fruit juice. He would not eat much during a race, usually just a little fruit.*

Excellent results followed on from his strict regime as he also won the Boulogne–Billancourt Grand Prix, to add to his victory in Paris–Evreux. He had infiltrated all of the breaks during the race and got away five kilometres from the finish with two others, whom he then proceeded to drop, to win alone by thirteen seconds. Jean Bobet commented that during this period Shay was so strong, and he seemed capable of doing whatever he wanted in a race, that he made other riders feel ridiculous.

Despite now living and racing abroad, he hadn't been forgotten back home, as he was selected to lead the Irish team in the Tour of Ireland in May, and the promoters hoped for a favourable reply to their invitation. But the Route de France was to start on the same day as the Irish race, and Shay had already decided to base his season around the French race. And in any case there was Weigant, urging him not to return to take part in his home tour. There was, however, the possibility of the Manx International event in June. Shay had also been selected alongside John Lackey, J.J. McCormack and Robert Erskine as part of the Ireland "A", and his schedule would allow him to travel to that race.

During the summer Shay's form continued to improve as he scored another top win in the Grand Prix de l'A.P.S.A.P. He dictated the pace of the race from the start, as he had initiated a break after 40 kilometres. They were captured at 135 kilometres, but he still had the strength to go again. With fourteen kilometres remaining, he attacked on an up-hill stretch, and only Orphée Meneghini and Christian Fanuel had the strength to go with him. He was easily able to outsprint them at the finish.

His name was now becoming familiar in France, as one reporter on French radio remarked: 'The Grand Prix de l'A.P.S.A.P was won this afternoon by the remarkable Irish rider Séamus Elliott, who escaped with two others, Meneghini and Fanuel, and beat them decisively in the sprint. Recently he won the Grand Prix de Boulogne by a lone breakaway

---

* Sports science wasn't very advanced at this time. Some riders, Coppi and Bobet, for instance, were making significant progress as regards the benefits of sound nutrition, but they were the exception.

near the finish, and his first great victory in Paris–Evreux was due to his qualities as a hill-climber. Elliott came to France to learn how to race. It seems to me he has come from Ireland to teach us.'

His name, and face, had also become familiar in the Passy district of Paris, where he was living with the Tchamassanians. When he returned there after his wins, many of their neighbours would be found leaning out of their windows to welcome him home.

A few days after his 21st birthday, Shay again took the start line of the Route de France, one of the few foreign riders to take part in the biggest amateur stage race in France. The first stage – 169 kilometres from Saint Pourcin to Langeac – went to perfection, and Shay said afterwards that it was possibly the easiest win of his career. He had chased after an initial four-man break. Another five soon joined this quartet. Then, with 20 kilometres remaining, Shay simply rode the others off his wheel. René Bianchi of the Champagne team set off in lone pursuit, but could not catch the Irishman. Shay came in over a minute clear of Bianchi, with the peloton another two minutes behind.

The following day, however, went very differently: only an hour into the race he crashed heavily on a steep descent, which left the skin on one of his kneecaps hanging loose. The race doctor had no option other than to cut it off on the road, which meant Shay losing a considerable amount of blood. In spite of all this he still managed to finish the stage, and with his team-mates helping him back to the bunch, even to hang on to the overall lead, albeit reduced to 26 seconds, as his rivals took advantage of his mishaps. Shay claimed that two French riders had deliberately caused the crash: out of view of the *commissaires* they had sandwiched him and brought him down. They were local riders and, Shay reckoned, none too enamoured of a foreigner winning. They claimed that it was unintentional, and no penalties were imposed upon them. What was not immediately obvious, though, was that this crash was going to rob the Irishman of his chances of winning the race overall.

The next stage was a 72-kilometre team time trial, which ACBB won convincingly, so that Shay was able to retain the race leadership and increase his overall advantage: he was now nearly two minutes clear of Gérard Saint. Saint was representing the Normandy team, and was considered by many to be the next big French star. Shay held on to his leader's white jersey for one more stage, but by then the wounds to his arm and leg were turning septic, and he was finding it impossible to pull on the handlebars. He had no option but to retire.

The injuries he sustained in the Route de France were going to keep him off the bike for a few weeks, so he decided to return home for a short while, his first time back in Ireland since he had gone to France at the end of January. While recovering at home, he took the opportunity to go to the Isle of Man week, where a record number of Irish cyclists had entered the island's races that year. In no small part this was due to Shay's successes in previous years. He had not only generated more interest in cycling, he had also shown Irish cyclists that they were capable of competing with their British and continental counterparts.

Monsieur Weigant had advised him not to take part in any races while he was away from the continent. Despite this, Shay had travelled to the island with his bike, just in case there were any withdrawals from the Irish team. He felt his injuries had healed sufficiently to take part in the mountainous time trial, but there were no late withdrawals and he missed out. One nice moment during the week came as Shay chatted with the French cyclist, René Abadie, who had won the mountain time trial, and his team-mates. Some of Shay's friends had not seen him for a while, and now they were really impressed that he was speaking French. His linguistic skills had improved rapidly.

Having not raced for a few weeks, Shay was concerned that he might lose his form, so he disobeyed Weigant's instructions and started the Dublin–Waterford–Dublin two-day race. But events proved Weigant was right: Shay was able to finish in eighth place on the first stage, but couldn't finish the return leg to Dublin. It was only two weeks after the crash and he had still not recovered sufficiently from his injuries.

Shay was to have returned to France on the following Wednesday, in advance of a big, one-day race he had been entered for with ACBB, but he delayed his journey by one day so he could take part in his home club's 100-kilometre race in Dublin's Phoenix Park. Despite trying several times to break away in the early laps, he was a marked man, and found it difficult to get clear. He tried again with four laps to go, but all the other race favourites were able to follow his wheel. So, there were nine men still in the leading group as it came into the finishing straight. Shay, however, had something in reserve and just managed to outsprint Jim McQuaid for the win. Clearly he was on the mend, and shortly after his return to Paris, he confirmed that his injuries had healed when he was narrowly beaten into second place by René Pavard in the Grand Prix Champignomistes – an amateur race of considerable importance.

Despite all his success during his season with ACBB, Shay continued to harbour doubts about making the jump to professional racing; he had heard about many outstanding amateurs who had failed when they moved up to that level. Madame Tchamassanian tried to convince him that he would not fail. 'Not since the days of Robert Charpentier has an amateur been as outstanding as you have been in 1955,' she told him. Charpentier had won three gold medals at the 1936 Olympics, including the individual road race title, but had never fulfilled his potential as a professional. Hardly an encouraging comparison, but, she insisted, there was an essential difference between him and Shay: 'Charpentier would have been a good professional had he been more serious in his training. You are serious, and, moreover, have won your races in every conceivable kind of way, sprinting, lone breakaways, uphill and down. You *will* be a success.'

Not only was Shay racing on the road, he was also appearing in a number of track meetings in Paris at both the Vélodrome d'Hiver and the Parc des Princes, where there was often an amateur omnium prior to the main events for the professionals. His club was based in Boulogne-Billancourt, not far from the Parc des Princes. After moving to Paris, Shay had kept in touch with one of his old club-mates from Dublin Wheelers, Jim McArdle, who would later go on to become the cycling correspondent for the *Irish Times*. McArdle was getting married that year and decided to combine his honeymoon with watching the end of the Tour de France. He asked Shay if he could organise tickets to the Parc des Princes to witness the final stage, and Shay duly obliged.* Prior to seeing Miguel Poblet take the final stage win, Jim saw Shay taking part in the amateur omnium. He hadn't seen Shay race since he left Ireland, and now there was his former club-mate winning a track event in front of 30,000 people. Together they watched the arrival of the 69 finishers in that year's Tour, including the two remaining survivors of the British Hercules team, Tony Hoar, the *lantern rouge*, and in 29th position, Brian Robinson, who was to play a significant part in Shay's professional career.

While Shay was racing in France that summer his family had decided to move out of Dublin to Kilmacanogue in Wicklow. His father sold the business so they could retire comfortably to the country. Kilmacanogue was a small village set in a picturesque location at the foot of the Wicklow Mountains. Nell decided to call the house 'Shaymallee' in recognition

---

* The Parc des Princes would continue to host the finish of the Tour de France until 1967, after which the site was turned into a football and rugby stadium.

of Shay's win on the Tourmalet stage in the previous year's Route de France. Around the same time as they made the move, Shay was selected, alongside Bart Sharkey and Tom Talbot, for the World Championships that were to be held in Frascati, near Rome.

This was to be Shay's third attempt at the race and although he'd been suffering from a bout of bronchitis, he had recovered sufficiently to travel in a confident mood. What he could never have foreseen was that the Championships would be the scene of a violent clash between the two Irish cycling organisations, the NCA and the CRE. The ensuing fracas made international headlines and was a thorough embarrassment for Irish cycling.

Two weeks prior to the race, the executive of the NCA, although no longer recognised by the UCI, decided they would send a team! So, two teams, both claiming to represent Ireland, turned up at the start, both wearing white jerseys with green and orange stripes. The Italian authorities did eventually remove the NCA riders, recognisable by their unofficial race numbers, from the starting area, but not before punches had been thrown, first at the CRE riders and then at the police.

Shay, sensing danger as the NCA riders came on to the circuit with shouts of, 'Make way for the real Irish team,' lifted his bicycle on to his shoulder and ran into the crowd on the other side of the road. Bart Sharkey, however, was not quick enough and was knocked down, while the NCA riders stamped on his wheels, saying that if they couldn't start, then neither would he. Sharkey recovered well enough to start (with changed wheels), as did Tom Talbot, even though he emerged with a visible injury below the left eyebrow.

When the NCA men rejected the Italian officials' peaceful attempts to lead them away, the Carabinieri closed in. One of the NCA's cyclists, Mick Christle, with his back against a fence, held them off for several minutes before being overpowered by sheer numbers, and was carted off to prison. The NCA had achieved its aim of publicising its grievance, but it's hard to imagine the members of the UCI would have known what to make of it. This bitter split in Irish cycling had its roots deep in Ireland's complex history, and would not be resolved for another 20 odd years.

These events somewhat overshadowed Shay's ride in the amateur race – nine laps of a 21-kilometre circuit, with 120 cyclists from 25 countries taking part. Because of his perfomances for ACBB during the year, Shay started the race as one of the favourites, but mechanical trouble saw him having to change bikes twice. It was while he was getting back to the peloton for the second time that three Italians escaped, to chase down a lone Danish rider who had escaped earlier. Shay won the bunch sprint but had to settle for fifth place, as the Italians took all the podium positions. Of the 48 who completed the race, Bert Sharkey finished in 43rd position; Tom Talbot did not finish.

With those World Championship kilometres in his legs Shay went back to France to win the prestigious Grand Prix de Boulogne – 25 laps of a 4-kilometre circuit in the western suburbs of Paris. Journalists the following day described Shay's performance in glowing terms. The following Sunday he was third behind two Independent riders in the Grand Prix de l'Equipe. As Independent riders were somewhere between amateur and professional this was a really good result, and he was in strong form again for one of his last road races of the season – the Criterium des Vainqueurs – where he finished second to André Lemoine. This race was open only to cyclists who had won at least one French classic during the season and Shay was beaten by a bare length by the Frenchman. All of this in the latter half of the season could only further improve his chances of securing a professional contract.

With the road racing season at an end, Shay continued to compete on the track. Before moving to France he'd done nothing more than a few races on a track at Lurgan in Armagh, but now, despite this limited experience, he achieved some remarkable results. In St. Etienne, he won two 4000-metre pursuit races on the same day. In fact, if he had achieved those times in the World Championships he would have claimed that crown. In one particular pursuit he clocked 15.0 seconds for the first 250-metre lap with a flying start. This was less than half a second behind the times of the top track sprinters of the day, Reg Harris and Arie van Vliet.

These kinds of outstanding track performances encouraged Weigant to persuade Shay to try to break the amateur 1000-metres flying start world record. The attempt was scheduled to take place before the annual Brussels six-day race at the end of November. Unfortunately, they were held up and arrived late at the Palais des Sports track, leaving Shay with no time to warm up. He had to go straight on to the track for his attempt. What's more, the track was not ideal for world record breaking – only 235 metres long, banked quite sharply, and with short straight sections which made it difficult for Shay to hold his line. But despite that, and despite his frequent wobbling on his green Claud Butler with its 48x14 gear, he still managed to knock 0.4 seconds off the world record time, which the Belgian Julien van Oostende had established just three weeks previously.* Afterwards, he was presented with a bouquet by seven-times world sprint champion, Jef Scherens, who told him, 'I've rarely seen a greater display of power than you've just achieved.'

Shay then went on to make an attempt on the amateur world hour record on the Vélodrome d'Hiver track in Paris, in what was to be his last appearance as an amateur. The one-hour record is known to be incredibly difficult and painful. The professional record has a great prestige attached to it and if Shay were to achieve the amateur version, it would crown his career in the unpaid ranks. At the time, the Austrian Franz Wimmer held the record at 43.337 kilometres (established the previous year, also at the Vel d'Hiv), but in a training ride of 20 kilometres, Shay had been seven seconds inside Wimmer's over that distance. Journalists covering the event predicted that he would go beyond 44 kilometres. Shay himself had trained intensely for the attempt and felt confident. For the first twenty minutes of his attempt, he was ahead of schedule. In the process he established new records for the world amateur five and ten kilometres, with times of 6'–34" and 13'–36" respectively**. However, the tide started to turn in the second half of his attempt, and his timekeepers began signalling that he was now going slower than Wimmer. After 50 minutes Mickey Weigant decided to call a halt to the attempt, as the record was no longer achievable.

Shay would hold on to the ten-kilometre record until 1957, when the Italian, Pietro Musone, knocked thirteen seconds off his time in Milan. On the weekend that Shay gained two world records he lost one when Willi Lauwers knocked 0.2 seconds off the one-kilometre time that he'd established a few weeks previously. On the Vélodrome d'Hiver he had ridden his last competitive kilometres as an amateur.

Shay was not the only Irishman with a connection to the Vél' d'Hiv, as the Vélodrome was more commonly known. The writer Samuel Beckett also left his native Dublin to pursue his career in Paris. At that time, one of the big French track stars was a man called Roger Godeau, and the story

---

* It was a bad night for van Oostende as he also had another one of his world records broken, when Pierre Brun beat his time for the five-kilometre standing start.

** As can be seen, his time for his second 5 kilometres was nearly half a minute slower than for his first 5 kilometres. He had started out too fast and was getting slower as his attempt progressed.

goes that one evening Beckett, out walking, found himself outside the Vélodrome. He asked a group of young boys what they were doing there. 'En attendant Godeau', they replied. And, if the story is to be believed, that is how Beckett found the title of his most famous play, 'Waiting for Godot'.

By now Shay had been assured of getting a professional contract for the following season with the Helyett team, which included the French stars Jacques Anquetil and André Darrigade. The top France clubs all had good relationships with the professional teams and the very fact that Shay had been signed up by a club such as ACBB meant there was a lot of faith in his talent and he was viewed as a gifted rider.

One consequence of Shay accepting this offer from Philippe Potin was that he would not be able to take part in the Olympics in Melbourne, the following year. Having finished as the top amateur in France in 1955, and fifth at the World Championships, Shay would have been one of the favourites to take Olympic Gold. He could very well have joined 1,500-metre winner Ronnie Delany, the first Irish gold medalist since 1932. But the Olympic Road Race was closed to professionals, and would remain closed until 1996, and Shay had no intention of jeopardising his chance of a professional contract by remaining an amateur for another year.

Shay arrived back after his successful first season on the continent to the new family home in Kilmacanogue, one week before Christmas. He'd left his bicycle in France, because he wanted a complete rest while he was at home, but he did bring home other items of luggage: a few bottles of red wine, two dozen escargots, and a number of his trophies. One of these was the 'Meilleur Amateur de France 1955' awarded to the best amateur in France; another was the 'Coupe la Varsaillaese' for the best amateur from a club south of Paris. He was also able to show his parents and Paul his race leader's jersey from the Route de France and his winner's sash from Paris–Evreux, the race which he still considered his best amateur win.

While he was at home Shay was interviewed by the *Irish Times* cycling correspondent, and spoke about how he wanted to take part in the following year's Tour de France. As soon as he'd signed his professional contract, there was talk of him riding in the Tour, either as a member of the French regional team, Ile-de-France, or as a member of the International team, which would be led by Luxembourg's Charly Gaul, who would go on to win the Tour in 1958. All this, though, would have to wait the coming season. How did cycling in Ireland compare with cycling on the continent the journalist wanted to know. 'There is no comparison,' Shay succinctly replied.

During that magnificent season he had established three World records, won six races, finished second six times and third once, in addition to finishing fifth in the World Championships. Mickey Weigant had been so impressed with Shay's performances, that he decided to try to unearth further talent from outside mainland Europe by placing invitations in Jock Wadley's magazine, *Sporting Cyclist*, for cyclists to apply to join his training camps, although they would be expected to pay for their own lodgings!

At the end of the year *L'Equipe* summed up Shay's season by saying that 'if a yellow jersey for amateur road racers had been given, Shay would have taken it right from the beginning of the season and kept it up to the end'.

5

Professional debut in Europe, a winning start

Despite the fact that he was returning to France to make his professional debut and would have to compete against the best cyclists in the world, Shay was not as nervous as he had been the previous year. He had already spent a year in the country, he had made some friends and was becoming more and more proficient in the language. His performances of the previous season also gave him confidence that he would not be out of his depth.

After meeting his new team at the traditional training camp on the Côte d'Azur, Shay was given his schedule for the season. He would start off with a couple of races in Algeria, before returning to the South of France. Weigant informed him that they were not expecting him to make an immediate impact, as it was only his first season.

During his first few weeks with the team Shay made the acquaintance of Jean Stablinski, the son of a Polish immigrant who had started work in the coal mines in Valenciennes at the age of 15. His father had been shot by the Germans during the war. After the war Stablinski's mother had to work long hours to keep her family fed. Unbeknown to her, a young Jean took it upon himself to advertise for a stepfather in a newspaper for Polish immigrants in France, and his ploy was successful, as his mother did actually marry one of the men who replied, a widower with a daughter. Not only that, Jean would end up marrying the daughter of his new stepfather.

Stablinski's actual name was Edward Stablewski. Stablewski became Stablinski, as French journalists found it too difficult to pronounce his real name, but where the Jean came from remains a mystery. He was not the only French cyclist of that era of Polish origin: there was also Roger Walkowiak and Jean Graczyk. Stablinski would play an important part throughout Shay's racing career, and in his private life.

Perhaps the most recognisable cyclist on the Helyett team was Jean Robic, who had won the Tour de France in 1947. He was well past his best by the time Shay became his team-mate, but would have had invaluable knowledge to pass on to the younger cyclists on the team, including Shay, the only non-Frenchman on the team. However, Robic had a notorious reputation for being cantankerous, and he was nearly as famous for his extensive knowledge of expletives as he was for his Tour win. His diminutive stature (1.61m, 60kg) and appearance was encapsulated in the nickname, 'the hobgoblin of the Brittany moor'. After fracturing his skull in 1944 he always wore a trademark leather crash helmet.

Shay's first race as a professional was the Criterium d'Oran in Algeria. It was not an auspicious beginning: he punctured and retired. The original intention had been that after this race the Helyett team would return to the South of France for a week's training, and come back the following weekend for two more races. Algeria had been a French colony since early in the nineteenth century, but now, with a growing independence movement, the OAS, it was considered dangerous for the team to spend unnecessary time there. By 1962 the OAS would blow up petrol storage tanks in the port of Oran, and leaving the city in flames. However, Stablinski, rather than going back to France for just a week, thought that cycling the 550 kilometres from Oran to Algiers would be better training, and Shay decided to join him. They forwarded their suitcases by train, carrying just the minimum on their backs, ate couscous, slept rough and covered the distance to the capital in two days. Stablinski spoke of this trip across the desert as the start of their friendship, as not only did he find the Irishman good company, but also that they shared a passion for hunting and fishing. And he was right about it being good training: at the weekend Shay won on the Saturday and Stablinski on the Sunday.

Shay and Stablinski were accompanied on their *cyclo-sportif* through the desert by the Belgian champion, Emiel van Cauter, and an Algerian cyclist, Mohamed Belkacemi. Van Cauter would never fulfil the promise he had shown early on in his career, when he won the 1954 World Amateur Championship and then the Belgian professional title the following year. He would later go on to establish a successful professional team in the early 1970s, before being murdered in Bangkok in 1975 (where it was rumoured that he'd upset some criminal gang).

More significant for Shay was the fact that he also made the acquaintance of Jean Bobet during his trip to Algeria. Jean was the younger brother of multiple Tour winner, Louison Bobet, and he and

Shay would go on to become firm friends. Bobet had studied English in Aberdeen, so he was one of the few members of the peloton who could converse with Shay in his first language. His first impression of Shay was that the Irishman looked more like a rugby player than a bike rider: 'He wasn't fat, but not thin either and this was an advantage for cold, rainy, poor weather conditions.' Within three months of having raced in Algeria, Jean Bobet would find himself back in the French colony, conscripted to the French army, and would spend the remainder of the year fighting in North Africa.

The 200-kilometre Grand Prix de l'Echo d'Alger was Shay's first professional win. Bernard Gauthier ('Monsieur Bordeaux–Paris' as he was known) had gone clear, and André Darrigade, the current French champion, went after him, followed by Shay and Jacques Dupont. They caught Gauthier after 140 kilometres, and Dupont was dropped soon afterwards. The other three stayed away until the end. Darrigade led the other two onto the cement track in Algiers, where Shay was easily able to come around him for the victory.

It was a victory that did not go unnoticed. In *Miroir Sprint* the famous cycling journalist, and founder of the Grand Prix des Nations time trial, Albert Baker d'Isy, tipped Shay to be amongst the protagonists in that year's Paris–Roubaix. And in the same magazine Charles Pelissier wrote glowingly of Shay, comparing him favourably to Pierre Brun. Brun had been one of the top amateurs in France in the preceding years, winning a number of important classics, but who'd not fulfilled his potential as a professional. Shay, however, would succeed where Brun had not, Pelissier felt, because he'd never seen a man so determined to succeed.

Three days later, back across the Mediterranean, Shay took part in the Grand Prix de Saint Raphaël. This was one of the oldest of the early season races, as many of the teams would be finishing their training camps nearby. At the time teams would generally have just one such training camp, unlike nowadays when teams have several camps, beginning before Christmas. It was another good performance by Shay. In a very close finish he was beaten by Jacques Dupont, but to most observers the Irishman was the moral winner. Shay had been in a 50-kilometre break with three others, and Dupont had only got across to them by taking pace from a fire engine. A group of six, including Dupont, had sat in behind the fire engine, which had passed the peloton and followed it all the way up to the break. In protest, almost all the remainder of the peloton had pulled out – there were only thirteen finishers. Jean Stablinski completed the podium. Amongst those who had withdrawn from the race was Louison Bobet, The triple Tour de France winner Bobet, reflecting on Shay's impressive early season performances, remarked afterwards, 'Elliott will give us all plenty of trouble this summer'.

The Press also took note of Shay's debut. After the Grand Prix St. Raphaël Michel Costes, cycling correspondent of the large circulation French daily, *Paris Presse*, spoke about the cycling world's enthusiasm for Shay Elliott's great showing in his first few races as a professional. 'In Elliott,' he wrote, 'Ireland has a professional cyclist of the greatest class.'

The following weekend Shay was again on top of the podium, winning the Grand Prix Catox. This was a 227-kilometre race run off in high winds in Marseilles, and he sprinted home, winning easily from Cieleska, at the head of a 17-strong group, which included Jean Robic, with the peloton nine minutes behind. This win was all the more noteworthy because it was Shay's longest ever race.

Shay's first big test of the year was Paris–Nice, a race which would become a successful hunting ground for Irishmen in later years: Stephen Roche won there, and Sean Kelly set an astonishing record of seven successive victories. It was generally considered by the top professionals that up until this point in the season all the races had been training races. In his first 'Race to the Sun', as Paris–Nice was nicknamed, Shay achieved some good stage placings – third on the second stage, and seventh the next day. The fourth day consisted of a 56-mile road race in the morning from Nîmes to Apt, where Shay finished third, in the same time as winner, Camille Huyghe, and a 32-kilometre time trial in the afternoon, where again he was third. On the final stage, however, he crashed when lying third overall, lost 20 minutes, and was denied a podium finish in Nice. He was not alone to suffer this misfortune: Jacques Anquetil, on whom the French press had been so focussed also crashed, on the third stage and abandoned the race.

When Shay started his professional career in the same team as Anquetil, the Frenchman was still part of the French Army. The army looked kindly on him, and gave him carte blanche to train and race as much as he wanted. His performances were good publicity for an Army which in recent years had been having a tough time. Morale was very low amongst their ranks. It was not that long since the German army had overrun their country, there had been a catastrophe at Dien Bien Phu in Indochina, and now trouble was starting in Algeria. The authorities felt that it would improve morale if the soldiers saw one of their own winning at the highest level.

The week after finishing Paris–Nice Shay travelled back up North to the capital to take part in a track meeting at one of the Vélodromes where he had performed so admirably the previous year, the Vél d'Hiv. Shay and his Spanish partner, Miguel Poblet, were narrowly beaten by the Swiss pairing of Oscar Plattner and Rolf Graf. In the 4-event omnium the Swiss duo beat Shay and Poblet by two points. They had won two of the events during the meet, the elimination race and the 10-kilometre derny race. Shay had ridden despite still suffering from the injuries he had received on the final stage of Paris–Nice.

Shay's impressive performances were helping the cause of Irish cycling no end, as in April an Irish team was invited to compete in the Route de France in late June. The Irish team did not include Shay, obviously, as he was now a professional, but the race organisers made it clear that the invitation had been issued because of his performances over the previous two years: 'the brilliant riding of Shay Elliott in the Route de France and his subsequent great form as an amateur and professional was the primary reason for the invitation to the Irish'.

Shay recovered sufficiently from his injuries to take part in Paris–Roubaix, as part of a field that included stars such as Fausto Coppi, Louison Bobet, Ferdi Kubler, Hugo Koblet and Stan Ockers amongst the 177 starters in the 252-kilometres race. A first-year professional in such elevated company, and riding for the first time on serious *pavé*, he would not be amongst the finishers of the 'Hell of the North'.

But he was back to winning ways when he took a win in a stage of the Tour du Sud-Est. This eight-day event served as a warm-up race for the Tour de France. On the third stage, from Avignon to Nîmes, Shay got away from the bunch with two others and sprinted in ahead of them at the finish. Perhaps partly as a consequence, it was announced a few days later that he would start the Tour de France as a member of the Ile-de-France team. Many experts considered the Tour de France to be too arduous for first-year professionals to undertake, and that it would do them more harm in the long run, as they could burn out. However, the management team were not concerned. Shay had shown that he was stronger than most new professionals, and they didn't believe it would be a problem for him. In his last race before *La Grand Boucle*, Shay finished a strong seventh in Paris–Bourges, a very competitive and tough event which attracted the top teams from France and elsewhere in Europe.

There was no clear favourite for the 1956 Tour de France as a number of previous winners, including Louison Bobet and Jean Robic, were missing due to injuries. The absence of Shay's trade team-mate Robic would give him more opportunities to race for himself, and while he was not expected to feature well in the overall classification, many felt he was capable of winning a stage. Unfortunately however, he went into the Tour with an aggravated knee injury stemming from a crash in a race in Copenhagen, shortly beforehand. On the opening stage from Reims to Liège, Shay was dropped and finished well behind the winner, André Darrigade. He struggled again the following day to Lille, getting dropped again.

Despite receiving treatment before and after each stage, his knee continued to swell and he finally abandoned 75 kilometres into the fourth stage. He said afterwards that without the knee trouble, he felt he could have done well. 'The Tour should suit me,' he added.

That year's Tour was won by the little known French rider, Roger Walkowiak, who some critics deemed to be unworthy of winning the yellow jersey. This unjust criticism affected him badly, and he retired a few years afterwards. He opened a bar shortly after his retirement, but became disillusioned when even customers claimed he should not have won the Tour. He sold his bar and started work in a factory, yet another of cycle racing's many sad stories.

Shay bounced back from his Tour disappointment in magnificent style when he won the Prix de Montsauche near Dijon later in July. One French daily described his win as a 'remarkable achievement' because he'd won after a 150-kilometre lone breakaway, which was made all the more difficult by the heavy rain and showers. The next day he was selected as the first ever Irish representative in the World Professional Road Race Championships. One of Shay's adversaries from when he had raced back in Ireland, Jim McQuaid, who was representing Ireland on the track, would also act as the team manager for the Championships in Copenhagen. Before the Worlds Shay scored another fine win in the French semi-classic Grand Prix d'Isbergues.

In his first professional World Championship road race, Shay finished a very creditable fourteenth, one place ahead of Fausto Coppi. The 283-kilometre race, which consisted of 22 laps of the narrow Ballerup circuit, was won by Rik van Steenbergen, with another Belgian, Rik Van Looy, in second place. Of the 71 riders who started the race, only half of them finished. Shay had put up a good performance, particularly towards the end of the race. He even got clear on his own on the sixteenth lap, but was reeled in a lap later by the bunch led by the Belgian team. At the finish he slipped back from the leading group of 11 riders who sprinted for the win in the pouring rain. The Belgians showed their dominance by taking five of the top six places.

Shay had originally intended to ride the professional pursuit race on the track also, but pulled out due to tiredness. So, his final appearance that season was at a track meeting at the Parc des Princes track in Paris. He won the 5,000 metres pursuit, beating Claude le Ber comfortably in a time of 6'–27".

He returned to Ireland at the end of the season, staying with his parents and spending a lot of his time hunting. He could be well pleased with his first year as a professional: he had amassed five wins and, over the course of the season, earned £1,500. He told the *Evening Press* cycling correspondent that his one major disappointment had been at the World Championships. He said that he had felt great at the start of the race, and been extremely confident until he punctured about 80 kilometres from the end and was given the wrong spare bike. 'I just couldn't ride it,' he said. 'And when the time came to make my winning break I missed it and accordingly, a much higher place than fourteenth.'

Shay was interviewed again by the *Evening Press* before returning to the continent after his Christmas holiday in Ireland. This time he spoke of his optimism for the coming season. His hopes included winning one of the really big classic races in France, and possibly the 550-kilometre Bordeaux–Paris. After that race, he hoped to take good form into the Tour de France which would start shortly afterwards.

*   *   *   *

At the beginning of 1957 Shay returned to France to spend time at a training camp in the south of the country, where the weather would be more suitable. He learned that he had been transferred to the sister team of Essor, which was sponsored by the bicycle manufacturer Helyett. Amongst his team-mates were André Darrigade, considered by many to have been the best French road sprinter ever, and Jacques Anquetil.

He also learned, at a meeting called by the management of the Helyett, about the strict hierarchy of the team. It was explained in no uncertain terms that every rider was there to serve the emerging star, Anquetil. After his excellent first professional season Shay naively felt that he might be one of the protected riders, but this idea was extinguished before the season had even started. Shay would not be going for the win in any race, unless he was to be given the green light by Anquetil.

In his first race of 1957 Shay finished third in the 104-mile Grand Prix de Monaco, behind Gilbert Bauvin of Belgium and former Tour winner, Louison Bobet. He did well in his next race also, just missing out on a podium place in the Grand Prix de Nice, which Brian Robinson won, ahead of Louison Bobet. Guests of honour at the start of that race were Prince Rainier and Princess Grace, who had married the previous year. The couple were introduced to some of the cyclists, and Princess Grace was particularly interested in speaking to Shay. She had a keen interest in sport, as her father was the celebrated rower and triple Olympic gold medallist Jack Kelly. Grace, whose grandparents had emigrated from County Mayo in the 1800s, was also intrigued by the fact that an Irishman was competing in this sport.

Although Shay finished well down on general clasification in his first big challenge of the year, Paris–Nice, the race was a great success for him. He helped his team-mate Anquetil win overall, and his own consistency earned him the green jersey for winning the points competition. Anquetil had just been discharged from the French army, where he'd been fulfilling his obligatory National Service, and he had started the race three kilos overweight. Shay, on the other hand, was in fine fettle: 'I felt on top of my form, and could have done better if the weather had not been as warm.'

Shortly afterwards Shay wrote to the *Evening Press* about his satisfaction with his early season form, but saying that he had not yet reached his peak. He also spoke of his expectations of winning one of the big classics. This may have been considered youthful exuberance by some, but given his performances to date, it would not have been too big a surprise to see the young professional pulling off such a win.

In fact, it seemed as if it might happen in the first classic of the season, the Het Volk. Shay was away in a race-long break with Brian Robinson, and it was only near the finish in Ghent that they were finally caught. There was some consolation for the pair: they won a lot of primes, and Shay still managed to hang for seventh place.

He was seventh also in the Tour of Flanders and, a week later, eighteenth of the 146 starters in Paris–Roubaix. He finished in the group sprinting for second place behind Fred de Bruyne, who, having won the week before, completed the Flanders-Roubaix double. Shay's form was good and he was learning all the time.

After this foray in the northern classics, Shay went back home to Paris for a short break and, while there, he won the Gentleman's Grand Prix in the Eastern suburbs of Paris. A Gentleman's race is a two-up time trial, usually over 25 kilometres, in which each pair comprises a professional and an enthusiastic (sometimes middle-aged) amateur. Shay and his partner were nearly a minute clear of the runners-up. Shay also had another couple of more serious wins, shortly afterwards, in the Grand Prix de Boussac and the Circuit de la Vienne.

His training rides were now steadily increasing in length in preparation for the marathon Bordeaux–Paris. Two weeks prior to the big race, he took part in Paris–Limoges, a race which, at 392 kilometres, served as ideal preparation for the Bordeaux race. He finished in seventh position, as part of a group sprinting for fourth place, just four seconds behind the winner, René Privat.

On the first Sunday of June, at 4 o'clock in the morning, Shay lined up alongside thirteen others for the start of the mammoth ride to Paris. The race was 551 kilometres in length, of which the last 258 kilometres, from Chatellerault, were ridden behind derny motorcycles. It was a race that all the top riders wanted on their palmarès, and it was really popular amongst the French public. It was estimated that two million people would line the race route, and 30,000 would pay to see the finish at Parc des Princes. The prize money was also good, with the winner taking home £1000, a huge amount of money at that time.

Shay was well to the fore during the first half of the race. In fact, after 320 kilometres, he, along with Brian Robinson, was only 40 seconds behind the leader, Albert Bouvet, and, in turn, 20 seconds ahead of the main group. This was the high point of the race for Shay; after that he struggled and finally dropped out at Ablis, having covered 480 kilometres. The Belgian classics specialist, Rik Van Looy, was also among those to abandon the race. Ten out of the fourteen starters would finish, and, for the fourth time, Bernard Gauthier finished first, in front of a large crowd in the Parc des Princes. It had taken him over fifteen hours to cover the route.

Brian Robinson reached Paris, but was unclassified, as he and Frenchman Nicolas Barone arrived after the gates to the Vélodrome had been closed. Shay was disappointed at not finishing Bordeaux–Paris. He had some slight compensation the following weekend when he won a criterium in Langon, but he would never again attempt the 'Derby of the Road'.

Shay didn't take part in the Tour that year. He would have been in the Luxembourg-Mixed team with Brian Robinson, if he had ridden, but he was discouraged by his team management. They felt he needed a rest after such a hectic season. In the end only one of the Luxembourg-Mixed team would make it to the finish in Paris. It was a pretty makeshift team: in January, Brian Robinson had resorted to placing an advertisement in *Cycling* magazine, looking for riders from Britain to join him in forming the mixed team to compete in that year's Tour de France!

Shay abandoned his next big race, and with his current lack of form decided he needed further rest and would not take part in the World Championships. The rest seemed to do him good because he bounced back towards the end of the season with some good performances, including a win in the Semaine Bretonne (Brittany Week).

Shortly after this, Shay again returned to Ireland for his winter break. While at home he presented the prizes at Bray Wheeler's club dinner at the International Hotel. He was also invited to Belfast as guest of honour at the Northern Ireland Cycling Federation's annual dinner and presentation of awards. In an interview at the awards, he pledged to do all in his power to help and encourage any Irishman, either from Ulster or the South, who wanted to try his hand in Belgium or France.

As in the previous winter, reporters from the local Press came knocking at his door. During one of his interviews he spoke about life in the peloton, revealing that the rider he admired most was Fausto Coppi, and he considered the Tour of Flanders to be the most difficult race that he had competed in, because of the cobbled hills and the quality of the field that took part in the race. He also spoke of his hopes for raising the popularity of cycling in Ireland by winning top races and by gaining lots of press coverage back home, in much the same way that Ronnie Delany had done for athletics after his gold medal in the 1500 metres at the 1956 Olympics.

Apart from the speed with which he had learnt the French language, Shay had also been quick to embrace other aspects of the country's culture. He appreciated French food, wine and music. His assimilation was also noticed at home. He called in on his old friend Billy Long during his stay at home. 'Shay parked outside in a big Peugeot, was dressed in a smart suit and looked every inch the star,' Billy remembered. He invited Shay in to meet his mother, who was originally from Lille. Shay engaged her in conversation – in French. She couldn't believe that this was the same Shay she remembered from before. 'He was such a gentleman,' she said.

That winter he was also involved in a crash with a van in Delgany in Wicklow. Both drivers claimed that the other was in the wrong, and they came to blows. The van driver was accused of assault, and when the case came to court his description of Shay was read aloud: 'He seemed like a kind of foreigner, but he spoke with a Dublin accent.'

Shortly after Christmas Shay returned to France. His pre-season training would typically start off with easy spins of 50 to 70 kilometres. He'd do this three or four times a week, at about 30kph. Only later would he build up the length of these training rides until he was covering distances of over 300 kilometres.

But first was the Simplex training camp on the Côte d'Azur. Jacques Anquetil, André Darrigade and Jean Stablinski were there, amongst many other seasoned riders. In that company Shay was confident that he could build on the successes he'd had in his first two seasons as a professional. Now, with added experience and strength, he was confident that 1958 would be his best season to date.

6

Love, near misses and glory

Shay's 1958 early season started very well as most years of his professional career would. In his first race he took third place in the Grand Prix St. Raphaël, followed by second in the Grand Prix de Nice, a race he more often than not excelled in. This was one of the tougher and more prestigious 'training' races, and although 'only' second this year he would take his revenge in the not too distant future.

Following these fine performances it wasn't surprising Shay had his first victory of the season in the Grand Prix Sigrand, organised three days after the Grand Prix de Nice and held on similar roads. Shay was on great form that day finishing 25 seconds ahead of his team-mate Joseph Mirando, who had won the Grand Prix Frejus six days earlier and was in the best form of his up and down career.

The on-form Irishman was then, not unexpectedly, selected for Paris-Nice. He showed good condition yet again and came close to a stage victory on several occasions. On the second stage Shay finished 5th to one of the world's fastest sprinters, the Belgian Willy Vannitsen, who also won the next day. However, the leading group on that second stage was very selective and was to have a great bearing on the final standings, with Shay now in the top ten in the overall classification. The next day's individual time trial, the first of two stages that day, was easily won by his team leader Anquetil, but the French star was out of contention overall. Second place went to Belgian classics star Fred De Bruyne who, although well beaten by Anquetil, took the race lead, which he never relinquished. It was the biggest stage-race win in his great career. Shay came close to victory in the afternoon when he finished second to Spanish fast-man, Miguel Poblet, as part of a four-man break, 38 seconds ahead of the peloton.

His aggressive form was still evident the next day, but he was just beaten again by the very strong French rider Fernand Picot. Shay finished ninth overall, just over eight minutes behind De Bruyne. This turned out to be his highest ever placing in Paris-Nice, a race in which he had come so very close to a stage victory on so many occasions, but the elusive win was never to be, despite the fact that he'd collected the points competition the previous year.

Shay's heart was set, however, on one or other of the biggest classics, the first of which was Milan-San Remo, taking place on March 19th, St. Joseph's day, and a very important national holiday in Italy at that time. On a cool Wednesday morning 215 riders set out from Milan to compete in *la Primavera* (nowadays the race is held on a Saturday, but still around the same date). Not unusually, and especially in such a very long race, an early break escapes for many miles. This edition was no different and a group went clear, but it gradually disintegrated as they tackled the climbs along the Ligurian coast until one man remained ahead, the Frenchman, René Privat, a consistent and talented rider, who on his day could beat the best riders around. Behind him, a group of seven riders, which included Shay and Belgian star Rik Van Looy, distanced themselves from the peloton and set off in strong pursuit of Privat. For a while it seemed like the race would be between the lone leader and the posse of pursuers. Unfortunately for Shay, the main field sensed the acute danger and chased all the riders down. The courageous Privat, left on his own, capitulated just four kilometers from the finish after being in the lead or part of the leading break for over 260 kilometers. This experience certainly helped him towards his day of glory in the race two years later. Just 69 riders came together at the finish on the Via Roma and, despite his earlier efforts, Van Looy still had the strength to win from two of the world's best sprinters, Miguel Poblet and André Darrigade. Shay finished in the bunch equal 10th, very disappointed, but confirming at least his very good early season form was still there.

Elliott and his team then moved on to Belgium to start their Northern classics campaign and on Easter Sunday assembled for Ghent–Wevelgem. Together with the following day's Het Volk, points would be awarded for finishers of both races, and the best points scorer overall would win the Trofee van Vlaanderen – the Flanders Trophy. There was also a King of the Mountains classification over the two races. These races would be further evidence of Shay's ability over the unforgiving cobbled roads of Flanders. These two major international semi-classics, although not as prestigious as the Tour of Flanders, were very important in their own right, as they still are to this day.

Before the start Shay was asked by Jock Wadley of *Sporting Cyclist* magazine, if he would attack. 'I hope so,' he replied, 'but with a field of

200 riders, a lot depends on how you get away.' He then took a newspaper from the reporter, and stuffed it under his many layers of clothing as additional protection against the bitter cold.

The Ghent–Wevelgem started on the main and very windy road towards the North Sea coast, and Shay got in an early break of 23 riders, which also included Raphaël Géminiani. They turned left when they reached the coast, which gave them a favourable tailwind. This helped the break to increase its lead to over two minutes. Shay was putting in big turns at the front as they headed towards the half-way point. The roads worsened as they passed through towns made famous by the tragic and futile battles of World War I, towns such as Passchendale and Ypres, but he often excelled in these difficult conditions.

Shay was riding strongly and feeling good and he took the maximum points at the top of the first big climb of the day, the Mont Noir, as well as the 1,000 francs prize that went with it. He had a decent lead at the top, and could have continued on a solo break. However, he needed the help of the others to reach the next hill, the Kemmelberg. Shay also topped this climb in first place. Heading towards the last climb of the day, the chasing group, including Rik Van Looy, was starting to make serious inroads into the lead of Shay and the others. Sensing the danger, the Belgian, Noël Fore, attacked out of the leading group on the last climb and stayed clear to the finish. Despite being caught by Van Looy's group, Shay still managed to finish seventh on the airfield at Wevelgem.

He started the next day in Het Volk as clear leader of the 'hills' classification, and could only lose if one rider from the early breakaway won all three primes, which wasn't to happen. Future Tour de France runner-up, Joseph Planckaert, broke away very strongly six kilometres from the finish to win the semi-classic, with Shay in the first group equal 12th place.

His very aggressive two days of work earned him over £150. By racing for the primes he may have scuppered his chances of winning either race. Equally, he may have decided that it was a safer bet to aim for the hills classification than risk trying to win the races, and taking home nothing. Cycling was a job, after all, whereby a cyclist had to maximise his earning potential, and in any case, there would be other days.

The money that could be earned from cycling in the late 1950s was nothing like it is now, and it was only really in the top echelons of the sport where earnings were substantial. Many lesser known riders could expect to earn no more than a few pounds a week, which was barely enough to live on. Shay of course would be more sought after by race promoters because of his fine performances, and he could expect to receive £40 or £50 starting fee for contracted races. While this was substantially more than an ordinary *domestique*, it was considerably less than the big stars received. Louison Bobet, for example, despite his very best years being behind him, was still a huge attraction to race promoters and could still command fees of £300 and upwards for starting certain races. Prizes for major races varied, depending on the stature of the event. For one of the big classics the winner could sometimes expect to receive between £400 and £500. He would often receive a victory bonus from his sponsor, which, depending on his contract, could be a substantial sum. Criteriums and 'exhibition' races would often pay very well. Usually a lot of the fees and prizes would be divided among the team in major races, or shared among the riders who accompanied the bigger stars to the smaller, but nonetheless lucrative races.

Shay's next major classic was Paris–Roubaix and it turned out to be the start of one of the most disappointing episodes in his career. He had managed to stay with the lead group over the infamous cobbled sections, and in the last hour of racing he had enough strength left to attack alone when team-mate Anquetil had been hauled back after a long solo breakaway. With about 10 kilometres to go Shay was still in the lead; then his saddle broke. He was forced to sit on the bare metal frame, but couldn't sustain this unorthodox position for any length of time, so he rode out of the saddle for the remainder of the race. This difficult position caused him, not unexpectedly, to cramp. Yet, despite this, he still finished a remarkable 20th, in the same time as the Belgian winner Leon Van Daele.

His misfortune continued the following weekend in Paris–Brussels. Again Shay was away on his own, with 40 seconds advantage on three others, and a sure winner with just one and a half kilometres to go. Then his front forks broke. The rules of the time meant that he was not allowed to change to a new bike from the following team car, and he borrowed a bicycle from a priest who was spectating, and finished on that, but not before the classics specialist, Rik Van Looy, had broken away from the chasers to take the win. A bitterly disappointed Shay finished in the peloton in 28th position, over a minute behind. There would have been no way he would have been caught with a lead as large as that, and with only 1500 metres left. In a matter of eight days Shay had come so close to wins in two of the biggest races of the year. A win in either would have elevated him to the ranks of the very best in the sport, in addition to leaving him much better off financially. He would also have received a lot more protection from his team in future races.

In the dressing rooms afterwards, where he was still within earshot of Van Looy's raucous supporters, Shay was inconsolable: 'I lost Paris-Brussels, 500,000 francs and my morale. I want to hang up the bicycle and return home to Dublin.'

Shay didn't return to Dublin though, and his good form ensured that he was selected as team captain for the Helyett-Leroux team for the Flèche Wallonne and Liège-Bastogne-Liège weekend. Flèche Wallonne took place on the Saturday, and Shay did not finish. The next day turned out to be a particularly tough edition of Liège-Bastogne-Liège, in which only 34 of the 189 starters finished. Shay did well to come home in 15th place in this especially tough edition of the race.

Despite the good form that he had shown all season, Shay still hadn't won much, but this would change in his next race. The Four Days of Dunkirk was a very hard event in Northern France which had quickly gained in prestige. On the first stage Shay missed the important breakaway which gained over a minute on the peloton, and it was his team-mate, André Darrigade, who took the leader's jersey. On the second, 234-kilometre stage, Shay this time did manage to go clear, in a small group which formed after only 18 kilometres and which stayed away to the finish. He punctured, but was able to regain this break. Then, with 40 kilometres remaining, he took off on his own, and hung on for a fine victory.

The following day he won again, and this time took over the leader's jersey. This third stage was known as 'the stage of the Monts (hills)' due to the number of difficult climbs the riders had to negotiate. On the historic Kemmelberg, a number of men went clear, and an in-form Shay bridged across to them. As team-mate André Darrigade was still overall leader when the stage started, he was able to sit in, and finally win the group sprint quite easily.

Although he now had an overall lead of nearly a minute, with only one stage left to race, Shay was resigned to not winning the race. Unfortunately for him, that final stage was a 77-kilometre individual time-trial, and he had no illusions that his two minutes advantage over his team leader, Jacques Anquetil, would be anything like sufficient. 'Jacques will take four or five minutes off me, and I can do nothing about it,' he said. If anything his prediction was an underestimate: he lost more than five minutes, despite Anquetil having to change his bicycle twice. However, Shay finished a fine sixth overall, and he did have the consolation of winning the points competition, while his Helyett team won the team competition.

In late June, after a good performance in the Grand Prix du Midi Libre, where he'd finished fifth overall (and second on one stage), Shay travelled north to Brussels for the start of the Tour de France. He'd been selected for the International team, and for company he would have three Britons – Brian Robinson, Stan Brittain and Ron Coe – two Portuguese, four Danes and two Austrians, one of whom, Adolf Christian, had finished third the previous year. He was to share a room with Brian Robinson during the race. The team wore plain white jerseys, Shay's with an Irish tricolour stitched on the front. It was a team without any clear leader, which, arguably, gave each of them more of an opportunity to race for himself. This was Shay's second Tour and his ambitions were to finish the race, and to win a stage. Both ambitions seemed strong possibilities.

If their team might have seemed to lack cohesion with riders from so many different countries, it would not be the only one. There was considerable friction within the French camp prior to the start of the Tour, and they were all of one nationality. Anquetil declared that he didn't want both Louison Bobet and Shay's future *directeur sportif*, Raphaël Géminiani, on the same team as him. The French manager, Marcel Bidot, gave in to Anquetil's demands, and selected Bobet. Géminiani was enraged, and prior to the start of that year's race, a fan presented him with the gift of a donkey. Gem named the donkey 'Marcel'.

Shay did complete the Tour, and if ever there was a race that really showed his true strength of character and his courage, the 1958 Tour de France was it. During the race he would crash several times, suffer umpteen punctures, and also come down with bronchitis and dysentery. He came close to the hoped for stage win on a number of occasions, but he was repeatedly denied: once he was pulled back by his jersey; another time he was delayed at a closed level crossing; and then there was more than his share of mechanical trouble. A weaker and less determined man might have used all these problems as excuses, but Shay never did.

In the early stages he took advantage of the freedom of not having to work for a team leader and showed his good condition. He comfortably took the bunch sprint for seventh position on the first stage from Brussels to Ghent, which was won by Darrigade, his trade team-mate. He'd fallen halfway through the stage, but luckily suffered only a cut knee. 'Maybe I'll feel it later,' he said, 'but I must say that today I hardly noticed it.' Coming into Ghent he jumped clear of the pack that was chasing a six-man break. 'Maybe, I won only a few seconds,' he commented, 'but I've an overall good position.'

The next day, back on French soil, Shay improved on his fifth place to finish third on the stage. He'd managed to get into a break which had gone clear at the day's feeding station, at Roulers. Together, his group built up a lead of two minutes until, shortly before Dunkirk, the same town where he'd taken two wins earlier in the season, they were held up at a level crossing and caught by the peloton. The commissaires had noted the time difference, and intended to allow the lead group to set off with their original lead, but the fast moving main bunch simply ignored the 'request', and Shay and his escape group found themselves back with the peloton – all their good work gone for nothing. However, shortly afterwards, another group went clear and again Shay, determined he wouldn't be shortchanged after his previous effort, joined the break, and this time they did stay away to the end.

It was a very hectic sprint finish with a considerable amount of switching and pushing, and Shay was beaten by Voorting of Holland and the Italian Baffi, both of whom were known as exceptionally strong sprinters. Afterwards, Shay complained that he'd been blocked by the Belgian and Dutch riders in the break, and had even had his jersey pulled to prevent him from winning. This was quite likely the truth: with Shay being on his own, and a non–Continental to boot, he would still have been treated as an outsider who hadn't weaved his way into the fabric of Continental cycling, despite his *palmarès*.

Jock Wadley, following the Tour and writing reports for his magazine, had known Shay from the time he had first moved to the Continent. He had observed his transformation over a number of years, from a shy Irish teenager to somebody who had adopted French culture so readily. Despite his immersion in all things French, Wadley noticed that Shay had not forgotten his roots, as he wrote of him after one particular stage: 'This cyclist who now never eats potatoes, or cabbage; who drinks red wine but seldom touches tea; who can't be bothered to speak anything but French – wasn't it nice to find him listening to the soft music from Radio Eireann, which by some happy chance was broadcasting "Mother Mo Chroi" (a traditional Irish song) as I peeped in to his room to say goodnight.'*

---

* As a teenager Shay had a fine voice, and Nell felt that he had a potential singing career, and should have singing lessons. Jim was having none of it, and wanted his son to concentrate on racing instead.

Shay came close again on the 223-km stage to Saint Brieuc. He escaped with twelve others near the finish, and after a tough last five kilometres, mostly uphill, he was passed by the very fast Belgian Martin Van Geneugden, almost on the line. This time he did lodge a complaint that he had been impeded by Van Geneugden and his fellow Belgian, Gilbert Desmet (1), who finished fourth. After studying a film of the finish the officials rejected his claims, and confirmed the standings.

On the 7th stage to Brest, the International team finally found success – through Brian Robinson. The Yorkshireman thus became the first English speaker to win a stage of the Tour de France. In a two-up sprint for the line he had apparently been beaten by Arrigo Padovan, but the judges deemed that the Italian had sprinted unfairly – this time it was too obvious to overrule. The Italian was relegated to second, giving the win to Robinson. An historic event in British cycling and one that Elliott was sure he would one day achieve for Ireland.

Robinson, true to his nature, was remarkably self-effacing afterwards: 'I am proud of being the first rider from across the Channel to win a stage of the Tour, but I really should have been the second. The journalists all tell me that Shay Elliott was fouled just as badly yesterday when he finished second at St Brieuc, but the judges wouldn't listen to his protest.'

It was, in fact, fortunate that Robinson had lodged his protest – he'd only done so after some journalist friends of his had urged him to. And, as well as being awarded the stage win, he also won 100,000 francs for being voted the 'most aggressive rider of the day'.

That should have been a cause for general celebration among the Internationals in their hotel that evening, but there was already some dissent among them. That very morning Robinson had been approached by one of the continentals, arguing that the prize money he and Shay had previously won should be divided amongst all the team. Robinson disagreed; he and Shay and the other Britons felt that the other members weren't pulling their weight. They hadn't won a single franc so far, and it didn't look likely that they would either. In fact they were a hindrance: the previous day one of them had been seen helping the peloton that was trying to pull back Shay's breakaway group. Robinson had to threaten to punch him to get him to stop.

Thereafter the Anglo/Irish contingent would eat at their own corner of the team's hotel dinner table each evening. Most of the Danes were eliminated early in the race, but not Hans Andersen, who later admitted that there had been no real cohesion in the International team. 'Elliott,

Robinson and Christian,' he said, 'wouldn't share the prize money with anyone but me because they knew me from previous races. They didn't believe in the other Danes, and I'd have none of that, so we all rode for ourselves.'

Shay performed poorly in the time trial the following day. He blamed it on a crème caramel he'd eaten that morning, too close to the start, which had made him feel sick on the first hill. But he also confessed: 'I hate solitary (time trial) races; they can put my morale down to zero.'

But the next day he bounced back. Still inspired by Robinson's fine performance, Shay got into a seven-man break on the road from Quimper to Saint-Nazaire – a stage of 206 kms. Fortunately this was the winning break; working very well together they gained ten minutes over the bunch. Coming towards the finish, Shay was keeping his eye on André Darrigade, the man he feared most. The group was really moving at the time, when Shay, pushing his 52 x 14 (probably the biggest gear generally used at the time), suddenly found there was no resistance to his pedalling. His free wheel had broken, a mere three kilometres short of the line. His Portuguese team-mate, Antonio Barbosa, who was also in the break, didn't stop to help him, which considering the dissent within the team was understandable. However, with the team car right behind, Shay changed his back wheel and set off after the leaders, but it was to no avail. He finished in seventh position, 12 seconds down.

He did take the 'most unfortunate rider' award, however, but it was very little consolation to the Irishman, and did nothing to alleviate his continuing frustration, for he really felt he could have won the stage and the team prize for the day, which would have amounted to 200,000 francs. Frenchman Darrigade would naturally have been considered a better sprinter, but the other very fast rider from France, Jean Graczyk, was also in the group. The two Frenchmen were both in contention to take the *maillot jaune* that day, and neither wanted the other to take the winner's time bonus. All this would have played into Shay's hands and allowed him some leeway. In fact, after the finish, Graczyk told him that he would gladly have let him win the stage. As it was, in Shay's absence, Darrigade won the stage, and took the yellow jersey. 'This is continuing the bad luck I've had throughout the season,' Shay shrugged.

Considering the season and it ups and downs, at least his form now was excellent and he wasn't going to give up his quest for a Tour stage win. Even if his luck didn't seem to match his good condition, Shay still had his mind on a stage win and he wasn't easily going to deviate from that aim. It wasn't surprising he continued to show his good form the next day, on the 255-km stage to Royan, when he got into a very dangerous break. So dangerous in fact, that the French team manager ordered his team, including Jacques Anquetil no less, to the front in an effort to defend Darrigade's *maillot jaune*. Marcel Bidot had become alarmed at the danger posed by the Irishman and some other possible threats in the break. At one stage Shay was not that far from being the race leader on the road. In the end he finished fourth, but more importantly had moved up to seventh overall. It must have been a difficult time for Shay, being so near to glory but not being able to take the final step up the podium.

As the race entered the Pyrenees, not unexpectedly, Shay started slipping back on general classification – probably as much due to various misfortunes as to lack of climbing talent in the high mountains. The 13th stage, 230 km from Dax to Pau, went over some historic tour climbs, and on the ascent of the Col'Aubisque he punctured. Not only that, he fell on the descent, fortunately only receiving some minor cuts and bruises that wouldn't prevent him continuing. On the Col de Portet d'Aspet he punctured again, only this time his team car was miles behind. The result was that he lost even more time, nearly twelve minutes, although considering the circumstances it was still a fine performance on a very hard stage.

His injuries from the fall came back to haunt him the next day. He struggled on all the climbs on a very tough 127-km stage to Luchon. Fortunately his morale was sufficiently high for him to make a joke of it: 'I climbed slowly and this had an advantage – I had time to look at the beautiful views all along the twisting roads.' Still suffering from his thigh injury, Shay dropped further down the standings on the next stage to Toulouse. Two more punctures didn't help his cause either, and he came in 25 minutes behind the leaders .

After the Pyrenees came two scorching hot days as the Tour traversed the south of the country, heading for what might truly be called a 'race of truth' – the time trial up Mont Ventoux, one of the most feared climbs in France. Shay was not alone in his anxiety about the amount of time that he might lose, not to mention the heat and exposure on this climb. Three years previously Ferdi Kubler had underestimated the Ventoux. After attacking near the start he was soon zigzagging across the road, with saliva dripping from his mouth. He took refuge in a café, and after emerging in a dishevelled state, he set off the wrong way down the mountain. Another rider on the Ventoux that day, Jean Mallejac, fell into boulders at the side of the road, lapsed into semi-consciousness and had to be transferred to a hospital in Avignon. And, of course, in the future it was to take the life of Shay's good friend, Tom Simpson.

Despite his aversion to hot weather, Charly Gaul won the time trial from Federico Bahamontes by 31 seconds; it was an indication of the superiority of these two men on the hardest climbs that third-placed Dotto was almost five minutes slower. Shay finished thirteen minutes down on Gaul and, like his team-mates, complained that their mechanic had put the wrong gear ratio on their machines. It wasn't really that important in the greater scheme of things, however, it was another little upset that could have worn down a lesser man.

As if his troubles hadn't been bad enough, the next day he punctured three times, and to add to his woes, also had a bout of bronchitis. But he wasn't in the mood for quitting. He rode the stage with a plaster on his chest, as he had a bad rash resulting from a fever. 'I don't want to drop out. I want to stay to the end to save the honour of Ireland,' he said.

On an epic Alpine stage from Briançon to Aix-les-Bains, Gaul edged closer to the lead. There was torrential rain on the stage and Shay arrived wet, muddy, with grazed arms and legs in torn shorts and a ripped jersey sticking to his skin, 35 minutes after Gaul's historic victory, which has since gone down in Tour legend. Despite a deep gash on his shoulder, Shay refused any medical attention after his fall. Remarkably he was still upbeat and smiling at the finish: 'Two punctures, a fall and a broken free wheel. I had to change one of the tyres myself as the car was a mile back. I crashed in the mist on the descent of the Luitel. It's a job to say how much time I lost, but I felt pretty good.'

Two days later, Shay, struggling with dysentery, had to stop repeatedly to receive medical attention. He arrived at the finish in Besançon in second to last place. 'I began suffering on the way up the Savine Pass. The doctor gave me some medicine, but it didn't do me any good. The other riders just left me alone behind. I could not accelerate any more,' he explained. 'I had to stop twice to take pills the doctor gave me. It was by far my toughest stage of the Tour – just horrible.'

Despite there being only two stages remaining he was still not confident of finishing the Tour as he spoke of the following day's time trial. 'If I don't feel better, I'll certainly be unable to do it. I may have to drop out, even so close to the finish.'

Shay naturally struggled in the final time trial, still affected by the bout of dysentery and his injuries, and he was caught by the Italian

Nascimbene, who'd started six minutes after him. The threat of inevitable sanctions didn't perturb him from taking shelter behind Nascimbene. 'That's the only way I could possibly have finished,' he said at the end of the stage. 'No strength in the legs at all. I'll be fined and penalised I know, but I'll finish the Tour. I hesitated about whether or not to drop out, but we are so close to the finish, I decided to stay. One more stage,' he grinned as he got off his bike.

Charly Gaul had won the time trial and also taken over the *maillot jaune*, which he held effortlessly the following day into Paris. Shay ended the race in 48th place overall, thus becoming the first Irishman to finish the Tour.

The final stage brought an horrific accident when in the sprint at the Parc des Princes André Darrigade collided with an official who'd strayed on to the track. The 70-year-old sécrétaire-général of the stadium, Constant Wouters, ran across the grass in the centre to prevent photographers encroaching on the track and Darrigade rode into Wouters as he, himself, stepped on to the track. Darrigade escaped relatively unscathed, but the official died in hospital eleven days later.

* * * * *

The month of August was taken up by more criteriums. Shay found himself travelling the length and breadth of France, with occasional sorties beyond her borders. One of those was not a criterium race but a track omnium near Brussels, in which he competed alongside the six-day specialist, Peter Post. The pair easily beat the Belgian duo of Rik Van Looy and Josef Schils, with Anquetil and Darrigade rounding out the top three. The following day he beat the same Belgian pair again, out-sprinting them in a criterium in Zingem. Shay was always great value in these usually well-paid events, and especially so when he felt on good form. He had a great knack for entertainment, and was very popular with the public wherever he raced.

However, competing in criteriums was never seen as ideal preparation for the World Championship Road Race, which at that time was staged at the end of August, or early September. Criteriums were often less than 100 kilometres in length; the World Championship race was well over twice that distance. The tiredness that came from all the travelling to and from the criteriums would not help a cyclist's preparation either. However, these races did ensure good money could be earned, and often it was the case that all your competitors would have similar schedules, so you were not automatically at a disadvantage. But there were always riders who missed out on some of the criterium contracts and trained specifically for the Worlds.

That year the Championships were held in Reims, east of Paris. The Italian Champion and Olympic gold medalist, Ercole Baldini, won the race, while Shay finished in 21st place. Baldini had broken away with three others, including Louison Bobet after only 20 of the 275 kilometres, and built a big lead. Shay had attempted to bridge the gap to the leaders with the help of his trade team-mate, André Darrigade, with three laps to go. However, the bad luck which had dogged him throughout the season struck again as he suffered a bout of cramp on the last lap. He dropped back to the main bunch, while Darrigade continued on, and eventually claimed the bronze medal.

After the Worlds Shay had been invited to London to compete in a one-day track meeting at Herne Hill in South-East London, which would see a team representing Italy taking on a team called 'The Rest'. The Italian 'big names' included the great Fausto Coppi (riding on the eve of his 39th birthday and well past his best, but still a massive star) and the very talented Nino Defillipis, while 'The Rest' comprised Shay, Brian Robinson and two Australians. Coppi had been paid £300, and the crowd of 12,000 had paid an entry fee of £1 10s, which was a significant sum at the time. They were also blessed by a Catholic cardinal prior to the racing, and during a 'tea break' the stars cycled slowly around the track signing autographs.

The day's event involved a pursuit race, a 5-mile points race, a 3-mile scratch race and a 10-kilometre motor-paced race behind Lambrettas. The meeting had been organised by a number of Italian businessmen based in London, and it was said that it was impossible to find an Italian café or restaurant open in the city that day as all the owners and staff had gone to see Coppi at the 'Hill'.

The capacity crowd saw the Italians hold the lead until the last race, the motor-paced event. Going into that final event the Italians were leading the Rest by 25 points to 20, but the Australian 6-day star, Reg Arnold, finished first with Shay second. Coppi just kept Robinson out of third place, but this was still enough for the Rest to overcome their deficit. This track meeting, known today as the 'Coppi Meeting', became part of British cycling racing folklore.

Afterwards, Fausto was taken to an Italian restaurant in London – one that was open. The waiter reported back to the chef that he had just served his last dish to Fausto Coppi; whereupon the chef burst into tears.

Shay was still living with the Tchamassanian family at this time, but he had been looking at a number of properties around Paris over the previous months. One in particular had caught his eye, and upon his return to France he decided to invest his hard-earned savings in a house on the banks of the River Marne. The house was in the high-class residential area of Bry-sur-Marne, and it was valued at more than £5000. The back garden of the house backed onto the river, and Shay even had his own moorings. However, there was quite a deal of work needed on the house, and Shay would not move in until the following year.

All in all it had been a disappointing season for Shay – at least by his standards – but there were at least two things to take heart from: he had ridden and completed the Tour de France and, when he had the form, had demonstrated his potential for future glory; and he was confident that he had what it took to win a single-day Classic.

And one other thing to take heart from – Shay had also started seeing a Parisian girl. An interviewer commented at the end of the season how well Shay spoke French (albeit with a slight accent) and how thoroughly he had adapted to French culture. Shay answered that he intended to remain in France after he retired as 'life was more pleasant there'.

Over the winter he was again somewhat troubled by a pain in his foot, caused by an awkward growth on one of the bones. It was the same injury which the great Italian, Gino Bartali, had suffered from. Of course he hoped the injury wouldn't ruin his 1959 season, as he knew there was so much more to come in his fourth year as a professional.

7

Belgium Classic glory,
'home' win in Isle of Man

At the start of 1959 Shay was determined to make amends for the bad luck of the previous season, when he had come so close to winning a classic. In February he attended a training camp in Nice with Brian Robinson and a group of British cyclists, who were all attempting to gain professional contracts. They were able to get some good mileage in their legs, with the help of the pleasant weather. Once again he would start off his year in North Africa. In his first race, the criterium de *l'Echo d'Oran,* Shay finished well down, but he made up for this with a win in his next race, the Criterium d'Alger.

Upon his return to France his good form continued as he won the Grand Prix de Nice, bettering his performance of the previous year, when he finished second in this race. Again, Shay had set a good ride in Paris–Nice as his first major objective of the season. The organisers of Paris–Nice had taken the unusual step of extending the race in 1959, and it became known as Paris–Nice–Rome, a change that would only last the one year. The winner of the race would be given the task of handing a personal message from the chairman of the Paris Municipal Council to his counterpart in Rome, and another to the Pope.

Cycling is a sport that has traditionally had strong links to the Catholic Church. It has always been popular in the Catholic countries of Europe, such as Spain, Italy, France and Belgium (Ireland being a notable exception) and there are a number of churches, including the chapel of the Madonna del Ghisallo in Lombardy, which are devoted to cycling. One British journalist spoke of cycling as a 'sport of unspoken Catholicism'. Shay would have been honoured to have met the Pope at the end of the race, and it would have given him extra incentive to do well in the race, not that he needed any. He had regularly attended Mass back in Ireland, although this racing schedule had made his more difficult on the continent.

In one of the early stages a bunch of eighty riders arrived together in Moulins, and it was Shay who started the sprint. The Italian rider Favero moved across the road and forced Shay against the barriers. He had to freewheel for 20 metres and take his hands off the bars to ward off Favero. If Shay had been more stubborn and not backed off, it could have resulted in a mass pile-up. He did hang on for fifth, however. Shay was clearly angry after the stage, but he did not lodge a protest. He felt that a protest would not benefit him, as the stage win would still not go to him, but instead to Belgian super sprinter Willy Vannitsen, who was second on the line. Shay said afterwards, 'I know that on form I can beat the best. That's a satisfaction in itself.' The French media praised Shay and criticised the race organisers for not penalising Favero, most probably for political and commercial reasons, as the race was to finish in Italy.

Two days later Shay started to feel feverish and he did not think that he would be able to finish the next day's stage. The following morning he did not feel much better as he had a very high temperature. However, with great difficulty, he managed to hang on though to the end of the stage.

Shay was eventually diagnosed as suffering from bronchitis. He started the next day's stage, against the advice of doctors, but he would eventually pull out after 45 kilometres of the stage. The race had by this stage turned into a battle between Shay's Helyett French team-mate, Jean Graczyk, and Gérard Saint – a the man many considered to be the heir to Jacques Anquetil. Graczyk, upon hearing the news that Shay had pulled out, said, 'What a pity. Elliott is a good team rider and would have worked hard for me, I know'. Shay rested for a few days, and then started training intensely with a view to putting in some good performances in the forthcoming Northern classics.

Paris-Nice-Rome was eventually won by Graczyk, by just fifteen seconds from Gerard Saint, whom Shay had raced against in the Route de France a few years previously. Saint would die tragically the following year in a traffic accident. Only 24 years old, he had already won races such as the Tour of Luxembourg, and finished ninth in the Tour de France and second in the points classification, despite not being a very good sprinter. His death was a sad lost for the French and cycle racing in general..

After Paris–Nice–Rome Shay rested for a few days, but was still feeling the effects in his first classic of the year, Milan San–Remo, and not unsurprisingly he finished well down.

It wasn't too long before he was able to start serious training for the forthcoming Northern classics, beginning with Easter Monday's Tour of Flanders. Starting in Ghent, the race travelled around West Flanders, and finished 242 kilometres later in Wetteren. Shay managed to get into the 18-man winning break which developed after the infamous Muur van Geraardsbergen. Unfortunately, classics specialist Rik Van Looy was also there along with four of his Faema team-mates. Faema marked every attempt by Shay and the others to break away from this group, and towards the end Van Looy went clear with two other Belgians and easily outsprinted them to take the win. Shay's group came in ten seconds later, and he managed to claim ninth place. 'It was useless murdering myself near the finish,' he remarked afterwards. 'I was the only one of my team in the group. Better to get a reasonable place today and hope for better luck next time.'

After Flanders Shay made Lille his base for the next few weeks as he would be racing around that region in all of the Spring classics. Shay's good form continued as he won the Grand Prix de Denain on the Wednesday after the Tour of Flanders. The 150-kilometre inaugural edition of this race was held in the town of Denain, not far from the *pavé* of Paris-Roubaix, and his friend Jean Stablinski was to take third place. Shay had finished alone, half a minute ahead of the rest of the field after a dominating performance.

The following Saturday Shay started Ghent–Wevelgem in a confident mood, only to suffer the misfortune of a broken frame, which forced his elimination. Not finishing Ghent-Wevelgem, however, did not disqualify him from the Flanders weekend; he was still entitled to start the next day in the 210-kilometre Het Volk. The newspaper *Het Volk* had established the race in the previous decade in response to rival daily newspaper *Het Nieuwsblad*'s sponsorship of the Tour of Flanders. Despite being eligible, Shay was uncertain about starting; he simply didn't feel comfortable on the only spare bike available to him.

But in the morning he decided to try out the bike again, by cycling from the team hotel at Courtrai to the start in Wevelgem, and found it more to his liking. He decided to go ahead and start the race at least. And how fortunate that he did.

There was heavy snow during the race, and only 64 of the 175 starters would make it to the finish. Shay, perhaps unexpectedly, found himself in great form, and when the race reached the steep climb of the famous Muur van Geraardsbergen, he was able to drop the entire field, bar one rider, the Belgian Fred de Bruyne. De Bruyne was one of the most formidable classics specialists in the peloton – a previous winner of Milan–San Remo,

Liège–Bastogne–Liège, Paris–Roubaix and the Tour of Flanders. Despite his strong sprint, Shay would clearly have been second favourite in this two-horse race, if the pair made it to the finish together.

Having escaped together, Shay and de Bruyne worked well to stay ahead of the peloton for the final 30 kilometres. Riders of the calibre of Rik Van Looy, Wim van Est and Rik Van Steenbergen were not able to make any impression on their lead. Coming into the finishing straight in Ghent, a few kilometers from De Bruyne's home town of Berlare, Shay managed to force de Bruyne to lead out the sprint. Despite the Belgian's speed, Shay was easily able to get around him to take his first ever classic win, albeit not one of the more established monuments. He had achieved one of his aims for the season, and was delighted after the race, as he talked about his win to journalists. He'd already shown that he was capable of competing with the best on the short climbs or *pavé* of the classics. Now this, he felt, was his breakthrough, and more classic victories would follow.

Shay's win in Het Volk was the first win for a non-Belgian. Fausto Coppi was first over the line in the 1948 edition, but was disqualified for taking a wheel from the Belgian Walschott, who was not on his team. Not only was it Shay's first classic win, but it was also the first ever for an English speaker.

The weekend after Het Volk Shay competed in the classic he most coveted, Paris–Roubaix, but he could only finish in 12th place, just over a minute behind the winner, Belgian Noel Fore. He would have only one more chance that season to win a Spring classic – in Paris–Brussels. However, it was not to be: he badly strained a muscle after a crash early on, in what turned out to be a very competitive race.

Shay's foot injury had resurfaced at this stage, and he underwent surgery to have the growth removed. The surgery was successful, and Shay was not off his bike for long. The rest did him good prior to his next big aim of the season, the Giro d'Italia. He was chosen by Mickey Wiegant to help Anquetil attempt to win the Giro d'Italia for the first time, and thereby become the first Frenchman to win the race. Shay had rested after the classics, and it did him good as he was sixth on the fourth stage. Two days later, on the road to Naples, he got away with the Spaniard, Miguel Poblet. Poblet had won Milan–San Remo earlier in the season, and was known for his fearsome sprint. Shay was not confident of his chances of outsprinting his breakaway companion, so three kilometres from the finish he attacked him. He was still leading 400 metres from the finish, but a sudden bout of cramp gripped his leg, and he was left helpless as Poblet overtook him.

Shay had further misfortune in Ischia a few days later when he suffered a wrist injury in a fall. He spent the remainder of the race riding exclusively for Anquetil. Anquetil could only manage second place overall at the finish in Milan, as the great climber Charly Gaul won the race. Shay finished in 40th place.

The week after the Giro finished Shay flew back home to Dublin to take part in a track meeting being held at Santry stadium. Billy Morton, secretary of the Dublin athletics club, Clonliffe Harriers, had conceived the idea of building a banked tarmac track at Santry, around the outside of the athletics track. This resulted in the track being particularly long at 515 yards. The Guinness brewery had helped to finance the project. Morton, who was noted as being a showman, decided that the opening of the track should be something to remember. He'd asked Shay to help him recruit some famous names to come over, and Shay had duly started signing them up. In addition to Shay there would be Brian Robinson, Fausto Coppi, Albert Bouvet, Roger Hassenforder and André Darrigade. The cycling events would take place over the first two nights, and the athletics events would take centre stage on the third evening. Coppi's efforts for the two nights would pocket him the tidy sum of £400, plus expenses. At this stage Coppi was living on past glories, and was a shadow of his former self. In that year's Tour of Spain he had been the first rider to be dropped every day, and race promoters were reducing the lengths of their races to ensure that he would finish. The other professionals would share £1100 between them.

One of Coppi's conditions was that he should receive payment in advance, which he did. Upon his arrival at Dublin airport he was driven to Groome's Hotel by Jim McQuaid. However, the hotel was not to his liking, as he would have to negotiate stairs to get to his room. The message was sent across to Billy Morton that 'Fausto does not walk up stairs'. Morton was enraged, reacting with, 'Well fuck that pigeon-chested Italian', but he knew he'd have to find Coppi a new hotel or he'd be off with the easiest money he would ever earn. Coppi had not been the only cyclist who had been demanding. Shay had originally persuaded multiple-Tour winner Louison Bobet to take part. Bobet had wanted his trainer and masseur to accompany him, and the organizers to pay their expenses! They agreed to his demands, but in the end Bobet decided not to come to Dublin, without giving any reason.

Gerry Duffin had loaned Coppi his car during his visit, in return for which, Coppi gave him one of his Bianchi bikes. In later years Duffin would sell the bike for £50, which he has always regretted doing. Shay, meanwhile, arrived in Dublin with Brian Robinson. He took the Englishman, his trade team-mate André Darrigade and Coppi to the family home in Kilmacanogue, where they met Jim and Nell. Nell later recounted that she felt weak at the knees when introduced to the great Fausto. Down in the country they also engaged in some clay pigeon shooting. Needless to say, they couldn't resist their competitive streak, and the shoot soon became a competition. Coppi beat Shay into second place, and Robinson was well off the pace.

On the morning of the day that the track was due to be opened there were two explosions at the stadium, which were heard all over North Dublin. They wrecked a portion of the stand and blew a hole in the track. Fortunately, there were no casualties, although some nearby residents were blown off their feet by the blast. Who had planted the explosives was never discovered, but the finger of suspicion pointed at members of the NCA. Shay believed that some of their members took exception to the appearance of the British rider Robinson at the meet. Workmen spent all day clearing the rubble, repairing the stand, and filling the hole in the track, so that it was ready for racing in the evening.

The big crowd was pleased on the first night of racing, when Shay won both the sprint and the pursuit, and failed narrowly to complete the treble when he was beaten by Darrigade in the points race. Darrigade won the final sprint to win the event by a single point. Shay was the clear winner of the pursuit, beating Fausto Coppi by fifteen seconds. In the final of the sprint he faced Robinson. With 200 metres to go Robinson tried to get away from Shay, but he hung on and managed to come around the Englishman at the finish.

The following night Shay again won the sprint race, beating Hassenforder in the final. Later, the professionals competed in the devil-take-the-hindmost race, in which the last man over the line at the end of each lap was eliminated, and this was Shay's fate on the third lap. Fausto Coppi won this event, pipping Jean Bobet to the line. Coppi and Shay had argued during the meeting, as Coppi felt he should win all the events, while Shay wanted a fair competition. In addition to the troubles outlined, Morton also took some stick from some of the cycling community, who argued that they weren't seeing the best track riders in action, but road riders competing on what to them was strange territory.

Morton swore that he would never promote any bicycle racing again, and the top professionals would not compete in Ireland again until the 1980s.

The Dublin public were fortunate to see Coppi in action, as he would be dead within a few months. In December Coppi was invited to Burkina Faso, or Upper Volta as it was known then, to compete in a criterium, and also go on safari while he was there. Jacques Anquetil and Raphaël Géminiani also joined him on this trip. After hunting big game they took part in a criterium on December 13th in Ouagadougou, where Coppi finished second, behind Anquetil. The criterium also saw Roger Hassenforder and Roger Rivière, amongst others, competing.

The cyclists then returned to Europe, and within a few days Coppi began to feel feverish. The doctors wrongly diagnosed his symptoms as being a cold. However, Coppi had contracted malaria, and he died on the 2nd of January. Even today, there are those who are suspicious of his death, and one of the stranger theories put forward, is that he was poisoned by locals who gave him a concoction, which contained poisonous herbs, to quench his thirst while hunting.

Directly after the second night of track racing at the Santry stadium Shay and the other professionals took the short flight over the Irish Sea to the Isle of Man to take part in the 160-kilometre Manx Trophy, which took place on the Clypse Circuit the following day. It was the first time that there had been a professional road race during the annual cycling week on the island, and it was probably the best field that had ever been assembled in Britain for a bicycle race. The start list included Fausto Coppi, Louison Bobet, Jacques Anquetil, André Darrigade and Roger Walkowiak. The organiser of the race, Curwen Clague, set up grandstands at the finish and despite charging £6 a seat, he filled them all.

A really strong wind was blowing during the race, and the continental professionals formed echelons to combat the wind, which the British riders were unused to. This resulted in many of the British independent riders being dropped early on. After a few laps a break of 14 developed, which included Shay, Brian Robinson, Coppi, Géminiani and Darrigade. Anquetil, who had been at the rear of the peloton since the start, missed out, and wasn't to be seen again for the remainder of the race.

On the last climb of Ballacarrooin Hill, the lead group splintered, leaving Shay, Robinson and four others out ahead. This reduced group stayed together for the remainder of the lap, and Shay, being the strongest sprinter, was a clear first across the line in Douglas ahead of the Dutchman

Jo de Haan and Robinson. It was seven years after his first Isle of Man win in the Mannin Veg race.

'I thought I might do it,' Shay said, 'especially when there were just six of us together coming up to the finish. But I was still worried about everyone who was there, particularly Brian. Then when de Haan started his sprint too soon, and I was on his wheel, I knew I could win.' The prize presentation was in the Villa Marina in Douglas, and the 2000 fans assembled gave Shay a magnificent cheer when he was presented with his prize of £150.

Shay's next event was the Tour de France, where he hoped to improve on his performance of the previous year. His Isle of Man victory certainly suggested he was capable of winning a stage. But his tour got off to a bad start: he missed the train from Paris and was late for the team presentation! While waiting for a lift from Mulhouse train station from his team manager, Shay struck up a conversation with a pretty young hairdresser from Mulhouse, Marguerite Geiger. Sauveur Ducazeaux, the team manager, also gave Marguerite a lift to her home. Shay was immediately attracted to her, and vowed to contact her after the race had finished. Marguerite would later say that it was his smile and accent that attracted her to Shay.

The International team also included cyclists from Denmark, Austria, Poland, Portugal and four Britons, Brian Robinson, Vic Sutton, Tony Hewson and John Andrews. Shay finished in 38th place on the first stage from Mulhouse to Metz. With two others he had broken away after 130 kilometres, and even lead briefly after dropping them, but they were all reeled in before the finish. Darrigade took the win, making it the fourth tour in a row when he'd won the first stage.

The next day followed a similar pattern with Shay making a valiant attempt to win the stage into Namur. He managed to get clear, and was still on his own with ten kilometres left on the twisty roads that led to the finish at the city's citadel. Once again, though, he was caught by the peloton, this time just five hundred metres from the finish line. It had taken the combined efforts of a number of riders, including Charly Gaul and Federico Bahamontes, to catch him, but he hung on to take tenth place.

'You can't imagine how sorry I feel. I felt I had the victory in my legs and I thought I was far ahead and alone. I looked behind often, but could not see farther than 20 yards on the twisting road,' he said afterwards. 'I made the mistake of straightening up on my machine when I saw the finish line ahead of me and this cost me the victory. A few whizzed past me and it was too late.'

On the eighth stage to Bordeaux, Shay finished third, and won the prize for the most aggressive rider. He had attacked early on from the bunch and was followed closely by a number of others. His team-mates helped his chances by trying to disrupt any efforts by the bunch to bring them back. Shay finished third from the group of nine at the city Vélodrome in Bordeaux, as he was outsprinted by the Frenchmen Michel Dejouhannet and Jean Stablinski in front of a large crowd. Shay earned 100,000 francs for the most aggressive rider award.

Shay's team-mate, Brian Robinson, had a very good day on the road to Aurillac. He took fourth place in the stage, but more importantly, he jumped from eighteenth to ninth place on General Classification. Shay, on the other hand, had a day of mechanical difficulties – puncturing twice, and further problems with the tyre coming off the rim, which forced a bike change. Robinson's move into the top ten would soon prove to be very significant.

Early on the fourteenth stage to Clermont-Ferrand, the very next day, the Englishman was dropped. It was an incredibly hot day in the Massif Central, and he was suffering from stomach pains and had hardly slept the night before. Shay, acting as a faithful *domestique* to Robinson, dropped back to accompany him to the finish. He stayed by Robinson's side sheltering him from the wind, splashing water in his face and encouraging him to continue. Robinson tried to get Shay to push on himself, telling the Irishman to 'bugger off', but he refused. Instead, he rode ahead of Robinson, stopping at cafés to obtain drinks for him. As Robinson caught up with the waiting Irishman, Shay recalled hearing some spectators saying, 'Look at Robinson, he's been doped' – such was his dishevelled state. At one point race officials caught Shay giving Robinson a push, and he was subsequently fined £2. Shay felt that they could have fined him £50 and they would still have underestimated the amount of pushing he did that day.

The Tour's doctor, Dr Dumas, recommended to Robinson that he pull out, but he refused. Shay had told Robinson that if he packed, then so would he, so through a combination of the threat from Shay and his own grit he continued. Shay twice stopped to repair Robinson's bike after punctures, and also administered medicine that was given to him by Dumas. Shay himself also had some trouble. A car splashed tar into his right eye and he had to be given a sedative to ease the pain. He had to keep his eye closed for most of the stage.

The two came in a full 47 minutes after the winner, just five minutes outside the time limit, which was set at ten per cent of the winner's time, and they were eliminated. 'It was a real disappointment for both of us,' Robinson said after the stage.

By the following morning, however, Robinson had been reinstated. There was an ancient regulation in the Tour whereby any rider in the top ten overall could not be eliminated by finishing outside the time limit, and Sauveur Ducazeaux, the International team manager, had found it. It was the first time in the 53-year history of the race that the rule had been used and it allowed Robinson to stay in the race.

There was no such luck for Shay, however, and he had to return home. He did win 150,000 francs as the unluckiest rider of the day, which was not much consolation to him. Returning to Paris on the night that he was eliminated he said, 'I'm not complaining. It's just one of those things that happen. I came in this Tour to help Brian. There are mountain stages ahead in which he can still do well. Good luck to him. I am going to Paris tonight, as I want Brian to forget all about me for the time being. He's a bit upset about my disqualification, and seems to think he put me out of the race.' Shay added that he did have one consolation: he would not have to face the mountainous stages which constituted much of the rest of the tour. 'The mountains are not really my place, and I hope to do better in the Tour de l'Ouest later this month.' He was already looking ahead.

Behind him he left a certain amount of controversy: Robinson, when told that he would be reinstated, but Shay would not, remarked, 'It's too unjust. Elliott helped me throughout yesterday and without him at my side I would have dropped out of the race. He took care of me like a mother.'

Dr. Dumas said later: 'Elliott's self-sacrifice was one of the most moving pages in the Tour's history. Despite his eye ailment Elliott could have finished the leg in time, but he chose to stay at the side of his friend to help and encourage him.' Shay's efforts in helping Robinson were described in the next day's *l'Equipe* as *'attentions de mère poule'* – the care of a mother hen.

But Jean Bobet recalled that not everybody saw what Shay's actions in this light. 'He got criticized a lot,' he said, 'because in this ruthless world an act of kindness could be seen as a weakness. So, as a racer, Shay was "weak", as hard and rotten as that might sound.'

Robinson was to go on to win the 20th stage of the Tour, arriving twenty minutes ahead of the peloton after a lone break of 80 miles. Early in the stage Robinson had been helping his trade team-mate, Gérard

Saint, in the mountains competition. However, Robinson was going really strongly that day and soon found that not only could Saint not hang on to his wheel, but everybody else had dropped behind as well. He told journalists afterwards, 'I won today's leg for Séamus Elliott of Ireland, who helped me so much when I was dragging behind last week. Poor Elliott was eliminated because of his assistance and his cares for me. I promised him that I would try to win a leg to thank him.'

Robinson's winning margin that day was so great that the 1947 Tour winner, Jean Robic, was eliminated from the race. It was said that the judges would have allowed anybody else to stay in, but Robic's foul mouth had made him few friends. Only three of the twelve members of the Internations team would finish the Tour, the Austrian Adolf Christian, Brian Robinson and Vic Sutton. At the finish of the Tour in Paris, Shay was honoured again for his efforts. The race organizers gave him an award for his 'courage and team spirit', saying that he had sacrificed his own chances to save his teammate.

After the Tour Shay had some time to himself, and finally made the move out of the Tchamassanian house into his own villa in Bry-sur-Marne. He would continue to pay regular visits to his adopted family though for the rest of the time that he lived in Paris. He would not forget the generosity and faith that the family had showed him.

Brian Robinson lived on the opposite side of the Marne, and the two used to meet up for training rides. Although Robinson considered Shay to be very friendly, he did find him a somewhat difficult person to get to know, and their conversations would tend to revolve around racing. In addition to training, they also used to cut down on expenses by travelling to races together. If there were a number of races in the South of France, they would find cheap accommodation down South and stay there for the duration of the races, rather than travelling back up to Paris. The two also used to meet and train with Jean Bobet as he also lived in the locality. Shay's break after the Tour also gave him some time to visit Marguerite, the girl he had met in Mulhouse before the start of the Tour. They had kept in touch throughout the race.

The World Championships that year were being held in Zandvoort, Holland. It was the championship made remarkable by Tom Simpson just missing out on a podium place after only three months as a professional. For Shay it was not a memorable race – he attacked a number of times, was chased down by the Belgians, and finished in 22nd. The real drama for him came after the race.

The night before the race a stranger had visited Shay at his hotel, saying he was a friend of Rik Van Looy, and offering him £700 if he helped the Belgian to victory. Van Looy, himself, was unaware of any of this, and ended up trailing in disappointingly near the back of the bunch, while the Belgian cycling federation suspended all but three of their team for non-aggression. Shay, of course, received no money, and nearly ended up getting kicked out of his trade team.

When he rejoined the Helyett team, Wiegant flew into a temper the moment he saw Shay and waved photos from the Championships in his face. 'Look at these.' he shouted. 'You rode for Van Looy and these pictures prove it.'

Shay didn't deny it. 'Well, why shouldn't I?' he asked. 'It was an open race and I was going to get paid for helping him.'

'Paid!' exclaimed Wiegant. 'A bribe, you mean. Your own team-mates were in that race and you were going to take money to help beat them. I'll get you sacked from the team for this.'

The row blew over though, principally because it was one of the Helyett team, André Darrigade, who had won the Championship.

Shay finished off his season in Italy where, first of all, he took part in the Trofeo Longines. This 31.4-kilometre team time trial took place in Rimini on the Adriatic coast, and Shay's Helyett-Leroux team were the winners – a victory that would have been due in no small part to Jacques Anquetil's time trialling ability. Darrigade, Graczyk and Michel Vermeulin were the other members of the team.

The Helyett team had had an excellent season. This was acknowledged in December when they were awarded the Trophee A.I.O.C.C., which was given to the team which was considered to have put up the best collective performances of the year. The organisation listed the events and winners of the seven races that counted in Helyett's favour: Four Days of Dunkirk; the Lugano and the Geneva time trials, both won by Jacques Anquetil; the National Criterium and the World Championships, won by André Darrigade, Paris–Nice–Rome, won by Jean Graczyk, and finally Het Volk, won by Shay. Despite being eliminated from the Tour, Shay could feel very pleased with how his season had gone.

On his way back to Ireland for the winter Shay would often call on Mick Byrne, a friend from his early days racing in Ireland. Like many Irishmen during those difficult economic times of the 1950s, Mick had moved to Birmingham in search of work. It was there that Shay would drop in on him to break the journey and to catch up on old times. Mick used to look forward to these visits, not least because of the good bottle of wine Shay would bring with him. He'd followed Shay's results avidly, and this year was able to congratulate him on his classic win. They both felt sure that Shay had finally overcome his run of bad luck and that the floodgates would now open for future classics wins. However, the 1959 Het Volk would be his one and only win in the big one-day races.

Shay with his father in their house in Rathfarnham

After winning a race in the early 1950s

Shay with the Dublin Wheelers, early 1950s

Shay winning a stage of the C.R.E. Tour of Ireland

Route de France, 1955, in the leader's jersey

1955 – Best amateur rider in France: postcard

Tour of Lombardy 1958

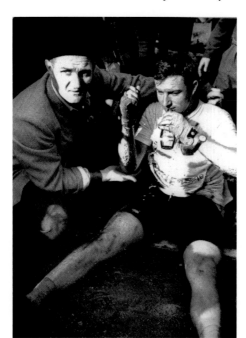

*An exhausted Shay
(date unknown)*

Paris–Roubaix 1959

Isle of Man 1959, with Brian Robinson

A guest of the Irish Club, Paris

Shay and Marguerite,
Wedding Day

Tour de France 1961

*Picking up a dropped
musette*

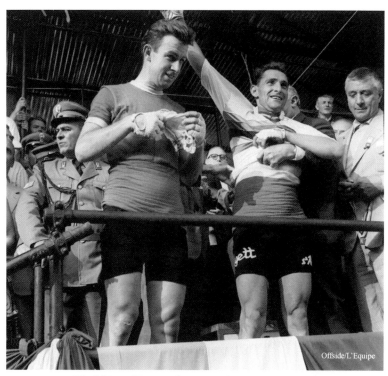

World Road Race Championship podium, 1962

A signed photograph sent by Shay to his friend John Cleary

Roger St Pierre

Tour de France 1963: the winning break: with Stablinski and Van Aerde on the road to Roubaix

PhotosportInternational

With Tom Simpson in the World Road Race Championship 1963

The first Irish yellow jersey

Offside/L'Equipe

Shay, Stablinski and Anquetil the morning after

Alan Ramsbottom, Shay and Tom Simpson; Grand Prix Corona, Crystal Palace, 1964

Chasing Stablinski, Paris–Luxembourg, 1965

IHS

In Loving Memory
of
MY DEAR HUSBAND
JAMES ELLIOTT
DIED 21st APRIL 1971
AGED 86 YEARS
ALSO HIS BELOVED WIFE
ELLEN ELLIOTT
DIED 3RD JULY 1989
TREASURED MEMORIES OF
A WONDERFUL HUSBAND AND FATHER
EDDIE ELLIOTT
DIED 29th AUGUST 2000

MY FOREVER FRIEND

R . I . P .

In Loving Memory
of
SHAY ELLIOTT
DIED 4th MAY 1971
AGED 36 YEARS

JUST WHEN LIFE SEEMED BRIGHTEST
IN THE PRIME OF HIS YOUTHFUL DAYS
SHAY'S LIFE ON EARTH WAS ENDED
BY FATES MYSTERIOUS WAYS.

ALSO TREASURED MEMORIES OF
SHAY'S DARLING SON
PASCAL
DIED 13th NOV. 1978, AGED 16 YEARS
AS A RESULT OF A ROAD ACCIDENT
INTERRED IN FRANCE.
IN LOVING MEMORY OF
MY DARLING SON, PAUL
AGED 45 YEARS
DIED 9th JANUARY 1986.
R . I . P .

IN
MEMORY OF
SHAY ELLIOTT
IRISH INTERNATIONAL RACING CYCLIST

ERECTED BY HIS FAMILY AND FRIENDS
IRISH WHEELMEN CLUBS
1971

8

Another historic first in Italy;
Father Shay

Shay found himself with a little more time to spend at home in Ireland and to relax prior to the 1960 season, because he didn't have any important track meetings to take part in during the winter season. These could be lucrative, but also very tiring, because the winter racing was always hard and wouldn't necessarily prepare you very well for the new road season. Shay was hoping 1960 was going to be another breakthough year and he wanted to be fresh for the road season. Furthermore, the authorities in Paris had decided to pull down the old Vel d'Hiv, the Vélodrome being a constant reminder of what had happened during the German occupation two decades previously. So, one of the few venues he might have ridden at was no longer an option.

The continental cycling world was still in a state of shock over Fausto Coppi's death when Shay returned to the continent, and there were many rumours doing the rounds. It was the main topic of conversation when Shay met some of his team-mates in Paris. They travelled together to the Côte d'Azur for their annual training camp, prior to crossing the Mediterranean for the start of the season. In 1960 there was a new addition to the Helyett team, Augustin Corteggiani. Shay and Cortegianni had raced together as amateurs with ACBB, and the signing of Corteggiani enabled the two to renew their friendship. This friendship continued even after the Frenchman's undistinguished career came to an abrupt end the following year. Some time afterwards Shay would have the misfortune of employing the untrustworthy Corteggiani and it was to cause him some major problems, but it was a recurrent feature of Shay's life to be let down by people he had instinctively trusted.

In February, in the Algerian city of Oran, Shay won the first race of the calendar, the Criterium de *l'Echo d'Oran*. The race had an extremely good line-up, including Federico Bahamontes, Charly Gaul, Rudi Altig, Louison Bobet and Jacques Anquetil, along with many other European pros, and with the remainder of the field made up by a number of Algerians and Moroccans. At the end of the race Shay was easily able to outsprint his two breakaway companions, in front of an estimated 100,000 spectators. But the annual trips to these races were not as enjoyable as they had once been because there were now tensions in Algeria. It was to be an explosive period in the country's history.

In the mid-1950s a guerilla effort fronted by Ahmed Ben Bella, an ex-sergeant in the French army, arose to oust the French from Algeria. The group was called the FLN (Front de la Liberation Nationale), and in 1962 independence was declared. Immediately about a million colonists left Algeria for France. This guerilla war and subsequent loss of Algeria as a French colony meant the end of these early season races, in which Shay had taken a number of victories over the years.

Shay returned to Europe to take part in Paris-Nice. His team might have been expected to win the team time trial on the second stage, but to the surprise of the majority of press and fans, Anquetil – of all people – had been dropped. This proved to be the beginning of the end in a race in which Shay had often excelled in the past, but although André Darrigarde and Jean Graczyk won a stage each, the race for the overall win for the team was never a realistic proposition.

However, Shay hoped he could improve on his showing in the forthcoming classics in Belgium and France, which he had earmarked as his targets for the early season. He finished in fifteenth position in the Tour of Flanders, and then eleventh in Paris-Roubaix the following weekend, over one minute behind the winner, Pino Cerami. That year's Paris-Roubaix was historic, as it was the first race ever to be televised live. Televising of races had started regularly in 1952, but these first broadcasts were mainly from a stationary camera at the finish line of a race. The last hour of this year's Paris-Roubaix was shown throughout Europe by means of a camera mounted in a helicopter sending a signal direct to the studio. This technological advance gave the sport even more exposure. Millions of viewers tuned in to see Tom Simpson on his own in the lead, and then to watch as he was caught at Hem just a few kilometres from the finish. But Tom's profile in Europe was enhanced considerably with his wonderful performance, and he eventually finished ninth with Shay eleventh, just two places behind in the leading but splintering nineteen-strong break.

Shay's classic performances were excellent, but he was quite disappointed, considering what he had shown himself to be capable of in previous years. In fact, despite being only 25, Shay's best years in the classics were behind him, which was surprising since it was often the older, more experienced riders who excelled in the Classics and the major one-day events.

The next big event for Shay was the eight-day Roma-Napoli-Roma, or the Grand Prix Ciclomotoristico as it was known in Italy, which consisted of split stages every day. Cyclists have always disliked split stages, and to take on sixteen stages over eight days would not have been appreciated by many, although it did give more opportunities to take a win.

Shay achieved some good placings in the first few stages. After the first stage he was lying in eleventh position, some two minutes behind Louison Bobet, who was riding out of his skin despite nearing the end of his illustrious career.. He improved his overall position to ninth the next day and then, on day three, he won the first of the day's split stages. On the 187-kilometre half-stage from San Giovanni to Manfredonia he finished nearly three minutes clear of Miguel Poblet, and took the leader's jersey in the process. However, he would only hang on to it for one stage as Louison Bobet took it off him after dominating the short afternoon stage, and he would hold it through to the end. It would be one of his very last major wins, and his last in a stage race.

Shay and the team drove back to France for the next big race of the season, the 'Grand Prix Peugeot-Stan Ockers', named after the Belgian road and track star, one of the very finest riders of his generation, who had been killed in a Derny race at the Antwerp Vélodrome in 1956. He'd been a highly successful and popular rider, whose palmarès included World Road Race Champion in 1955, second in the Tour de France in 1950 and 1952, and winner of both Liège-Bastogne-Liège and Flèche Wallonne in the same year, 1955. For a number of years the organisers had been trying to put the race on a par with some of the smaller classics, but, as with similar memorial races, they had never successfully achieved that status. Nevertheless, the 'Stan Ockers' was an important race which attracted a top class entry; it was always hard fought and to win it a major accomplishment.

This 253-kilometre event, starting from Rennes on Mayday, was a very aggressive affair over difficult terrain. Eventually Shay managed to break away with three others. Two of them, Frenchmen Privat and Graczyck, were currently major contenders for the Super Pernod Prestige competition (World rankings at the time, and another reason why this event was so prestigious) but seemed more concerned with beating each other than winning the race. Shay took advantage of their personal rivalry to jump away near the finish and claim the win in Brest, a second ahead of the talented all-rounder Belgian Jos Hoevenaers, who had won the Flèche Wallonne the previous year.

The following day Shay travelled west across Brittany to take part in the 121-km Grand Prix du Tregor in Plougasnou. Many of the riders who had competed in the Stan Ockers race also took part, so it was a strong field for the short but tough race. Shay scored another victory, attacking on his own and finishing over a minute clear of World Champion André Darrigade, who later told *L'Equipe*: 'Shay has ridden like a real champion these last two races. When he has this kind of form he is almost impossible to beat.' Six days later he finished second to superstar sprinter Miguel Poblet in the Prix Argentan, again in France, with a young and very fast German Rudi Altig just behind him in third place. His form was very good and he hoped for some great opportunities in the following month of May.

Shay's hopes were realized when Mickey Wiegant informed him that he would be on the Helyett team for the Giro d'Italia, in a very serious bid to help Anquetil win the famous Italian Tour for the first time. Directly prior to the start of the race Wiegant had briefed each of the team in Rome. 'You're a strong finisher,' Wiegant said to Shay. 'We will often need you as a *domestique* when things get bad. But normally you will be free to help yourself to a stage win or two if all is well.' Shay was, of course, more than happy to ride his first Giro and to have confirmation that he should be given the opportunity to win a stage.

A total of 140 riders lined up at the start of the Giro, comprising Italians, Belgian, Dutch, Swiss, French, Spaniards, and one representative of Great Britain, according to the Italian newspapers. Although Shay was used to hearing himself being announced as 'British', he patiently pointed out to the organisers that he was in fact Irish – and very proud of it. Jean Bobet, brother of Louison, and a former professional himself, wrote that in France Shay was considered a 'Briton', although he also expressed the view that the French were ignorant of both geography and history.

On the opening stage to Naples Shay lost thirteen minutes, as he dropped back to help the valued climber Louis Rostollan, who had punctured. Due to his *domestique* duties and a very hard fought race Shay wasn't to get that many opportunities for personal success, and with Anquetil taking the overall lead again on the fourteenth stage, after leading for three days earlier in the race, these became even more limited. Despite his hard work for the team Shay's form was good and on a very tough 18th stage from Trieste to Belluno, he felt strong enough to take a real chance at a stage win. The stage of 240 km was the longest of the Giro, and the route through the Dolomites took in some very difficult climbs, including the Mauria Pass. Shay was able to get clear with some breakaway companions, but the very talented Graziano Battistini, who went on to gain second place in the Tour de France later in the summer, held a short lead a few kilometres from the finish. However, the Italian fell on a corner and Shay, who was flying, took the lead and never looked back. Battistini finished 43 seconds behind Shay, who said after the race: 'Sure, I'm glad to see that line.' It had evidently been a very tough stage.

So, Elliott became the first English speaking rider to win a Giro stage and only the second, after the British pioneer Brian Robinson, to win a stage in a Grand Tour. Anquetil rode brilliantly to win overall by just 38 seconds, so becoming the first Frenchman to win the Giro, while the future winner of the Tour de France that year, Gastone Nencini, was second and the previous year's winner, Charly Gaul, was third, nearly four minutes behind. Shay finished in Milan in 68th place, but a happy man after his stage win and with his team leader victorious.

After the Giro Shay returned to the Isle of Man hoping again to win the Manx Trophy as he had the year before, but he could only finish in fifth place, as French cyclists took eight of the top nine positions. Shay came in fifth, 42 seconds behind the winner, French World Champion André Darrigade.

Shay had originally been pencilled in to ride the Tour de France, but by this stage of the season, he was quite fatigued after his heavy schedule, and felt he was losing his form. After consultation with Mickey Wiegant he decided not to participate. Wiegant was not particularly keen on Shay taking part in the Tour anyway, as he would not have been riding for the Helyett team. At this time *extra-sportif* sponsors were not able to get maximum exposure in the Tour as it was still contested by national teams. It meant the Giro d'Italia tended on occasions to have a better field, until the Tour regulations were altered in 1962. Belgian Rik Van Looy, for instance, took part in the Giro three times in those years, but never took part in the Tour. However, financial considerations were probably more important to him and perhaps many others at this developing stage of commercial cycle racing in Europe .

Shay had been selected for the British team, and when he withdrew his place was taken by twice amateur World Pursuit Champion Norman Sheil, who wasn't a stranger to road racing, but not at the top level. It was to be a disappointing Tour for the team as a whole, as only two,

Brian Robinson and Tom Simpson, would finish that year. They both rode well, with Tom coming very close to the yellow jersey and finishing third twice on stages and 29th overall and Robinson three places ahead of Britain's future World Road Race Champion. Shay's absence from the Tour gave him the opportunity to spend a lot of time with Marguerite in both Mulhouse and Paris. Their relationship was flourishing at the time and Shay decided to propose. Marguerite accepted and they planned to get married prior to the start of the following season.

That year's Tour was won by Gastone Nencini, but his victory was overshadowed by the serious crash of Roger Rivière, who tried to follow him on the descent of the Col de Perjuret. The unfortunate Frenchman fell down a ravine and broke his back. It later emerged that he had taken Palfium on the climb, and the painkiller had numbed him to such an extent that he was unable to brake on the descent. Rivière was confined to a wheelchair and would die a broken man at the young age of 40. Nencini would also be accused of doping, as the medical chief of the Tour, Pierre Dumas, found the Italian receiving a blood transfusion in his hotel room, after one stage.

The rest of Shay's season wasn't that fruitful. His form hadn't disappeared and he rode well in most of the criteriums, but he only recorded one victory – a 125-kilometre criterium in Gouesnou. The nearest he got to another win was a second place behind his team-mate and good friend at the time, Jean Stablinski. What Shay wanted now was a good performance in the World Championships, which were being held in East Germany that year. He did ride well and finished with the leaders, albeit 17th and last of the group, but he had shown himself capable of sticking with the best in the race. As so often in World Championship races where loyalties can be in conflict – trade team versus national team – there were post-race rumours about some riders, and the fact that Shay, with generally a powerful finishing sprint, had ended last in the group caused some eyebrows to be raised.

He rode well again in Paris–Tours but although aggressive, he eventually finished in 12th place, two seconds behind the very fast Dutchman Jo De Hann. This race more or less terminated his competitive season and according to his friend, Brian Robinson, Shay was optimistic and looking forward to the following year.

1961

Over the winter there were to be some changes to Shay's team. The team split in two, with André Darrigade joining the Alcyon-Leroux team, while Shay, Anquetil and Stablinski stayed with Helyett, who had been joined by the Italian drinks company Fynsec as co-sponsor. Shay and Marguerite married early in 1961, and Jean Stablinski was best man in a low-key affair. However, the happy couple did not have much time to spend together, due to Shay having to attend the traditional early season training camp.

In 1961, for the first time in his professional career, Shay didn't start the season in Algeria. Instead his first race was Het Volk, where he finished in equal 24th position as part of the main bunch. Shay's next appearance was Paris-Nice, which team leader Anquetil had clearly stated he wanted to win.

There was a second Irishman on the start line in Paris. After making his professional debut in Genoa-Nice. Peter Crinnion was offered a place in Margnat's starting line-up for Paris-Nice, and it would be the first time that Shay would have a compatriot competing with him in a professional race. Shay rode particularly strongly in helping Anquetil to the overall win, chasing down a number of dangerous breaks, including several involving Tom Simpson, who was a big threat to Anquetil, and in helping St. Raphaël to win the 23-kilometre team time trial. Crinnion also did well to finish, as only 53 of the 96 starters completed the race. He had initially been offered a three-month trial contract with Margnat, so it was very important that he did well in every race that he started.

One of Crinnion's most vivid memories of that race was the strong leadership that Shay showed during the race. In an era long before telecommunications links with the directeur sportif, Shay would cruise up and down the bunch issuing orders to team-mates and discussing their tactics for the race. He didn't let any national loyalties get in the way of his job, and he had no hesitation in chasing down Crinnion in races. In fact, it took a while for the two to become good friends, and this only really happened after Crinnion had moved from Marseilles to Loctudy, when the two became closer.

Shay's next stage race was the Tour de Champagne, which was run in the region to the East of Paris. Shay finished fourth on the first stage, in the same time as winner, Joseph Verachtert of Belgium. He then took over the lead on General Classification on the second day. The day's racing consisted of a split stage. In the morning's 51-kilometre team time trial, Helyett-Fynsec won to give him the lead after a typical strong performance, but Shay slipped well back after the afternoon's stage. It was another of his team, French climber Louis Rostollan, who was the eventual winner of the race, and Shay finished well down. The race was also notable in that Britains latest promising export, Alan Ramsbottom, held the lead for three days, but lost it on the final stage.

A few days later Shay started in another French stage race, the prestigious Four Days of Dunkirk, a race he had often performed very well in. He dominated the second stage, beating French star Jean Forestier, a previous Tour of Flanders and Paris-Roubaix winner, in a two-up sprint, 14 seconds ahead of the main group. This was a hard fought victory and taken in good style; it promised a lot for the coming season. In fact, it turned out to be something of a false dawn. By the end of the year he had achieved few personal successes, although of course he continued to work conscientiously for the sake of the team.

Not surprisingly, Shay was chosen as a member of the Helyett-Fynsec team to help Anquetil in his attempts to retain his Giro d'Italia crown. Shay got off to a promising start, finishing in sixth place on the first stage. He came closer on the 11th stage, to Teano, where he finished third.

He worked hard for the team, but the third place would be as good as it would get for him, and he would fail to finish in Milan, as would many others. It was a particularly difficult Giro, which was exemplified by the 20th stage to Bormio. Charly Gaul's winning time that day was close to eleven hours. Amongst the climbs they had to endure that day was the 2,757-metre Stelvio Pass. Anquetil having led the race for four stages earlier eventually finished second in the race, won by the fine Italian climber, Arnaldo Pambianco.

Shortly after the end of the Giro, *L'Equipe* announced that Shay would ride the Tour de France with the Great Britain team. He rested up after his exertions in the Giro, and one of his only significant races was the Manx Trophy again, on The Isle of Man. Shay finished well down, but he was delighted with the chance to meet with his brother Paul, who was also racing that day in the Manx International, competing for the Ireland A team.

In the weeks before the start of the Tour de France there was some doubt that the big hitters who would be riding on the Great Britain team would in fact take part. Brian Robinson had initially been reluctant to compete, but at the start of June he won one of the biggest pre-Tour events, the Dauphiné Libéré. Robinson had taken over the lead on the third stage and kept the lead through the following mountainous stages. This excellent win changed his mind.

Tom Simpson had also been a doubt, as he had been hoping to have Robinson's support in the race. When Robinson announced that he would ride, Simpson decided that he too would ride for the British team. Ian Moore from Northern Ireland was also selected to ride for Great Britain, thereby making him the second Irishman to start the Tour.

Shay started off well, finishing in fifth place on the first stage, and moved up to fourth place overall after the time trial on the afternoon of the first day. However, that first stage would see his only top ten placing. He said afterwards, 'I did not want to go all out this morning but our manager urged me to, despite the fact that I wanted to shine in the stage to Roubaix tomorrow. Now, of course, I am very pleased to have got fourth place.'

After the stage to Charleroi his mood was still upbeat, as he told reporters afterwards that he hoped to win a stage very soon. During these first few stages Shay was suffering from a bad cold, and his hopes of a stage win weren't helped by the medication he was taking.

It was a disappointing Tour for the Great Britain team as only three of the twelve starters would finish. In fact, as early as the fifth stage their numbers had been reduced to four – eight of their riders having already abandoned. On the stage to Roubaix both Robinson and Simpson had fallen in a massive pile-up, but both were able to continue. However, Simpson abandoned the next day, complaining of a sore knee. He said after pulling out, 'You can say I abandoned because I could not pedal any more.' Shay, on the other hand, still held high hopes for the race if he could recover properly, saying at the stage finish in Charleroi, 'I hope to win a stage very soon'. The other Irishman, Ian Moore, abandoned on the same stage as Simpson.

Shay impressed his less experienced team-mates with his shows of strength. On one particular stage he punctured, and Vin Denson and a few others on the team dropped back to help him regain the peloton. However, such was his speed, Shay dropped them all on the chase back to the bunch. When they eventually got back, they found Shay sitting at the back of the group laughing.

Shay moved back up to fourth place following the sixth stage to Belfort, and was only six seconds from being in second place. He put in a particularly strong effort on the stage as Marguerite's family had travelled from nearby Mulhouse to see him race. Some of his in-laws watched the race as it passed over the Ballon d'Alsace, and others watched the finish in Belfort. This was as close as he would get to the yellow jersey for the time being, but his dream was still very much alive.

He slipped another place overall as the race moved south. After the stage to Saint Etienne he insisted his morale was still good as they faced the Alps. He expected to lose some time in the mountains, of course, but hoped to limit his losses and was feeling more confident about his climbing ability. Shay's team-mate and friend Brian Robinson helped him out during the stage by sharing water from his bottle, thereby saving Shay some time at the water fountains where the riders stopped to fill their bidons.

However, Shay slipped down the General Classification following the ninth stage to Grenoble, due to the misfortune of breaking his forks on the 1,134-m climb of the Granier, and then suffering two punctures. Led by Gaul, the main leaders' group had been quite small at that stage, but Shay was still hanging in there. He had declared prior to the start of the stage that, for the first time in a number of years, he felt really a lot more confident entering the mountains. After the finish of the stage he told reporters: 'Without all those mishaps, I'm sure I would have finished with Jacques Anquetil' (who finished second, 1.40 behind Charly Gaul, who was on one of his good days).

Lady Luck deserted the following day when he crashed on the descent of Mont Cenis, and finished 22 minutes behind Guy Ignolin of the Ouest-Sud Ouest team. He fell further behind on General Classification on the eleventh stage, which passed over three major mountains between Turin and Antibes.

He was pragmatic after the stage saying, 'All I want now is to finish the Tour and perhaps, if I'm lucky, win a stage along the way.' Shay had finished 68th on the stage. He added, 'I am glad to get those mountains behind me.' During the stage he had performed more as a *domestique* than a team leader. In the village of Cuneo he had stopped at a roadside café, 'stolen' a bottle of water, and then ridden off and shared it with his team-mates.* As the race arrived back in France he said, 'The Tour de France is decidedly no race for me. Next year, I shall stay at home.'

---

* One of the customs of the Tour de France, which was still practiced at the time was known as 'la chasse a la canette', whereby *domestiques* would raid cafes, taking whatever came to hand. The Louis Malle documentary 'Vive le Tour' which followed the 1962 Tour de France, showed riders carrying bottles of beer and ice cream which they had gotten their hands on. Riders would also steal apples, oranges and peaches from orchards which they would pass by during a day's racing.

He suffered more the following day to Aix-en-Provence as he was hampered again by a chest infection. The race doctor ordered him not to ride too hard during the stage. To add to his misfortune he also broke his front wheel soon after the start. So much for the luck of the Irish.

Despite his difficulties Shay's form started to improve later in the race. On the stage to Toulouse he made numerous attempts to get away from the peloton, but was chased down each time by the French team, usually by Robert Cazala. The only break that he missed out on was – surprise, surprise – the winning one, made and won by the very promising Italian Guido Carlesi, who went on to finish runner-up in the Tour. However, he did win £143 for being unanimously awarded as the most aggressive rider of the race that day – a prize he richly deserved as he had tried nine times to break away to put himself in a position to win the stage that day.

After he was presented with his prize Shay was placed in a baby's pram with his winner's bouquet and paraded over the finishing area alongside Anquetil. Smiling, he said, 'I was considering giving up the race just a day or two ago, as I was really tired. Now, after getting this prize, I'm determined to see it through.'

Less determined was his team-mate Ken Laidlaw, who, during the stage, had drifted backwards to the rear of the peloton. When asked what was wrong with him he said that he was 'cheesed off with nobody to talk to', referring to the fact that both Shay and Robinson spoke French at the dinner table with their team manager, who couldn't speak English. The Scot was feeling isolated, and allied to other troubles he was enduring, this lack of communication was making him seriously consider dropping out of the Tour. However, he was persuaded to regain the peloton and finish the stage. That was a typical problem at the time – learn the language or be damned. Tough times and, of course, a million miles away from the situation today but back then it could be very demoralising.

Shay's efforts must have spurred on his two remaining team-mates, as the following day all three made attempts to break away, even though none was successful. It was Ken Laidlaw, whose main talent was climbing, who won the team another daily aggression prize. He had actually hung on with the climbers over the big climbs of the day, and broken away on his own near the end. He was caught close to the finish. On a rainy and windy stage, however, Shay and Robinson had been dropped on the tough Super-Bagnères climb.

The following stage was very tough, maybe the toughest in the entire race, and Shay was dropped early on as once again he suffered with his bad chest. He struggled to breathe as they raced at high altitudes over the Peyresourde, the Aspin, the Tourmalet and the Aubisque. He said that his legs would 'just not respond'. Laidlaw also struggled as he paid for his remarkable efforts of the previous day.

The following day Shay felt better as they came down from the mountains to Bordeaux. He tried to go clear with André Darrigade but failed, and they both eventually finished with the peloton. On the final time trial of the race, won by his trade team leader, Jacques Anquetil, he struggled again on the rain soaked course.

Anquetil dominated the Tour that year, finishing over 12 minutes ahead of Guido Carlesi in second place. His French team controlled the race from start to finish, suppressing all dangerous attacks. The director of the Tour, Jacques Goddet, was extremely critical of the Frenchman's rivals, and in a famous editorial he called them 'repulsive dwarves' who were 'satisfied in their mediocrity'.

Shay was finally to finish the race in 47th position overall, despite suffering bouts of bronchitis throughout the race, with Brian Robinson (53rd) and Ken Laidlaw (65th) the only other finishers for the team. He had ridden an aggressive Tour, making many attempts, when his health was good, to break away in an attempt to win a stage. Most of the time, however, he was chased down by members of the French team, despite being a trade team-mate of Anquetil's. This did not seem to faze Shay, as he said, 'Of course, this time Jacques and I were in opposition and naturally he sent André Darrigade or one of the others after me every time I tried to get away.' However, Shay finished this Tour in his highest position ever, and again showed that he was a very fine rider who probably just needed a little extra good fortune to make a real impression in the race with a stage win or two, and maybe with a chance of glory by wearing the yellow jersey for a day or so.

The Great Britain team came last of the eleven teams in the prize list. Their winnings of £488 were a long way short of the French team's total of £13,031. It turned out to be Brian Robinson's last Tour de France. Robinson was the first English speaker to be really successful on the continent, but had grown weary of the travelling involved. He decided to return to England with his young family and concentrate on the family building business.

Robinson's responsibility for his family was something that Shay would have noted with special interest, as during the Tour Shay had received some great news. Marguerite informed him that she was pregnant.

His season had been very tough, having competed and ridden hard in both the Giro and the Tour and it finally told on Shay. He decided to finish his season early, except for some criteriums, and his only win was in Macon. When he returned home to Ireland that year, he was honoured by the Bray Wheelers club at their Annual General Meeting, when he was elected President of the club, with Peter Crinnion being elected Vice-President.

Shay took stock of his performances both good and bad at the end of the year and realised that without the misfortune and sickness he had suffered, he could have done a lot better in the Tour. Whereas in the classics, he had no doubt he had underperformed. The following season would definitely see a shift in priorities and ambitions for Shay. Despite his difficulties in the 1961 season he seemed as positive as the year before and was again looking forward to the following season. 1962 would turn out to be one of the most significant of his career.

9

Spanish triumphs;
a 'stolen' Worlds

At the end of the 1961 season, the St. Raphaël drinks company made the decision to increase its level of sponsorship, and set the team the main objective of winning the following year's Tour de France. The Tour organizers had finally relented and allowed the change from national teams to sponsored teams. One of the main reasons for this was that riders were becoming more and more tempted to be loyal to their trade team-mates rather than their national team. The trade teams' *directeurs sportifs* were officially not supposed to be part of the Tour entourage, but they could often be seen at the start and finish of stages exerting their influence over 'their' riders. Apart from the two years of 1967 and 1968 the Tour's policy to this day has been to invite trade teams and, of course, the decision to permit the change in the race structure had enormous implications.

St. Raphaël had been sponsoring and supporting teams, both big and small, for a number of years but, despite gaining a good many important victories, they had not achieved the success they desired. Jacques Anquetil (who had already won the Tour twice) was the man they felt they needed to help increase awareness of their brand – and Anquetil would insist upon an extra strong team to support him. But as well as the Tour itself, St Raphaël wanted a line-up to have a real chance in other major races and classics. So, the decision was taken to develop a squad that is now often accepted as being the first commercial 'super team'.

The next step was for the St. Raphaël organization to approach Felix Potin, Fynsec's boss, to whom Anquetil was still under contract in the Helyett-Fynsec team. Fynsec had become co-sponsors of the Helyett at the start of the 1961 season, but had been unable to meet their financial obligations to Heylett. As a result, Felix Potin had personally helped to fund the team for the rest of the season. The St. Raphaël-Gitane would be an amalgamation of the Rapha, Helyett and St. Raphaël-Géminiani set-up, taking the best riders from each; it would become one of the first teams to employ so many top riders in one squad. Raphaël Géminiani was to be the new *directeur sportif* and would share the management responsibilities with Paul Wiegant, (although the partnership of these two strong personalities would, not unexpectedly, cause some problems later in the season).

When Jacques Anquetil learned of the likelihood of this new sponsorship deal he was apprehensive. He had always been very superstitious – utterly convinced, for instance, that he would die at a younger age than his father – and felt this could be an unlucky team for him. Nobody else could really understand this, but to his unique way of thinking he had good reason, because St. Raphaël had been the sponsors of the great French riders Gérard Saint, Roger Rivière and Raphaël Géminiani, all of whom had been affected by tragedy. Saint, a very talented young star, had been killed in a car crash in 1960; the same year Rivière, who had replaced Anquetil in the French Tour de France team, had been vying for the lead with the eventual winner, Italian Gastone Nencini, when he crashed while descending the Col de Perjuret and broke his back – his career was over. Pills found in his jersey pockets were rumoured to be Palfium – an analgesic which could help to dull pain, but could also slow reaction times. Rivière later revealed that he was taking up to 40 tablets per day. Rivière's shattered lumbar vertebrae were eventually mended and he was able to walk again, albeit with difficulty, but he never really recovered mentally or physically and died at the early age of 40 from cancer. Géminiani, who had come second in the 1951 Tour and third in 1958, had been on that infamous racing/holiday trip to Africa in 1960 and had contracted the malaria that was to prove fatal to his friend Fausto Coppi. Géminiani recovered, but didn't race much again and retired at the end of the season. Yet, despite all these forebodings and his personal reservations, Anquetil agreed to the new sponsorship and advised Géminiani also to hire Shay; he knew his value as a rider and team-mate.

With this change in sponsorship it seemed possible that Shay might have had the opportunity to race alongside Tom Simpson, whom the team really wanted to sign from the existing Rapha team, and with whom he had developed a good friendship. However, Tom had his own ambitions and, with his star on the rise after winning the previous year's Tour of Flanders, decided he would have to move on. For all that he was on quite good terms with Anquetil, he didn't want to be his *domestique*. He knew he could have earned good money riding on the French star's team, but he also knew that he wouldn't get the opportunities to win as many races, nor have the chance to lead the team in major races. So Tom signed with the Gitane-Leroux team for the 1962 season.

The Saint-Raphaël-Helyett team was eventually finalised, with Shay very happy to sign for them, and it was to prove a very successful period of the Irishman's career.

Shay began the season slowly enough, but his form started to come good in time for his first big objective of the season, the Vuelta a España. One downside of his participation in the Vuelta was that he would be unable to take part in many of the spring classics, where he had come close to victory on a number of occasions. Prior to joining his team-mates for the Spanish tour he showed he was in good form by finishing second in Paris–Vimoutiers (now known as Paris–Camembert).

On the 27th of April Shay felt confident as he lined up for the start of the 2,843 kilometres and the 17 stages of the 1962 Vuelta. He had trained hard and had every intention of using this form to aid Anquetil, although he was probably thinking he might get at least one chance for the personal glory of a stage win. The French star was the clear favourite for this race, and nobody else was really expected to seriously challenge him. Anquetil was aiming to become the first rider in history to win the three big tours – the Tour de France, Giro d'Italia and the Vuelta a España. To try to ensure this, his team manager Géminiani had put together a particularly strong team. In addition to Anquetil and Elliott, it contained Rudi Altig, Jean-Claude Annaert, Albertus Geldermans, Jean Graczyk, Marcel Janssens, Jean Stablinski and Michel Stolker, all very talented and established riders.

Shay wasn't long in displaying his fine form, second to the Spaniard Antonio Barrutia of the KAS team on the opening 90-kilometre stage, which finished on Montjuic, the hill overlooking Barcelona. On the next stage, 185 kilometres to Tortosa, Shay was seventh, another good effort, while his German team-mate, Rudi Altig, who had all the makings of a major star, claimed the yellow jersey after a very impressive win. This was to be the beginning of a show of dominance by the St. Raphaël-Helyett team. However, only Altig and Shay would wear the leader's yellow jersey for the rest of the tour, which, to say the least, was hardly what Anquetil had planned.

Not long after the start of the 141-kilometre fourth stage Shay, feeling very strong, broke away with KAS rider Martin Piñera. The stage was from Valencia to the coastal resort of Benidorm, where he easily beat the Spaniard in the sprint for the line, over two minutes ahead of Nino Defilippis, the Italian star who had won the previous stage, and was to win the Italian national title later that year. In the process Shay convincingly took the yellow jersey, thereby becoming the first English speaker to wear the leader's jersey in any of the three big tours. It was a remarkable achievement for the Irishman, who had now won stages in two of the three grand tours with 'only' the Tour de France remaining.

The St. Raphaël team showed their strength again in the following day's stage, a 21-kilometre team time trial, beating the Spanish Ferrys team into second place by two and a half minutes – a massive gap over such a short distance. Of course Shay was still race leader after the TTT, but lost the jersey to Rudi Altig on the seventh stage to Almería, where the German won his second individual stage. Shay, however, regained it two stages later when he finished fourth after a very hilly ninth stage into Córdoba, after Altig had punctured. The German was very irate after the finish of the stage, as no member of the team had offered up their bike to him; one might imagine that maybe this was on the instructions of Anquetil and the manager, who were getting very concerned at his increasingly dominant position.

At this stage St. Raphaël held the first five places on General Classification. Anquetil, it seemed, had been quite happy at first to see his team-mates swap the lead, as he did not want to have the stress of holding the leader's jersey at such an early stage in the race, but he was now getting more and more worried about the 'sprinter' Altig. During his stint in the leader's jersey Shay had even managed to get into some dangerous breaks which could have increased his lead, but his loyalty prevented him from contributing any effective help. Despite the good form he was in, his priority as ever was to help Anquetil win the race overall, and Anquetil had planned to take over the jersey by winning the Stage 15 time trial. However, considerable discontent was growing within the Saint Raphaël team, and Shay was stuck in the middle of the emerging divide.

The next five stages saw four victories fall to Saint Raphaël riders, while Shay was to hold on to the overall lead without many problems until the 15th stage – the all important long time trial. Altig's confidence prior to the time trial was sky high: he categorically asserted that he would be the overall winner of the race. Although Shay maintained a slim lead over Altig going into the 82-kilometre time trial from Bayonne to San Sebastian, all of the talk amongst the journalists was about whether Altig or Anquetil would win. Shay was not even being considered as a potential overall winner, even though it is well known that race leaders have often excelled in time trials because of the confidence that wearing the leader's jersey gives them. Time trialling, however, was not a particularly strong point for Shay, despite the earlier promise he had shown on the track.

In the end Shay did lose the race leadership after finishing a disappointing 10th (albeit in peculiar circumstances), losing seven and a half minutes to Altig. During the time trial from Bayonne to San Sebastian he had fallen on the descent after crossing the French-Spanish frontier. A thunderstorm had left the roads very slippery and his crash had badly damaged his handlebars and front wheel. He needed to change bikes, but his team car had been held up by the customs officials, who were intent on making a drug search as the authorities started to acknowledge the drugs problem within the sport. It meant Shay had to wait a long time for a replacement bike. When the car eventually turned up he lost his temper. 'Where have you been?' he shouted at them. 'Held up at customs,' came the reply. 'You liars,' Shay shouted. 'You've held back because you don't want me to win.' He lost valuable time, and with it any possibility of winning the Vuelta. It's impossible to know if he really thought he could do a good enough ride in the time trial to stand a chance of outright victory: he would have needed a time very close to that of Altig and Anquetil on that crucial day. Nor is it possible to determine whether the crash and subsequent delay would have accounted for the seven and a half minutes he lost. Others have taken a different view, however. Stablinski, for instance, later said he thought that, without the mishaps, Shay could have won the race overall, and one of Shay's best friends, Peter Crinnion, when interviewed for the film 'Cycle of Betrayal', also felt sure he could have won. But in reality that was probably unlikely, although second overall behind Altig would have been a possiblity.

As things turned out Altig was to win the 82-kilometre time trial by just one second from 'team leader' Anquetil, and take the leader's jersey from Shay, which he held until the finish of the tour in Bilbao two days later. Shay reverted to his normal role as *domestique* to help protect and support the overall leader, Altig, during the final two days, although there were no significant threats to his position. Altig would later say of Shay 'Often when I said to him during a race: "now I need you to work" he would nearly break the bike so hard did he push it. A worthy team-mate and good on the bike, but I also appreciated him as a person.'

Rumours were rife in the peloton and the Press that Anquetil was so extremely displeased with the outcome of the race that he failed to start the last stage. The race doctor announced that he was suffering from gastroenteritis, and upon his return to Paris he visited the Pasteur Institute where the real reason behind his sickness was diagnosed. He had been suffering from viral hepatitis. Many of the journalists and others, though, were unconvinced, and remained of the opinion that it was his ego that was injured rather than his body. Rudi Altig, for example, in an interview decades afterwards, said, 'He wasn't interested in second place and so quit, which was bad form for the team riders who missed out on the prize money because Anquetil didn't finish. He was saying: "I cannot win so I'm off!"'

Altig and Anquetil were never comfortable in the same team and eventually, after the end of the 1964 season, they went their separate ways. Altig explained: 'I was three years in Anquetil's team and as a rider he was very selfish. Once we had a row because our agreement was that I would work for him in the stage races and he would work for me in the classic races. In Paris–Nice I worked for him, and he won. Three or four days later was Milan–San Remo and normally he should have worked for me, but 50 kilometres after the start he dropped out of the race. In my opinion he did not respect our agreement and after that the mood in the team deteriorated and I eventually quit. Sometime later we renewed our friendship, but not in the same team. As a human being he was a great guy, but as a rider he was very selfish.' *

Anquetil's withdrawal, for whatever reason, elevated Shay into third place overall. The 1962 Vuelta was a long way from being the most mountainous Tour of Spain, but even so, Shay's final position on the podium was historic in the realms of English-speaking professional cyclists. He also finished second in the points competition. For all the team's internal problems he was able to take a great deal of satisfaction from his own performance, which was seen as brilliant by many in the Press. Shay had proved himself an even finer rider than many people had imagined. He

---

* Vin Denson, who rode for Anquetil between 1965 and 1967, offers a somewhat different view in his book *The Full Cycle*. 'So long as you worked for him in the races he wanted to win he would let you do well in those races he wasn't interested in.' André Darrigade, on the other hand, seems to share Altig's assessment that while Anquetil was generous in his private life he was a selfish rider: 'Anquetil was a friend, but he was more a taker than a giver. The team-mates all worked hard for him but he didn't like to work for them, to reward them.' But Anquetil was a champion, and in Jean Bobet's opinion we shouldn't expect anything else: 'He wasn't generous and that's one of the reasons why he was a champion; all the great champions are friendless, egocentric and really selfish! They only think of themselves, otherwise they couldn't be a champion.'

had ridden strongly and unselfishly, first in support of Anquetil and then Altig, and did not have one bad day in the entire race.*

As for the team, they won the team classification, together with twelve of the seventeen stages, altogether a remarkable team performance, despite the controversy between Altig and Anquetil. St.Raphaël were so dominant in fact that the manager of the KAS team, Dalmacio Langarica, was heard to claim that St. Raphaël were the 'Real Madrid of cycle racing', a great compliment since Real Madrid had won the European Cup in the five consecutive years from 1956 to 1960.

Shay and the team won plenty of money as Altig collected 250,000 pesetas for the overall victory (approximately £1500). A lot of other cash and prizes the team won were also shared among all the riders. Altig's performance was all the more impressive given the fact that this was his first real season racing on the road. His background was predominantly on the track, where he had won the World Pursuit Championships as an amateur in 1959, and twice as a professional in 1960 and 1961 – and he would go on to be World Road Champion in 1966.

The friction caused by Altig's Vuelta win continued to have repercussions within the Saint Raphaël camp. Mickey Wiegant resigned over the way the team had been managed by Raphaël Géminiani, and Anquetil, feeling he had been double-crossed by the German, stated that he would have nothing more to do with Altig. But the indisputable fact was that Altig beat him in that final time trial. For sure, Anquetil had planned that to be where he would make his major move for race leadership, but he had already left himself with far too much to do: it was doubtful that Altig could lose five minutes to Anquetil that day, even if he'd tried. The truth is that Anquetil had not ridden a good race. Their differences were supposedly resolved by Daniel Dousset, who was manager of both men. Dousset, it is said, convinced Anquetil that he had only lost the Vuelta because of his sickness, and persuaded him that Altig would be no threat to him in the Tour de France, as he was not strong enough in the mountains.

---

* On the same day that Shay was finishing the Tour of Spain, his younger brother Paul was winning the Route de Cill Manntain, held on a tough route around the Wicklow Mountains and organised by the respected amateur club Shay would join when he retired, the Bray Wheelers. Paul became the first holder of the trophy which Shay had presented to the promoters. Years later, the race would be renamed the Shay Elliott Memorial, and it is still being fought out to this day.

Due to his racing schedule Shay was unable to spend much time in Paris after the Vuelta. Just a few days later he had to travel to take part in the Grand Prix du Midi Libre, where he finished a very creditable 10th overall. After the Midi Libre he had a longer break, where he could spend more time with his wife and son Pascal at home in Paris.

Despite his good form, in June he had a major blow to his hopes for the season as he found out that he would not be riding in the Tour de France that year. He had been amongst the original fifteen riders on the St Raphaël shortlist, which the team had been required to send to the Tour organisers by 1st of March. The reason for him not being selected stemmed from the fact that when the Tour reverted back to trade teams one of the stipulations was that each team could only contain three foreigners. Shay felt confident that, despite this, he would obtain one of the places on the St. Raphaël team. Of the seven foreigners on the original provisional list, Brian Robinson was not having his best season and had retired, Dutch star Johan De Roo was more interested in trying to win classics later on in the season than burning himself out in the Tour, and Marcel Janssens had just ridden the exhausting Bordeaux–Paris (where he finished third). That left Geldermans, Altig, Elliott and Stolker to fight for the three final positions. Rudi Altig deservedly was offered one of the positions, having won the Tour of Spain, and eventually more than justified his selection by taking three stages and the Tour's points jersey. The two remaining positions were given to the Dutchmen, Albertus Geldermans and Mies Stolker. Geldermans amply justified his selection as he helped Anquetil win the race again, and managed to finish a remarkable fifth overall himself, in addition to holding the *maillot jaune* for two days, but the fact is there was a lot of commercial politics in the selection, which centred especially around St Raphaël making a new sales drive in the Netherlands. Whatever the reasons for his non-selection, Shay, after his great performance in the Vuelta and his well known loyalty to his team leader, had every reason to feel very disappointed at missing out on the Tour.

All the more so because at the last minute he did almost find himself on the starting line. Géminiani had informed his team that Jacques Anquetil would be the sole leader, a decision to which Rudi Altig objected. As World Pursuit Champion and Vuelta winner, he argued that he should get preferential treatment in the team and be joint leader. Géminiani told him that if he didn't accept Anquetil as team leader, then his place would go to Shay. Unfortunately for the Irishman, Géminiani did not have to make good his threat.

There was a particular irony to Shay being dropped from the Tour team in that his friend Brian Robinson had been campaigning for years to have trade teams instead of national teams in the Tour, and Shay had supported this. In the past he felt that Robinson had never had adequate support from his British or International team-mates. Then, when they were finally introduced, Shay didn't get a place.

Shay's own view, which he later revealed, was that he'd been dropped from the Tour because of the events at the Vuelta a couple of months earlier. He suspected that some of the other members of the team believed that he had plotted with Altig (they were room-mates in Spain) to bring about Anquetil's downfall, but this was pure speculation.

As it turned out he missed quite a controversial Tour. Twelve riders pulled out of the race sick in a single day, many of them from the same team. The riders and their *directeurs sportifs* insisted they had eaten bad fish at their hotel. The hotel proved this not to have been the case, and Dr. Dumas concluded that they had taken a badly administered cocktail that included the pain-killer, morphine. The incident led Dumas to organise a conference on drug prevention at Uriage-les-Bains the following year. This produced France's first law against drugs in sport, passed shortly after a similar law in Belgium, although it would not be until decades later that tests started to become anywhere near effective.* Shay also missed out on seeing his friend Tom Simpson become the first English speaking rider to wear the yellow jersey in the Tour, which he took on the stage to Saint Gaudens and held for just a day.

Financially Shay also suffered from Géminiani's selection. He calculated that he lost £800 by not riding the Tour, and over £2000 due to missing out on a number of the lucrative post-Tour criterium contracts. In this era of cycling many riders did not receive particularly high salaries from the team sponsors (sometimes very little, if anything) and often had to live on their prize money and any other income they could generate. This was why the post-Tour de France criteriums were important: they offered them a chance to earn substantially more money through appearance fees and prize money at the many, very popular local races held throughout France, Belgium and Holland, and some of the other major cycling countries. These criteriums usually consisted of many laps of a short circuit based around a village or town, and the race would generate a carnival atmosphere in the locality. A good performance in the Tour would help riders to negotiate better appearance fees.

---

* Even with today's scientific advances they are still not 100% effective.

114

The contracts for racing in criteriums were organized through agents, and three in particular had control over many of the top cyclists and criteriums throughout Europe at this time. They were Jean van Buggenhout of Belgium, and the Frenchmen, Roger Piel and Daniel Dousset. After Dousset's riding career petered out in the 1940s he turned his attention to management, and went on to manage Anquetil, Stablinski, Aimar, Simpson, Roger Rivière and Shay, amongst others. Cyclists relied on these agents to ensure they received appearance money for riding in the post-Tour criteriums and other races throughout the season. If they were not contracted to one of the agents involved in this cartel, it was nigh on impossible to make any money on the potentially lucrative circuit. The agents, of course, would ensure that they also got a healthy percentage of the appearance fees.

The money for organising a criterium was usually donated by the local *comité-des-fêtes* out of the profits made from their own fete day, and by local businesses. Income would come from a combination of public entry fees to the criterium, raffles where goats, cows or cheese, amongst other prizes, could be won, fees paid by the travelling fun fairs which would inevitably be in the town at the same time, and often an evening ball organised in the local dance hall.

The commentator, or *Monsieur le Speaker*, at the race would also generally get somewhere between five and ten per-cent of the total. A good speaker was usually able to persuade both spectators and the local businesses to donate more money for primes on various laps. The more that was donated the more both he and the riders would receive. The importance of criteriums has decreased since then, due to salaries increasing significantly in the 1980s. There are far fewer events now, and they can be a lot smaller, but they can still generate a good and sometimes great payday for the cyclists. In 2004 it was rumoured that Lance Armstrong pocketed €110,000 for appearing in a criterium in Prague.

Although he had missed the publicity from competing in the Tour, Shay went through a purple patch in some of the more important post-Tour races he did ride. He was second in the Circuit de la Vienne, third in the Grand Prix d'Orchies (both big French races he won at different points in his career). In addition, he won the Ploneour-Lanvern Criterium (not far from where he would later establish a hotel) and followed this up with wins in the Chateagiron Criterium, the Aubusson Grand Prix and the Felletin Grand Prix. However, he was also training hard to build up his stamina as he had bigger ambitions for the rest of the season.

And while Shay was enjoying these successes, a second Irishman was making his name in the cycling world. Peter Crinnion achieved what had escaped Shay when he won the 9-day Route de France, becoming the first foreigner to win the race in its 22-year old history. He had over four minutes to spare over his nearest rival when the race finished in Besançon. This was a remarkable performance, and a very promising future was predicted for Peter. It didn't work out that way, but he was to have a close relationship with Shay and to play an important part in his life.

Earlier on in August the Irish cycling association affiliated to the UCI, Cumann Rothaíochta na hÉireann (CRE) had confirmed the names of those who would be representing Ireland in the World Championships. Obviously, Shay was nominated to take part in the professional road race. His brother Paul, John Lackey and Sean Dillon would represent Ireland in the 200-kilometre amateur event. Shay faced a problem prior to the start of the race, as he was told he would not be able to ride unless a fine imposed on the CRE by the UCI be paid. Fortunately, Philippe Potin of Shay's former club, ACBB, stumped up the £50 required. Stephen Lawless of the CRE later explained the situation in a letter to the press: 'This association regrets any inconvenience or embarrassment caused to Elliott in this instance, and the matter is being taken up with the governing body.' The intervention of Potin would prove to be very important. Presumably Shay would have paid the £50 required by the UCI, but perhaps he was digging his heels in, as the fine had been imposed on the CRE and was therefore not his responsibility.*

In the couple of weeks prior to the World Championships Shay decided to forsake the guaranteed income from the criterium circuit. After missing the Tour he was determined to put in another really good ride in a major race, for fear his reputation would start to slip. So he started training intensively, often behind a Derny. This kind of training had long been deemed a beneficial method of helping riders to peak for particular races. When Stablinski heard of this he joined Shay and also started training behind a Derny. Before they left for the World Championships Géminiani told the Irishman that he was in better condition than Stablinski, and, furthermore, that the Frenchman knew it. Shay was also said to have been warned by Géminiani to look out for his trade team-mate and 'good friend', Stablinski.

---

* He may well have been trying to call the CRE's bluff, but it obviously helped that Potin stepped in and paid the fine.

Shay and Stablinski travelled together to Salo in Italy, beside Lake Garda, where they met up with Shay's brother, Paul, and the other members of the Irish amateur team. Shay was obviously a very keen spectator of the Amateur Road Race Championship, which took place on the Saturday, the day before the professional event. Unfortunately, none of the Irish team finished. In Salo Shay shared a room with the French team manager, Marcel Bidot, for the two nights before the race. Some people saw this as an indication that Shay was effectively an extra member of the French team, but perhaps it revealed no more than that Shay wanted to save a bit of money. According to his one-time coach, Gerry Duffin, Shay could sometimes be a bit 'tight'. But then, most professionals were, as they had to work so hard for their money.

The professional race on the Sunday started under blue skies and the temperature would soar as the day progressed. The good weather and the prospect of an Italian win produced a massive crowd, estimated to be at least 200,000. The course, almost 300 kilometres long, was considered to be very tough. The riders would have to face the climb of the Taormina Wall, which had gradients of up to 12 per-cent. The heat would make the race all the more difficult and would eventually cause many to retire.

As was the norm with the World Road Professional Championships a number of lesser known riders went clear early on, but, also as usual, this caused little concern to the big hitters. The race would only really get going and take shape after some 180 kilometres. Somewhere after this point in the race, on the sixteenth of the 23 laps, Shay managed to get away in a small group, which also contained Stablinski. The seven other members of the break were the German star Rolf Wolfshohl and his team-mate Horst Oldenburg, Jos Hoevenaers of Belgium, the Italians Franco Cribiori and Arnaldo Pambianco, Dutchman Huub Zilverberg and Stablinski's French team-mate Joseph Groussard. As the race progressed a number of these riders were dropped.

A few from the main peloton did get close to bridging across to the leading group, including Britain's Tom Simpson, who got to within 50 metres of the break, but no closer. Rik Van Looy, who was favourite to win the Championships for the third year in succession, made a valiant effort to join them four laps from the end, despite his team-mate Hoevenaers being in the group, but he also was unable to close the gap.

Going into the last couple of laps Shay, Stablinski, Hoevenaers and Wolfshohl were the only survivors in the front group. Of these, Shay, with his pedigree, would quite rightly have been considered the fastest finisher.

He said afterwards, 'I thought the big moves in the race would come after about the fourteenth lap, so I sat in the bunch and waited until I thought a big break was starting. Jean on the other hand was chasing most of the breaks, except the smaller early ones.'

Two laps from the end Shay was in conversation with Stablinski, who persuaded him to attack; the Irishman, he claimed, was capable of winning the race. Shay attacked in an attempt to drain the Belgian and German of their energy, and stayed out on his own for the best part of a lap. Many in the crowd were now convinced that they were watching the new World Champion. If he won it would easily have been Shay's most important win by far, and would change his life and career forever. However, Hoevenaers and Wolfshohl were working together to haul him back. When Shay was finally caught, Stablinski made a classic move between 'team-mates' and counter attacked just before the start of the final lap. Now it was the Frenchman out on his own. Although Wolfshohl and Hoevenaers had worked very hard to catch Shay, they made no effort to try and bring back Stablinski. Shay later recounted that he asked the other two in the break what was going on, but they just grinned back at him without saying a word. It would later transpire that Stablinski had paid the other two to work for him against his friend. Looking at the archive footage from the 1962 Worlds, at one point, when Shay is leading the break, you can see Wolfshohl behind, reaching over to shake Stab's hand. Was this the point where the deal was being made, literally behind Shay's back?

On the final lap Stablinski punctured and, with no team car in sight, had to borrow a bicycle which was several sizes too big for him. Despite that, the others made no inroad into his lead. The race was now effectively over: Stablinski finished nearly a minute and a half clear of Shay, who, easily stronger than the other two, jumped clear towards the finish to claim the silver medal. The Irish star had lost what would turn out to be his best chance ever to win the World title, ironically to his very calculating 'best friend'.

After the race Shay said: 'It was a very difficult race because of the heat and the hills, but it was my biggest success ever. I suppose, in one way, it is disappointing to finish second, but considering I was the only Irishman in the race and had no national team support, I shouldn't complain.' He went on, 'I thought I could win when I got away on my own near the end. When the others caught me I wanted to try again, but then Stablinski went, and he went like a flash. At the time that Jean broke away I wasn't feeling too good, a little sick in the stomach. Perhaps it was something I'd eaten, or perhaps it was from not eating. I can't say. But in the two or three minutes that I felt not quite right Jean attacked. I could not have caught and passed him, so I concentrated on holding off the others. We had agreed that one or the other would take the title. I'm not supposed to say that I helped Jean, since the race is an individual one, but if it could not be me I am glad it was Stablinski who won. He is my team-mate in Paris and my best friend in professional cycling, and is godfather to my seven-month-old son.'

The rainbow jersey was presented to Stablinski by the Italian President of the UCI, Adriano Rodoni. Podium photos from that day show the disappointment etched on Elliott's face. It seemed that after all the silver medal was not much consolation. Afterwards, Stablinski swore that some day he would repay his debt to his friend.

A few months later Shay heard the rumours that were circulating about how Stablinski had won, but couldn't or wouldn't believe them. He summed up Stablinski's cunning by saying, 'Even if there had been only the two of us left for the final sprint, Jean would have thought up some plan and beaten me.' Only years later would he allude to the well founded view that Stablinski had paid off Wolfshohl and Hoevenaers. During a television interview with the Irish state broadcaster RTE, after his retirement, he explained how he had lost the race: 'Actually, I was outnumbered. There were four of us with two laps to go, and I regret it to this present day. I still think I was the strongest of the four, but I was outnumbered three to one. Even if I had been twice as fit as I was the force of numbers meant I would have been beaten'. When asked to expand on this, he replied, 'No, I wouldn't like to elaborate on this, but it is true due to the fact that there were four of us in the breakaway, four different nationalities. Stablinski, who won the Championships, wouldn't normally have the German or Belgian riding for him, but a little coaxing, and a promise of cash on his behalf got them back over to his side of the fence.'

Despite being best friends with Stab at the time, Shay didn't have the Machiavellian streak that his friend had in abundance. In fact, he was known within the peloton to be a very loyal friend and an honest man. Jean Bobet reckoned that 'Shay was more of an amateur cyclist, not cut out for the rough and tumble of the professional world because loyalty had more value to him than anything else. Loyalty and naiveté prevented him from fulfilling his true potential.'

His true potential included the possibility of becoming World Champion that day. André Darrigade, for one, remains convinced of that. But he was up against Stablinski: 'Stab was very clever. He knew how to race, knew when to attack and could read a race with his eyes, winning with both his cunning and his legs. But they were close friends and Stab also happened to be the Godfather of his son. They trained together, preparing for the championship behind a motorbike and I'm sure Elliot could have won that day. He should have been World Champion.'

A number of years after those World Championships Stablinski would join the Mercier team, coincidentally the team to which Shay went after he left Anquetil's camp. There Stablinski would become a team-mate of Barry Hoban, the English cyclist Shay had raced with in the Mercier team. Hoban would be a similar victim of Stablinski's craftiness in a big single-day race on the border of France and Belgium, the Circuit de la Frontier. They were both in the leading break towards the end of the race, and Stab indicated to Hoban that he was going to attack and that Hoban should mark Arthur De Cabooter, as he was the danger-man. The implication was that de Cabooter would probably chase Stablinski, which would then give Hoban the chance to counter attack and maybe win.

As Stablinski disappeared up the road, Hoban, sitting on De Cabooter's wheel, realised that the Belgian had probably never posed any real danger. De Cabooter had been a great cyclist at his peak, winning the Tour of Flanders in 1960, but his greatest days were behind him. Hoban trailed De Cabooter over the *pavé* at what he described as a snail's pace. Stablinski had wanted to gain some ground on Hoban as he knew the Englishman would win if it came to a final sprint. By the time Hoban eventually realised he had been duped, Stablinski was too far ahead and took the win.

The former French champion, Henry Anglade, agreed with Hoban's opinion of Stab, saying 'Stablinski was a fox. He was impossible to outmanoeuvre. The English would have called him Sherlock Holmes due to his ability to work out everything, and he had great race intelligence.'

Towards the end of the 1962 season there was more success for St. Raphaël and Shay played the team-mate's role to perfection in helping his Dutch team-mate, Jo De Roo, to a great victory in the classic Paris–Tours. At the end of the season Shay finished in equal eighth position (ironically, equal with Stablinski) in the Super Prestige Pernod competition – the forerunner of the World Cup, Pro Tour and UCI rankings – whereby riders received points based on their finishing position in the very top races. It was a measure of the consistency he had shown throughout the year. Although not up to the same standard as more contemporary and comprehensive competitions, it was the only ranking system at that time. He finished ahead of team-mates, Jean Graczyk and Jo De Roo, and also cyclists of the calibre of Federico Bahamontes and André Darrigade. Not surprisingly Jacques Anquetil won the competition, and his prize was two million francs, which equated to about £1500. The 1962 season saw Shay make history yet again for English-speaking professional riders on the continent and, not least, Irish cycling history.

10

The wonderful road to Roubaix; at last Shay shines in Yellow

Prior to the start of the 1963 season, while Stablinski, Anquetil, Graczyk and their wives had enjoyed a winter holiday in New Caledonia, in the South Pacific, Shay, as usual, returned to Ireland. After his best season to date, he received the honour of being the first CRE cyclist to win one of the Caltex awards, given to the best performer in a number of different sports. As Shay had returned to the continent, Jim collected the award on his son's behalf from the Taoiseach, Seán Lemass, and managed to get his photo on the front page of *The Irish Times*.

On his return Shay's training was set back by particularly unkind weather in the South of France. He met up with Stablinski and Tom Simpson in Narbonne, but they soon became snowbound; they even had difficulty getting out of their accommodation to replenish their stocks of food. According to Simpson their training consisted of digging out the snow and going out to shoot ducks to eat, and that if Shay hadn't proved to be such an excellent marksman they would have starved! The trio were eventually able to escape Narbonne and start training in Nice, where the weather was somewhat better. This delay in his training programme would turn out be somewhat fortuitous as it meant that Shay's best form would not come until later in the year. This was to prove significant because Anquetil had already guaranteed that Shay, after his performances in the previous season, would be one of the three foreign riders in the St Raphaël team for the Tour de France.

With his principal season's target of helping his team leader win the Tour, Shay made an inauspicious start to the season at the Tour of Sardinia, where he retired on the final stage. He also had a relatively quiet Paris–Nice, although he rode well enough to contribute to Anquetil's convincing overall win. Raphaël Géminiani's general team policy for the season was for Anquetil to be team leader for the bigger stage races, and Altig and Stablinski to lead St Raphaël in the one-day races, with Shay taking his chances whenever the opportunity presented itself. Altig had also been a member of the team that helped Anquetil to win Paris–Nice, but three days later, in Milan–San Remo, Anquetil pulled out after only 50 kilometres. It was the beginning of the end for Altig with the St Raphaël team.

At this time Shay was also helping his younger brother settle into Paris. Paul Elliott had decided to go to the continent in a bid to follow in his brother's footsteps. He became a member of ACBB, where Shay had raced as an amateur eight years previously. 'I hope first to become an independent semi-professional and then a full professional like Shay,' he said, adding, "there is a very big jump in standard between amateur and professional cycling, but I'm taking the chance and I hope it works out all right.'

Shay's Classics season was disappointing, and he had no results of any note except a third place in the 260-km Boucles Roquevairoises in a bunch sprint finish behind Paris-Roubaix winner Emile Daems. This was a prestigious race at the time and suggested Shay's form was progressing in the right direction. His next big race was Ghent–Wevelgem, which resulted in a controversial finish although it did not directly involve Shay. His group had come in over two minutes behind the winner, the Belgian Benoni Beheyt.

Beheyt (who would unexpectedly win the World Championships later that year) very narrowly out-sprinted Tom Simpson for the win, and there were rumours afterwards that Beheyt had paid off Simpson. Photographs of the sprint published afterwards showed Simpson with fingers on his brake levers well before the line; this was a rumour that Simpson denied.

Not long afterwards both Shay and Peter Crinnion were formally announced as being among the early provisional list of starters for that year's Tour de France. Crinnion was a member of the Margnat team, and would have been riding in the service of one of the other main favourites, the great Spanish climber, Federico Bahamontes, winner in 1959.

Shay's form improved somewhat in April and he achieved some good results: second yet again in Paris–Camembert, and seventh in the only German classic, the Grand Prix of Frankfurt. Following on from these results, he was once again selected for the Vuelta a España. Shay's last race before travelling to Spain was Paris–Brussels, which was won by his team-mate Stablinski, with Tom Simpson finishing second, five seconds behind. On the same day he was racing in Paris-Brussels, his brother Paul achieved a good result by finishing 11th in one of the French amateur classic, Paris–Evreux. For a time it seemed just possible that the younger

Elliott might follow his brother into the paid ranks, although it has to be said that at a similar stage in his career Shay had been far more successful. In the end it proved not to be; Paul wasn't able to follow in his brother's footsteps and returned to Ireland.*

Jacques Anquetil had again decided to attempt the Vuelta-Tour double and also to become only the third ever French winner of Spain's national tour. This time there would be no Rudi Altig in the race which had caused so much friction in St Raphaël's camp the year before. And this time Anquetil did not wait to stamp his authority on the entire race.

The Vuelta began with a road stage on the first morning, followed in the afternoon by a 52-kilometre time trial into the northern town of Gijón, which Anquetil won with ease. By the end of the opening day the Frenchman was in the leader's jersey, and he never relinquished it. For him and the whole team it was to be a very successful race.

Shay also started the race well and managed to get in the winning break on the third stage, a mamouth 249 kilometres through the Basque hills from Torrelavega to Vitoria. The very fast Spaniard, Antonio Barrutia, managed to get clear of the three others in the break to win the stage. Shay came in second, 34 seconds behind, and climbed to ninth place overall, which would be as high as he would get on General Classification during the race that year.

The St Raphaël team was every bit as powerful as the year before, and defended Anquetil's lead without any real difficulties. Shay was riding strongly but, as the race wound its way south beside the Mediterranean, with only three stages to go before the finish in Madrid, he was still without a stage win. He hadn't given up hope though, and on the longest stage of the race, 252 kilometres into Valencia, he finally achieved the win he'd been seeking when he finished two seconds clear of Sebastian Elorza, of the KAS team. It was a fine win and would have helped his chance of getting into final team selection for the Tour de France.**

In addition to winning overall with Anquetil, St Raphaël would also collect the team prize together with six stages, and their Dutch rider, Bas

---

* Some Irish friends of Shay and Paul considered Paul to have even more natural talent on the bike than his older brother. But Paul's first love was hunting, and if he had a choice of training or going hunting, the bike would lose out.

** Shay's prize for winning the stage was a Luigi-Franchi shotgun. This was the gun that would be involved in the tragedy of his death years afterwards.

Maliepaard, would win the points competition. Shay could not repeat his fine third place overall of the previous year, but he seemed more than happy with his role in supporting his team leader in a race that proved to be a much happier experience than the previous year. This time there was only one absolute leader and the overall winner, Anquetil, was on track for the first Tour/Vuelta double in history.

Not long afterwards Shay managed to get his second victory of the season when he won the Grand Prix de la Trinité, shortly before the start of the Tour de France. This was a very small race but showed his condition and form was still progressing just in time for his main objective of the season, the Tour de France. St Raphaël selected only two foreigners for their Tour team, even though they were entitled to three. Anquetil had been true to his word and Shay was given one of the slots; the other went to Dutchman, Albertus Geldermans who, having finishing fifth the year before, deserved his place, but under the strict understanding he would support Anquetil for the overall victory.

The 1963 Jubilee Tour de France was scheduled to start in Nogent-sur-Marne, not far from the Elliott family home in Bry-sur-Marne. This gave Marguerite the rare opportunity to see her husband, as she had driven the short distance from their home to the start with their son Pascal. The presence of wives at races was usually frowned upon, but Géminiani turned a blind eye on this occasion.

Shay's primary objective was obviously to help his team leader win a record-breaking fourth Tour de France. In the weeks before there had been speculation that Anquetil wouldn't start due to illness caused by a tapeworm, but the Frenchman was able to take his place alongside the others. Shay also had his own personal ambitions for the race, as he still hoped to win a stage. If he did so he would become the first English speaker to win stages in all three major tours. Although his first duty was to Anquetil it seemed likely that he would be given a chance to get some personal glory if circumstances allowed.

Even though the Tour was not the global event it is today, it was still massive in Europe in 1963. The cavalcade that followed the race consisted of over 1,000 people, and highlights of the race would be watched by millions on television every night. The official prize list for the race was £50,000, a very considerable amount of money at that time. A stage win for Shay would also mean he could negotiate substantially better contracts for the criterium circuit after the Tour. Shay had now passed his 29th birthday and knew he did not have too many more years left at the top in the sport. He wanted to earn enough to set himself up in a business to support his family for the rest of their lives.

On the opening 152.5-kilometre stage to Epernay Anquetil fell and cut his left hand, but without any really bad injury. Shay and the rest of the St. Raphaël team paced him back to the peloton without any major problems. One of Anquetil's main rivals, the great Spanish climber Federico Bahamontes, winner of the Tour in 1959, had shown his intentions were serious even at that early point in the race by getting into the winning break of four. The stage was won by the Belgian Eddy Pauwels from his compatriot, Edgard Sorgeloos, with Britain's Alan Ramsbottom a fine third and Bahamontes in fourth. Eddy Pauwels, now with the yellow jersey, was a possible outsider for the overall and Bahamontes had gained some valuable time on Anquetil. It had not been a good day for the St Raphaël team.

Rik Van Looy won stage 2A after 185 kilometres, which ended in a big bunch sprint. Stage 2B was a team time trial where, although it was known that Anquetil was off his game, St Raphaël were very disappointed to finish in only fourth place. Pelforth were dominant that day with Ramsbottom, still in excellent form, leading them over the line. The French 'super team' lost nearly a minute, and Pauwels kept the yellow jersey.

The third stage from Jambes to Roubaix was over some very difficult roads and a number of riders were to crash out of the race. After 70 kilometres a group of 12 broke away, with two of Anquetil's team-mates, Shay and Stablinski, up in the break. Because they were in the team of the race favourite, and also because the break contained two danger men, Henry Anglade and Gilbert de Smet, neither of the St. Raphaël men were obliged to work. Yet despite their non-participation, the break's lead jumped to nine minutes. Shay was to puncture twice over the cobbled roads, first after 150 kilometres and again 30 kilometres later, but each time, with Stablinski helping him by slowing the group down, he got back to the break. After one of his punctures Shay was so impatient for his team car to arrive that he had jumped off his bike and removed his back wheel, not realising it was actually his front that he had punctured.

Six kilometres from Roubaix Stab led the group onto a cycle lane at the side of the road. Everybody followed, except Shay, who jumped clear on the cobbled stretch, while his team-mate helped the cause by again deliberately slowing the break. The narrow lane made it difficult for the others to get around Stablinski, and this was all the chance Shay needed. When he attacked he gave it his all, as he had done in many races before, but the bad luck he had suffered so often was not going to prevent him from gaining glory on this day. Shay was clear, and arrived into the Vélodrome at Roubaix half a minute ahead of his breakaway companions. He took both the stage and the yellow jersey. He was the second English speaker to wear the yellow jersey as Tom Simpson had worn it for a day the year previously. This stage win made him the first and only Irishman to win stages in all three major tours.

Shay was mobbed by reporters when he crossed the line, before setting out on a lap of honour around the Vélodrome. He said: 'I'm very happy to have won this stage. I hadn't done much in the stage until the Paris–Roubaix [cobbled] section. Today is a sort of revenge for me on this great classic route.' This was in reference to his Paris–Roubaix ride in 1958, when a broken saddle just ten kilometres from the finish denied him final victory.

He went on to say that he'd been instructed by the team to go to the front. 'It was Anquetil, after seeing that I was strong in yesterday's stage, who told me to ride at the front today and control the breakaways, and that's how I managed to jump into the good break. Our mission was clear. We had to make sure that the break didn't take too much time, and then mark the most dangerous opponents in the finale. I was in perfect condition and I knew that I was going to do well, but I didn't think it would be such a victory…I am very happy, because it means something in the life of a cyclist to wear the yellow jersey, particularly for Ireland. Now people will realise that cycling also has its place elsewhere than on the continent. In those final kilometres I was thinking of my son Pascal. I wanted him to be proud of what I was doing.'

Whether he would try to defend the yellow jersey would depend on the course of the race he told the reporters he was careful not to sound too ambitious, although it was very unlikely he would cause friction in the team since Anquetil would not feel the Irishman represented any real threat, although a number of journalists suggested he might be.

In a scene reminiscent of what had happened to Harry Reynolds all those years ago in Copenhagen, the brass band at the Roubaix Vélodrome played 'God Save the Queen' during the prize presentation, instead of the Irish anthem 'Amhran na bhFiann'. They obviously had not been expecting a win by Shay. It was not the first time that he'd encountered confusion over his nationality. In fact, throughout his career, many race commentators and journalists had described him as British. He never got overly upset by this, merely pointing out every time that actually, he was Irish!

After the stage Jean Stablinski said, 'Séamus was best placed on General Classification, and it was completely normal that he should attack and I should protect him. For my old friend Séamus, I am as happy as he is.' Then he added, somewhat ironically, 'I remember the World Championships in Salo last year.'

Anquetil was equally delighted to see his loyal team-mate take the win, but disappointed that he had lost time to Anglade and De Smet. Henry Anglade won the prize that day for most aggressive rider, and was not particularly happy with the passive role Shay and Stablinski had played in the break, although he later admitted that the two St Raphaël riders had been right to ride the way they did. The day after he had taken the yellow jersey a French cycling magazine tried to help readers to pronounce the name 'Séamus' by outlining the French phonetic spelling of it thus: '*Sé-a-musse*'.

Shay was to hold on to yellow for the next two stages into Rouen and then into Rennes as the race continued westwards. The stage to Rouen was raced in appalling conditions with strong winds and rain, and misfortune struck him not long after the start. On the cobbles, six kilometres into the race, he was involved in a big crash which also took down Henry Anglade. They both escaped unscathed. Shay attempted to break away after 60 kilometres and gained a minute on the peloton, but the audacious effort proved futile and he dropped back to the bunch. Only Shay would have attempted such a move, but whenever he was in this kind of form he was difficult to control.

Marguerite, prominent in a pink suede coat, appeared again at the stage end in Rouen to embrace Shay, after travelling with Pascal from Paris. 'I congratulated him by telephone yesterday,' she said. 'Today, I decided to do it in person.' At the stage end Shay spoke to reporters of his chances of winning overall: 'Naturally, I know my chances of winning the Tour are very slim, as I am not good in the mountains and there are still seventeen days left, but the nine minutes between me and Anquetil and Van Looy raises my hopes.' In retrospect this comment surely has to be taken with a pinch of salt, with Shay throwing a scrap to the beguiled press.

The Irish Press, showing their naiveté about the sport of cycling, ran with the headline, 'SHAY CAN WIN THE TOUR'. They discussed his possibilities with Shay's father, Jim. 'At this stage I'm not sure what to do, but if Séamus keeps this up, I'll be there,' Jim said. 'It all depends on whether his team decides to give him their full support. At the moment they are committed to supporting their number-one rider, Jacques

Anquetil. If Anquetil fails to find his form, however, they will back either Jean Stablinski or Séamus. Whichever one is in the strongest position will undoubtedly get the number-one spot. I think Séamus will, however, try for another stage, even if Anquetil or Stablinski is in the lead.'

He remained upbeat even when asked to discuss the suggestion that Shay's climbing abilities would possibly let him down later in the race: 'When Séamus won a stage in the amateur Route de France, it was over the most mountainous course in the whole race. He might drop some time in the mountains, but I don't think it will seriously affect his chances. Besides, it's the descent I'm worried about rather than the climbing. It is during mountain descents that most accidents occur, especially when they are trying to make up time.'

But, as has been shown time and again, a great amateur climber does not necessarily make a dominating climber when he turns to the cash ranks. He relies more on his strengths and natural talent than he might exhibit later in his career. Shay was surely an outstanding professional rouleur, but neither mountain climbing nor time trialling were his strongest attributes.

Jim, although not a French speaker, had been following the Tour on the French radio station, Europe 1 (there being no live radio coverage in English during the 60s). 'I do the best I can, and most of the time I can make out the position by listening to the names of the riders when they are read out,' he explained.

Stage 6b in Angers was a 24.5-kilometre time trial, and it was hoped that Shay, with over a minute advantage on both Anglade and de Smet, could put in a good enough ride to maintain his lead. 'I'll have a go,' Shay was to say on the start line of the stage, 'but how I hate time trials.'

Unfortunately, he lost nearly three minutes to Gilbert De Smet who took over the lead, as Shay slipped back to third. Disappointing though this was, he had several days of glory in the bank, and the assurance of more lucrative criterium contacts. And in any case, Shay was first and foremost a team player: the most important feature of the day, he said to journalists afterwards, was that Anquetil had won the stage convincingly: 'I never hoped to do more than hold the jersey for more than a few stages. Now I will be going all out to work as a team member with Anquetil, and try and place him on the winner's podium in Paris on July 14th.'

Shay had worn yellow for four stages, and that feat is all the more impressive if you consider that this was more than some cyclists who actually went on to win the race outright, including Charly Gaul, Jan Janssen and Jean Robic. Other greats, such as Rik Van Looy, Tom

Simpson, Rik van Steenbergen and his former mentor Charles Pelissier, wore the jersey for fewer days than Shay. His exploits were unique in Ireland's sporting history, yet they didn't make the impact they should have done. They were overshadowed by something momentous taking place in Ireland itself.

Following directly on from a European tour, which included a visit to Germany where he made his memorable 'Ich bin ein Berliner' speech, the American President, John F. Kennedy, was making an emotional journey to his ancestral homeland. Hundreds of thousands flocked to see JFK, the first American President to visit Ireland, and his visit occupied the headlines of every newspaper for days. This meant the greatest days of Shay's career, in that year's Tour de France, were unfortunately generally confined to the sports pages – the four days of the President's visit virtually coinciding with Shay's four days in yellow. It was perhaps typical of Shay's often untimely bad luck that the presence of JFK would understandably displace almost everything else newsworthy from the headlines.

After four glorious days in the yellow jersey his more characteristic misfortune – on the road – hit him on the eighth stage, when he punctured three times. 'I finished very tired,' he said afterwards. 'It was a stage in which I wanted to take it rather easy in view of the big efforts when we begin climbing mountains, but puncture troubles forced me to make a big effort in catching up.'

On the stage to Grenoble Shay once again showed his worth as a team-mate. Louis Rostollan injured his hip in a fall and was struggling behind the peloton. As he was a strong climber, and therefore very important to Anquetil's overall chances, Shay dropped back to help him get back into the bunch. But Rostollan's injuries were slowing them to the point where they both faced the possibility of elimination, and 50 kilometres from the finish Géminiani instructed him to leave Rostollon to his fate and ensure he finished within the time limit. There would be no repetition of the incident with Brian Robinson in the 1959 Tour.

The following day St Raphaël would lose another rider when Stablinski dropped out (as did one of the pre-race favourites, Charly Gaul, and the great French sprinter, André Darrigade). Stablinski had crashed heavily during the stage, and once again, Shay had to drop back to nurse a stricken team-mate, again to no avail as it turned out.

Anquetil would go on to win the race, despite being put under some severe pressure by Bahamontes. After the departure of two of the team due to injury it was left mainly to Shay and Guy Ignolin to protect Anquetil and leave him in a position whereby he could take the *maillot jaune* from Gilbert de Smet on the 19th stage time trial to Besançon, which he duly did. If Shay had been thinking about another stage win his chances were now very slim; he had more than enough work on his hands simply protecting Anquetil.

The final stage finished in the Parc des Princes in Paris, and Shay finished the tour in 61st place, nearly two hours behind the winner. 'I am not too disappointed with my placing,' he said. 'It doesn't make any difference if you finish 20th or 60th. You have to finish in the first ten or higher. After that, people are more likely to remember you because you have won a stage or worn the yellow jersey. And I did both.'

St Raphaël were to take the team prize and they also won the largest amount of prize money – the equivalent of £8,294 – which, following tradition, was divided amongst all the members of the team. The real money was not from the prizes, but from the lucrative contracts for the post-Tour criteriums, and here Shay stood to do well, thanks to his stint in the yellow jersey and the superb stage win.

He achieved a series of good placings in some of these races, culminating in a win in the Grand Prix de Vayrac, where he finished 20 seconds ahead of Raymond Poulidor. Shay then helped Anquetil to win the Felletin Grand Prix, one of the tougher races on the circuit which he had won the previous year. Afterwards Shay, Anquetil and a number of the other competitors travelled to Clermont-Ferrand to take part in the 205-km Circuit Vergongheon d'Auvergne, a tough road event rather than a criterium. They arrived late at the hotel, and after a feed of pasta, steak and dessert, Raphaël Géminiani ordered a bottle of champagne to toast Anquetil's victory in Felletin. While most of the riders, including Shay and Rik Van Looy, went off to their rooms, Anquetil's night was only starting. He continued to feast on eggs, which he washed down with whisky, as even more champagne was ordered.

At three in the morning he drunkenly phoned Marcel Bidot, the French manager for the forthcoming World Championships, and requested his presence in Clermont-Ferrand for a meeting after the race. Bidot obliged despite the seven hour journey.

At five o'clock Anquetil finally called it a night. Two hours later, Géminiani was knocking at his door waking him for the race start. Anquetil wouldn't budge from the comfort of the bed until Géminiani reminded him of the fact that he had requested Bidot's presence, and he would look pretty foolish if he didn't even turn out to race.

Anquetil eventually arose and joined the rest of the peloton at the start line. He punctured after a few kilometres and tried to seize this opportunity to abandon the race. Géminiani, however, was having none of it, and persuaded him he could win the race. Anquetil rejoined the group and gradually started to feel a bit better as the laps passed. At the same time the peloton was steadily diminishing on the very tough circuit until there were only a handful left, including Anquetil and Shay. With two kilometres left Anquetil attacked the remaining few and soloed home to win, while Shay claimed a fine third place.

Anquetil thrived on the reputation he had developed for living life in the fast lane, although many of the stories had been grossly exaggerated. He once told a young fan that 'to prepare for a race there is nothing better than a good pheasant, some champagne and a woman'.

After taking part in the many post-Tour criteriums, mainly throughout France, Shay looked forward to the World Championships in Renaix, where he hoped he could go one better than the previous year, although he still had his trade team commitments to consider. However, it wasn't only the Frenchmen in St Raphaël – Anquetil and Stablinski – who were hoping to be able to enlist Shay's support: Tom Simpson, knowing the British team would not be capable of giving him much help in his quest for the gold medal, was also hoping he could recruit his friend Shay and the only other Irish selection, Peter Crinnion.

There were no major moves in the race until Shay attacked halfway around the eleventh lap, and was quickly joined by Henry Anglade and Italo Zilioli. The Belgian team were content to leave Shay and his companions out front, aiming to reel them in towards the end. On the fifteenth lap the leading trio were reinforced when Simpson joined them.

Then, with only three laps to the finish, Simpson broke clear with Shay and the pair gained about a minute on the peloton. But, for all the Englishman's urging, Shay seemed only half-committed to the break, and eventually Simpson concluded that Shay was only there to mark him. Inevitably, with a lap to go, they were recaptured by a chasing group of 26 riders.

The race was eventually decided by a group sprint, won by Belgian Benoni Beheyt. He finished half a wheel ahead of his compatriot and the crowd's favourite, Rik Van Looy, who had promised the Belgian team a bonus of £1000 each man if he won. But the 22-year old Beheyt, who lived near Renaix, seemed less impressed by the money than by the prospect of a rainbow jersey. In the final moments, as they surged towards the line, he appeared to lean on Van Looy, although in fact Van Looy had moved across during the sprint and Beheyt, in trying to avoid crashing, had placed a hand on his shoulder. The race officials first announced Van Looy as the winner, but when the photo-finish picture was developed it was clear that Beheyt's wheel had crossed the line first, and he was pronounced the new champion. A storm of booing greeted the announcement, while Van Looy called it 'treachery'. The Belgians debate the result to this very day.

Afterwards there were allegations that during the race Simpson had offered Shay a considerable amount of money to buy his help in winning the race, but that Shay had turned it down. Simpson confessed to these allegations in the British Sunday newspaper *The People* two years later:

> Elliott and I were away together and I could smell victory. With help, I knew I could hit the jackpot. 'Come on,' I said. 'Work with me and I'll pay you!' Shay looked at me and waited. He knew he was committed to helping his Saint Raphaël team-mate, Anquetil and, in retrospect perhaps naively again, his 'best pal' Stablinski.
> 'Five thousand francs,' I said, and that meant more than £350.
> 'No Tom,' said Shay.
> 'Ten thousand,' I almost shouted.
> Again Elliott declined. I could see the Championship slipping through my grasp.
> 'All right, 15,000 francs!'
> I was offering the Irishman £1,100. For seconds, I reckon, temptation pressed him sorely. But then he replied, 'No Tom, I can't. I've given my word. I've got to support my leaders. After all, I don't ride for Peugeot.'

Simpson knew what he meant and realised that there would be a lot of angry men in Shay's team if he had helped him. 'And that was that,' concluded Simpson, 'I didn't win the Championship and as things turned out, neither did Anquetil nor Stablinski. I cursed Shay then but in retrospect I admired him.'

Late in September, with the season's end in sight, Shay won the criterium at Vayrac, after riding away from Raymond Poulidor. It was his final win of this great season. A week later, in the first week of October he lined up for the classic Paris–Tours, mainly to support Dutch star and team-mate Jo De Roo, who was trying to win the year's final two classics (the other being the Tour of Lombardy) as he had the year before. Shay rode strongly for De Roo, who won the race convincingly from Tom Simpson and Raymond Poulidor after an elite group finished nine seconds ahead of the peloton. Shay finished in equal 15th position. De Roo went on to win the Tour of Lombardy thirteen days later, therefore completing a unique double/double.* It was a satisfying end of season for Shay and the St. Raphaël team who'd had a remarkable year.

With the year almost at an end Shay joined Anquetil, Anglade, Baldini, De Roo and Simpson on another trip to New Caledonia. A substantial number of French ex-pats lived on the island, and for several years some of the businessmen there had arranged for the cycling stars to travel over for a number of races. When they weren't taking part in the races, the cyclists spent their time spear fishing, hunting turtles and visiting some of the smaller islands. It was an amiable end to a great year for Shay. Winning a stage in two of the three major national tours and holding the yellow jersey for a few days in THE Tour ranked him amongst the best in the world.

At the end of December, Shay donated his yellow jersey from the Tour to an auction for charity, organised by the Dublin Press Stage Children's Charities Committee, and held in the Mansion House in Dublin in January. Amongst the other donations were a signed football from Stanley Matthews and £10 from Jacques Anquetil. Shay's yellow jersey was won by Ned Sweeney, who proudly keeps it to this day.

It was a measure of Shay's friendship with Jacques Anquetil that he and Marguerite were invited to the Frenchman's holiday home in the Alps that winter, for a skiing trip. In fact, Shay and Marguerite were to spend a number of winter holidays skiing with the Anquetils. While downhill skiing was mainly for fun, cross-country skiing was a popular training method amongst cyclists during the off-season as it complemented cycling so well. Prior to the start of a new season there would be a cross-country ski race in Saint-Gervais in January in which a number of top cyclists, including Anquetil, Graczyk and Henry Anglade, would take part. It was a sign that the new season would soon be upon them.

---

* Philippe Gilbert almost repeated it – completing the double victory in 2009 and going on to win at Lombardy again the following year.

11

A fallow year

Shay's first big race in 1964 was the Paris–Nice, where he competed alongside another Irishman, Ian Moore from Belfast, who was riding for the small German Ruberg-Caltex team. Shay hadn't exactly started the early season with a bang; he'd had some respectable results but nothing really significant, except a seventh place in the Boucles Roquearoises in which he had finished third the year before. He rode well again in Paris-Camembert, but had to protect his Dutch team-mate, the promising Arie Den Hartog, who won from Rudi Altig, another St. Raphaël rider who was making a strong start to the year. Moore, who had been making a good impression in the opening of the season, finished 13th, one place ahead of Shay. After taking part in the 1961 Tour de France as a member of the Great Britain team, Moore had raced for a number of seasons on the continent. Despite his obvious talent, which had brought him some really good amateur results, including a win in the Essor-Breton in 1962, he never reached the same level of success as Shay. Like a lot of riders from the British Isles at the time he couldn't really cope with the European racing scene and with living abroad.

St Raphaël were not at their best in Paris–Nice. Shay's best performance was a second place in the team time trial stage. He, Anquetil and Altig were the first three in the team to finish this important stage, which indicates his condition must have been relatively good. However, in the end his team-leader Anquetil came a very disappointing sixth overall, one place behind the British rider Alan Ramsbottom, who produced one of the finest performances of his career. Ramsbottom's team-mate in the Pelforth-Sauvage squad, the new Dutch star Jan Janssen, who went on to become World Road Race Champion later that year, won the race overall. To cap it all, Pelforth-Sauvage also won the overall team prize. Some small compensation for St Raphaël was that Rudi Altig won the individual 34-kilometre time trial, but it wasn't the most auspicious start for their team. From Shay's point of view he had the satisfaction of knowing that he had performed well enough throughout most of the event.

After Paris–Nice came the Northern classics, and this season's campaign would prove to be even more disappointing for Shay than the year before. Rudi Altig dominated the Tour of Flanders to keep the team in the major classics spotlight, but Shay didn't excel individually even though he gave his best for the team, as he always did. It really did seem as if his ambitions were now fully focussed on the Tour de France, where he hoped he would gain more glory for himself and his team which, would again be led by Jacques Anquetil.

Near the end of May came the prestigious Tour preparation race, the ten-day Dauphiné Libéré. Always a very tough event, much of this year's race was to be held in the Alps, making it a very difficult and mountainous course. Shay showed he was coming into good form and rode aggressively thoughout the race. He achieved some good results, including fifth on both the first and the final stages – a promising sign for the Tour. His fellow Irishman Peter Crinnion had also been selected as a member of the St Raphaël team. He had started the season with Margnat-Paloma, but due to another new ruling which limited the number of foreigner riders any team could have, he'd been released from his contract. St Raphaël, taking advantage of this, had recruited him. In the weeks prior to Dauphiné Peter's preparation had consisted of short races, mainly criteriums where he could earn money more easily, so he wasn't well prepared for such a tough race and consequently abandoned on the third day. In the absence of Jacques Anquetil, who'd ridden and won the Giro that year, the race was eventually won by the up and coming Spanish rider, Valentin Uriona, from the KAS team, and a previous stage winner in the British Milk Race. France's favorite, Raymond Poulidor, finished runner-up, and, although nearly two minutes down, his performance indicated that he was going to arrive at the Tour in optimum condition.

Eleven days after the finish of the Dauphiné in Grenoble Shay was a surprise entry in the Manx Premier Road Race – a race he had won five years previously. At that time, and until its sad demise in the 1970s, the Manx Premier on the Isle of Man was the only British race that would consistently attract a World class professional field: Jacques Anquetil, André Darrigade, Tom Simpson, Rudi Altig, Eddy Merckx, Fausto Coppi, Louison Bobet and Lucien Van Impe were amongst those who'd finish on the podium over the years.

In 1964 Shay lined up with three other previous winners, Simpson, Darrigade, and his team-mate Altig, together with other major stars from Europe and most of the top riders in the British home 'cash' ranks, for the very tough 165-kilometre race. For Shay of course, this was like a home race, a chance for his many Irish and British fans to watch him, and he wasn't in the mood to let them down. For most of the ten laps of the energy sapping Clypse circuit, Rudi Altig led. Only in the last two laps did the German seem to tire and was brought back to the six-strong leading group. After constant attacks from most of the seven leaders, it was Shay who put in the decisive move two miles from the finish, and stayed ahead to win by 100 metres from Altig who, despite his earlier impressive efforts, still had the strength to outsprint the talented first year professional Barry Hoban for second place. Barry was the new British kid on the block at the time, and with his powerful sprint had won two stages in the Vuelta back in May in his first season as a pro and in his first major Tour. However, the day belonged to Shay, and his convincing and popular victory again confirmed he was getting near to his best form for the Tour.

Afterwards he explained that his team's plan had been for Altig to get away and, if he wasn't able to stay clear, it would then be each St Raphaël man racing for himself. With Shay taking advantage of the fact that Tom Simpson had missed the crucial break and with Altig finishing second it was a great day for the two St Raphaël riders, who capped a fine team performance.

Shay then returned to France to complete his preparations for the Tour de France. The rulings of previous years that limited teams to just three foreigners had been relaxed, which helped ensure Shay of his place in the team that year. His main purpose would be to help Anquetil to a record-breaking fifth victory. Anquetil, however, had been left shaken by the news that an astrologer working for a Parisian newspaper had predicted that he would die during the fourteenth stage of the Tour and, being superstitious enough already, this prediction played continually on his mind. To make matters worse many of Poulidor's fans sent him copies of the article to try and upset him further.

This was Shay's sixth Tour and, despite his careful preparation and the excellent form he'd shown prior to the race, it was to prove a disaster. Other than the heat, which dogged the riders especially in the second week, there was no obvious explanation for what was the Irishman's worst Tour performance in his career. As early as the third day he was dropped during the team time trial and finished way behind his team in 99th place. Then there was further disappointment when he lost 18 minutes on the first mountainous stage to Briançon. His poor form, coupled with bad luck, continued during the following day's stage to Monaco. He was the first to be dropped on the Col de Vars, the first big climb of the day, and then suffered more as he punctured three times, eventually finishing forty minutes behind Anquetil, who had narrowly out-sprinted an impressive Tom Simpson on the the cinder track.

As the race moved further south it was run off in a heatwave, and Shay suffered badly in the heat. Even when they reached the Pyrenees the temperatures were still high and his Tour came to an end on the difficult 14th stage: after crashing, puncturing several times and then climbing the Port d'Envalira into Andorra, he finished outside the time limit and was eliminated.

Anquetil would go on to win the Tour in an epic and historic battle with Raymond Poulidor. It would be his final Tour victory, although not the last he would ride. For Shay, however, it would be, and indeed the last appearance of any Irishman in the race until Sean Kelly took part in his first Tour in 1978.

Shay seemed to recover quickly from the Tour, because shortly after he travelled to Britain to take part in the Grand Prix Corona, a race around the motor racing circuit at Crystal Palace in south-east London, which was sponsored by the soft drinks manufacturers who were major supporters of cycle racing in the UK. In front of more than 12,000 spectators Shay lost by just half a length from, not unexpectedly, Tom Simpson. The pair of them, together with Alan Ramsbottom, had broken away from the field of 60 and had lapped most of them by the finish. The gulf in class between the continental-based pros and the other British cyclists was clear to all. Billy Holmes, a previous Milk Race winner, who had been the last man in the decisive seven-man break in the Manx Premier, was again the best of the home-based riders.

On his return to the continent Shay wasn't long in winning his second race of the season, the short Circuit du Morbihan – only three stages long but difficult all the same, with many of the French riders out to demonstrate their form before the forthcoming World Championships. Shay took the overall lead after St Raphaël won the team time trial on stage 2, and his team had no real difficulty in controlling their main opponents on the final day. His victory confirmed that he was recovering well from his difficulties in the Tour.

In August came the unexpected announcement that the St Raphaël drinks company would end their sponsorship of the iconic St Raphaël-Géminiani team at the end of the season. It is a reflection of the popularity and impact of that team that forty years later one of their original team cars is still a popular sight in the publicity caravans of some races. When Anquetil heard the news he started to look at his options, one of which was joining one of the big Italian teams. Anxious to prevent that, Géminiani was quick off the mark in seeking out a new French sponsor. It didn't take him long: he had good contacts in the giant motor firm Ford-France, and by the middle of September senior representatives of the car makers had put pen to paper to sign a sponsorship deal. Shay, along with most of St Raphaël's riders, would be retained by the new Ford-France team. The one notable exception, which came as no surprise, was Rudi Altig. Altig and Anquetil were becoming increasingly distant, with Altig feeling he was not receiving enough support from the team for a rider of his talent.

Throughout August Shay had had some good results in the post-Tour criteriums, at the same time as he was training hard for the World Championship. Those shorter criteriums were no real preparation for the 290 kilometres of a World Championship ride. This year he wouldn't be the only Irishman in the professional race; he would have Peter Crinnion for company. Shay had initially been somewhat frosty towards the newcomer when he arrived on the continent – did he fear his thunder might be stolen now he was not the only Irishman in the peloton? – but by this stage their relationship was improving and they were to become the firmest of friends.

The World Championship race, held on Sunday 6th of September in Sallanches, not far from Mont Blanc in the French Alps, saw the professionals competing over twenty three laps of a very tough eight-mile circuit, with the road wet or damp throughout the day. Shay rode well enough and again found himself in attacking positions, but his efforts weren't rewarded. He lost his chance in the final laps and finished 19th, in the main bunch, 38 seconds behind the winner, Jan Janssen of Holland, who out-sprinted Adorni and Poulidor for the title. Fourth was Tom Simpson who had ridden a typically aggressive race and a particularly courageous final lap, which enabled him to come close to winning the race and eventually at least contesting the final sprint for the rainbow jersey.

One of the final races of the season was at the prestigious criterium in Alençon in early October. It resulted in a clean sweep for St Raphaël with Anquetil winning, Shay immediately behind, after gifting his team leader the win, and Stablinski finishing ahead of the rest in third place, 25 seconds later. It was a fine way for the team to finish their legendary sponsorship by St Raphaël. The Alençon event wasn't a race of major importance, but it was another dominant performance in front of tens of thousands of spectators celebrating the great Jacques Anquetil's record-breaking fifth Tour de France win. A 1-2-3 finish for St Raphaël was a fine way to bow out. Shay had been a really important part of his team leader's success that year and this should have been a time when he could bathe in his team's glory, but his own season had been unexceptional and his unfortunate Tour de France very disappointing. All in all he was far less happy than at the end of the historic previous season in which he had enjoyed so much more success.

It was around this time that Shay started considering what he might do after he retired. Although he was not especially close to Anquetil, he certainly admired his business acumen and felt he could learn a lot from him. Anquetil's earnings from cycling were estimated to be in the region of £30,000 per year (a very considerable sum in that era), yet, though a full-time cyclist, he was still able to operate a number of businesses which further supplemented his income. He owned a farm, a large house in St Adrien, a hotel in Rouen and other properties in the North of France, and a gravel pit! But Shay, of course, didn't have anything like Anquetil's resources, so any business plans he had would have to remain on hold. For the time being he would concentrate on cycling. After all, he had kept his place in cycle racing's greatest team in its new format; he had a good contract in his pocket, and was determined that 1965 would be a year to look forward to with Ford-France.

12

Betrayal in Luxembourg;
end of a friendship

Although Shay did not know it, as he was preparing for 1965 in the blue and white colours of the Ford-France team, this year would prove to be one of the most significant and dramatic of his career. By the end of the season he would leave the only professional team with which, under different sponsors, he had raced since his professional debut and he would also be betrayed for the final time by a team-mate and supposed best friend.

As was more often than not the case, Shay started the early season in good form, and in one of his first races, the Grand Prix of Monaco, he claimed a second place to the fast Tour de France stage winner, Italian Antonio Bailetti. Two weeks later Shay would record his first victory in one of the harder opening races. Having already achieved a second place in 1956, and a third place in 1958, Elliott finally managed to win the 164-kilometre Grand Prix St Raphaël, in a sprint with seven other riders who finished over three minutes ahead of the peloton. The season was starting well for the Irishman and he was optimistic that it would prove to be his best to date.

He decided he didn't want to take part in Paris–Nice that year and, after some heated discussion, the team management agreed. He really wanted to excel in the Spring classics and do a lot better than he had done in recent seasons. His hunger to win a major classic, a 'monument', was all too evident, but he felt that time might be running out for him and that Paris–Nice would tire him out too much. Anquetil would evidently be going all out for overall victory and Shay would, as ever, be required to work very hard for the French superstar. Having come so close to a major classic win and a World Championship earlier in his career had possibly left him a little embittered. Being from outside mainstream Europe, Shay was still considered an 'outsider' and was never given the support he deserved, and also, as suggested by Jean Bobet, he was not selfish enough to fight his corner as hard as he might.

Anquetil duly won Paris–Nice from their former team-mate Rudi Altig. Meanwhile, Shay was seemingly in very good form for Milan–San Remo after his fine start to the season. The Italian classic took place only three days after the finish of the famous French stage race. However, he was to have a disappointing ride in the Italian classic, and didn't even finish the race. Unfortunately, most of his spring campaign went badly. The one good ride he had was in Ghent–Wevelgem where he was fourth, finishing second in the bunch sprint that contained some of the very best classic specialists battling for third place.

In the middle of his Northern Classics campaign Shay was selected to take part in the four-day Tour of Belgium. He ended up well down, having expended his energies helping Stablinski to overall victory at the finish in Brussels. Stablinski won again shortly afterwards in the 222-kilometre World Cup event, the Grand Prix of Frankfurt*, a new race designed to be Germany's big international classic. The race attracted a really classy line-up and would go on to become very well established, with many of the world's top riders fighting for victory, especially in the 1970s and 80s. Once again Shay worked his heart out for Stablinski, and the fact that he was able to hold on to fourteenth place was truly creditable after the effort he had put in to defend the Frenchman's winning move.

Shay in turn was helped by Stablinski when he won the Tour de l'Oise at the end of May, after dominating and winning the first stage, but this was a relatively minor race in Northern France – not much of a payback for the big races in which he had helped the Frenchman win that year, and not counting the many other wins he had helped his 'best friend' win over the years. It was beginning to look like a rather one-way relationship,

At the end of May Shay went over to London, having been offered a contract to take part in the marathon 445-kilometre London–Holyhead race which, at the time, was the longest unpaced event in the world. Surprisingly, he hadn't originally been contracted for the race, but two continental riders pulled out a couple of days prior to the start, and Shay and his Ford-France team-mate, Vin Denson, were drafted in as replacements – to the delight of their fans.

---

* At this time the World Cup was a team event taking in many of the biggest races. It was a competition and carried considerable status and substantial prize money. In recent years the GP Frankfurt has lost much of its prestige, although it is still one of Germany's biggest one-day events.

The London–Holyhead saw one of the rare occasions when a bad word was spoken between Shay Elliott and Tom Simpson. Shay had been upset that Tom had been attacking so early in such a long race, and he gave him a piece of his mind. One photo shows Shay leading the chase behind, shaking his fist in anger at Tom, but it was quickly forgotten after the race.

One problem for the riders in a race of such length is that they are more likely to require a toilet break. At one stage during the race Shay had dismounted, and as he said afterwards, he 'popped into the bushes for a bloody big crap'. This was a lot more dignified than the method taken by one of the visiting riders in the race who, for fear of being left behind, performed the task on the move. Roger St. Pierre, the cycling journalist, recalled afterwards: 'It was awful. It went all over his bike, all over his spokes, and because they were going downhill at the time and the wheels were turning quite fast, the stuff sprayed up everywhere.'

The winning break of eight eventually developed with about 80 kilometres to go. It was made up of Shay, Simpson, Denson, Hoban, and some of the top home based pros – including Albert Hitchen, the evergreen twice Milk Race winner Bill Bradley, and the talented young Peter Gordon, together with the Belgian René Van Meenan, like Shay a previous Het Volk winner. The break worked well together, although the ambitious young Hoban, sensing it was the crucial move and feeling particularly strong, kept attacking. All his efforts, however, were countered, and coming towards the finish they were still all together.

In the sprint finish Simpson very narrowly edged out Shay, with Albert Hitchen not far behind in third. Hitchen had not originally been included in the continental riders' plan, and evidently joined the combine on the understanding that he could secure third place on the podium, so long as he had the strength to be there at the end. He rode very strongly, but despite the deal, seemed intent on winning the race for a second time. Shay, finishing second, took home £120 for his efforts (plus whatever extra he may have earned from his alliance with race winner, Tom Simpson).

There were suggestions that Shay had sold the race to Simpson. Photographs of the finish clearly show him with his fingers over his brake levers before they had reached the line. Afterwards, Mick Byrne would ask Shay about this incident and whether he had blocked Hitchen to prevent him from winning. Shay just looked Mick in the eye without saying a word. Mick read into this that he was basically saying, 'Mick,

I know you're not stupid, you know what happened but I'm not saying anything,' as he maintained his professionalism to the last.

Later, however, Vin Denson would confirm that a deal had been made long before the race leaders reached Holyhead. The fact was that Simpson had felt it was important for him to put on a good show on home soil in an effort to try and get a major British sponsor to back a team, with him as leader, of course. He therefore spoke to Shay, Vin and others and they planned for Simpson to take the win. However, Hitchen sensing the possibility that he might get past Simpson in the final sprint, reneged on the agreement. What is shown in the photo, according to Vin Denson, is not so much Shay holding back from overtaking Simpson, but probably the consequence of keeping Hitchen in check.

Whatever the truth in the various stories about the 1965 London-Holyhead, the fact remains that the result was hugely popular among British fans. Their own greatest road cyclist had won, and Ireland's greatest cyclist (who had a considerable following in Britain) had come second. Who could wish for more than that?

Shay returned to the continent and had some good results, including a solid performance in the Tour of Luxembourg. He ended 11th overall and made sterling efforts in defence of his friend and team-mate Vin Denson, who was leading the race. It was not just the Irishman's heart and legs to which the Briton was indebted, but also his tactical nous. As Denson recalls, on the final day 'there were plenty of attacks, but this wasn't Solo [Vin's previous team]. This was Ford-France, and the team would normally defend their overall leader like mad, especially in a race like this. I was going really well myself, and I was itching to chase down any move off the front. It was Shay Elliott who put a stop to that; he was forever telling me off and dragging me back by my jersey. "You sit there," he'd say. "I'll get him back.". I had a lot to thank Shay for that day, and on other days.'

Sadly, Shay's return to Luxembourg a couple of months later would be a much less joyful occasion, both for him and for Ford-France.

Shay's next major race was likely to be the famous, partly Derny-paced, Bordeaux–Paris classic, which Tom Simpson had won two years earlier. He was in the running for one of the places awarded to Ford-France, and in preparation for the marathon race he and Jean Stablinski trained along the Mediterranean coast. Their preparation included a 300-kilometre round trip from St Aygulf, near Cannes, to Marseilles and back. They covered the distance in two days, with a change of clothing in their haversacks. It was just like the old times back in Algeria, when they had camped together during their long training rides. Then came the deeply disappointing news that Shay wasn't named for the race. One of the two slots available for supporting Anquetil went, naturally enough, to Stablinski, but Shay's form up to that point of the season had been good but not outstanding, so he was not selected. That was according to the team management's public statement, but it caused some eyebrows to be raised. It was well known that Bordeaux-Paris was a race that Shay had long wanted to take part in, so did the team management feel that his loyalty to Anquetil would be in question, or compromised, by the presence of Simpson? Both scenarios seem somewhat on the unlikely. Whatever the reasoning, the fact remained Shay did not get the ride and it was his good friend, Vin Denson, whom he'd helped to win the Tour of Luxembourg, who was selected as Ford-France's third man.

Earlier in the year Anquetil had made the decision not to compete in the Tour de France. When the route had been announced he felt that the race had been designed for his big French rival Raymond Poulidor, and that there was not enough time trialling (in spite of the fact that the total length of the time trials was exactly the same as it had been 1964). Anquetil also didn't think he would have much to gain financially: he had won the Tour five times and if he was defeated he would lose more than he could gain. He even went on to call the race the 'Tour de Poulidor' when speaking to journalists; sour grapes seem to be on the menu and part of another game he would play when it suited him. He didn't, however, want to lose any personal prestige and, in response, Géminiani put to him the idea of going for the very unlikely double of the Dauphiné Libéré and Bordeaux–Paris. The Dauphiné was one of the hardest stage races in Europe and Bordeaux–Paris, at 600 kilometres, was the longest single-day race in the World – and there would be practically no time between them.

Anquetil thought that if he succeeded it would quite rightly be a unique and historic accomplishment, all the more remarkable as Bordeaux–Paris started in the early hours of the morning, after the Dauphiné-Libéré finished on the opposite side of the country. Anquetil duly dominated the Dauphiné, beating Poulidor after a very tough battle. He not only won the time trial stage, as would have been expected, but the two toughest mountain stages as well.

The logistics were not easy, but such was the French superstar's standing in France Géminiani managed to charter a plane supplied by no less than the French President, Charles De Gaulle, to fly Anquetil across the country to the start of the marathon. The success for the Ford-France team, especially with Stablinski taking second place behind Anquetil and Tom Simpson finishing third, after a brave attempt to win for a second time, created massive media coverage, which would largely justifiy Anquetil's decision not to ride the Tour de France that year. His performance was quite astonishing and is still talked about to this day – and rightly so, because no rider today would accept such a crazy challenge.

Anquetil's decision, however, greatly reduced Shay's chances of starting the Tour, as he had always been one of Anquetil's first choices for the race. Lucien Aimar, who was selected as team leader of the Ford-France team, did not see Shay in the same light. In the end it was a disappointing race overall for Géminiani's squad, with Aimar retiring before the finish.

Shay was selected, however, as part of the Ford-France team (which included Anquetil) to travel to the Isle of Man, where he'd won the year before. The Manx Premier took place on the same day that the Tour started, and was won by Anquetil ahead of Eddy Merckx with Shay, in his customary support role to his team leader, in a good sixth place. Shay had never become especially close to Anquetil, despite being at his side for many of his big victories, sharing many bottles of wine while celebrating these wins, and even their wives becoming good friends. Although he was a loyal *domestique* to the Norman for years, he was never particularly happy about his role.

Years later, after his retirement from cycling, Shay told his friend John Flanagan that in hindsight he felt that some of the lesser wins that he notched up throughout his career had been assigned to him by Stablinski and Anquetil simply to keep him in check and to dampen his ambition for the bigger wins. It's a question that will remain unanswered as to why the Dubliner never left Anquetil to become leader in a more modest team, as he certainly could have done. Had he become just too comfortable in the team and so was reluctant to risk a move, or was it the money Géminiani offered him? And he needed the money: Marguerite's friendship with Anquetil's wife had given her expensive tastes which Shay could barely afford.

It was around this time that Shay started to give some serious thought as to what he wanted to do when his cycling career finished. His father suggested to him that he should open a pub in Dublin. Jim thought that having a pub named after the famous cyclist would be a big draw and prove very popular. Gerry Duffin, who had helped Shay all those years before – giving him the best of equipment and training advice – was living back in Dublin and running a guesthouse in Blackrock, and knew of a pub in Talbot Street that was up for sale. Jim felt that Shay should offer the position of pub manager to Gerry, who also had experience of running a pub.

So, the process of purchasing the business began, with Shay placing a considerable deposit on the pub. In the end, however, this proved to be wasted money. In the latter half of the racing season Shay's form finally started to come good, and he was offered a two-year contract with Raymond Poulidor's Mercier team. This was an offer he didn't want to turn down, and the question of what he might do after his racing days was postponed. He backed out of the pub venture in Dublin. Apart from the difficulty of trying to juggle a racing career on the continent and a business in Ireland, Marguerite, having now spent some time in Dublin, was quite adamant that she would not live there. Shay lost two thousand pounds in the venture as the deposit was non-refundable.

Despite not having taken part in the Tour Shay, because of his popularity and fine palmarès in these events, was still offered some worthwhile contracts for the post-Tour criteriums. He achieved some very good results in most of those he took part in and was often on the podium. In one of France's bigger events, early in August, the three–day stage race he'd been victorious in the year before, the Tour of Morbihan, he had little chance to pursue a repeat victory, as team-mate Guy Ignolin was in wonderful form. However, Shay gave full support to the local boy, and three times Tour de France stage winner, who won all three stages, with Shay giving up his best chance of a win on the final stage to ensure his team-mate's hat trick, and with it the overall victory. Despite not being given a chance by the team to win the race again, and despite all his hard work for Ignolin, Shay still finished third overall in a race that featured most of the best French riders. He had good reason to feel pleased with his form.

He was then selected as part of the team for Paris–Luxembourg, a race that was to be pivotal in Shay's career, as well as making a huge impact on his personal life. Jean Stablinski stole the 1965 Paris–Luxembourg from Shay, and this was to provoke the disagreement between the two men who had hitherto been firm friends. It also indirectly resulted in Shay leaving the Anquetil camp and prompted his move to Mercier.

Paris–Luxembourg was a short lived but very prestigious event that carried major points for the season-long Super Prestige Pernod trophy (the forerunner to the world ranking lists). It was a race that featured most of the world's top riders who were toning their form for the World Championships, as well as the top ranked stars trying to win the Super Prestige Pernod. Organised by Shay's old training partner and friend, Jean Bobet, Paris–Luxembourg had been increased from a two-day race to a four-day race for the first time, and Shay knew that a good ride in this would be viewed very favourably. Anquetil also had decided to enter because of the Pernod points on offer. Shay had trained like a maniac coming into the race; as it had been a poor season by his standards, a good performance wouldn't do any damage in helping him to renegotiate a more favourable new contract, and also help his preparation for the upcoming World Championships.

Shay started the race well and finished the first stage of 206 kilometres from Paris to Arras in eighth place. A break had gone clear with eleven riders, and as it included three from Ford-France – Shay, André Darrigade and Gérard Thielin – the onus was not on the Ford team to chase. The break gained over eleven minutes on the peloton. That night the atmosphere in the team's hotel wasn't good. Stablinski had an argument with Thielin, after Thielin had claimed it was pathetic of Stablinski and Anquetil to have allowed the break to gain so much time.

Shay was to seize the leader's jersey on the second stage. Stablinski, in his argument the night before, had told Thielin that he would attack from the gun the next day, and this he duly did. He got into a break alongside three Belgians, including new-pro Eddy Merckx, Noel van Clooster and Bernard De Kerckhove – a Tour de France stage winner and yellow jersey holder that year. De Kerckhove eventually won the stage after a fine solo effort, with Merckx 44 secs behind. They gained over two minutes on the peloton, with Shay finishing the stage in fourth place, but more importantly taking the overall lead. Stablinski, however, had been dropped before the finish, alleging that it had been his tactic to drop back to become the target of the peloton. This seemed a strange explanation though, since if he had become the target for the chasers, as he claimed, he would have drawn the chasers nearer to the break.

Even though Shay now wore the leader's jersey, the next day Anquetil and Stablinski went on the attack. They finished over a minute clear of the rest, including Shay. Stablinski outsprinted Anquetil at the finish, after a disagreement between the two of them as to who should take the stage.

Stablinski would claim later that Shay had been feeling weak on that 165-kilometre stage from Jambes to Charleville, and that he had struggled even to finish. Back at the hotel that evening the mood in the Ford-France camp was even worse than it had been the previous night. Shay was pretty angry with what had happened with two of his team-mates openly attacking while he held the overall lead. After all the magnificent work Shay had put in over the years for the two Frenchmen, and the sacrifices he had made on their behalf, he felt he'd been stabbed in the back by the two men he'd thought of as friends. Furthermore, Anquetil and Stablinski were not speaking to each other either, despite the fact that they were sharing a room. To say the position was complicated would be something of an understatement.

Stablinski claimed that in the hotel on the way to the bathroom he overheard Shay speaking to Rik Van Looy, saying 'You know Rik, Stab and Anquetil, they're assholes. At the World Championships in Spain I'm going to ride for you, not them.' Some might say this was simply Stablinski trying to justify his actions of that day and the next. According to Stablinski, Jean Graczyk had heard that Shay had been conspiring with Van Looy, and was livid. Graczyk had allegedly said to his masseur, 'tonight, you massage my arms, not my legs' – the implication being that he wanted a fight with the Irishman.

In spite of all this, going into the last stage of the race from Charleville to Luxembourg, Shay still held a comfortable lead over Pelforth's strongman, André Foucher. It should have been a formality for Shay to hold on to win overall. He was also five minutes clear of Stablinski. The Ford *directeur sportif*, Louviot, reassured him before the final stage, saying 'there's nothing to worry about, you're going to win', adding 'there's no need to try so hard. You're using up too much energy trying to keep the jersey.' Shay would naturally have read into this that he would be getting the full support of the team, most of whom, including Jacques Anquetil, had told him originally that they would support him to the hilt. All this – the backing of the team riders and management – added to Shay's confidence of final victory.

However, early on in the 210-kilometre stage a break went clear and Stablinski later bridged across to the them. Normal race etiquette would mean that he would not work in the break, as his team-mate was race leader, and indeed, when the break developed, Stablinski initially appeared to hesitate, as if undecided what to do. However, when the three surviving riders gained time on the peloton – the other two being Belgian sprinting stars Ed Sels and Guido Reybroeck – Stablinski started to work hard. He couldn't possibly suggest he was just going for the stage victory as he would have had very little chance of dropping two such classy riders, nor of beating both of them in the sprint. It could mean only one thing – that Stablinski was aiming to take the overall lead and the two Belgians could fight it out for the stage victory. When Shay realised what was happening it was already too late. He tried chasing down Stablinski, but the group stayed away and Stablinski took the overall lead, the trio having gained an advantage of nearly eight minutes.

The lack of action by the rest of Ford-France might have been due to Stablinski's influence in the team, or perhaps there was money changing hands. The Frenchman again claimed that Shay had been struggling all day, sitting at the back of the peloton, and that even before the break went he'd been shouting at him to get up to the front. He then said that after getting into the break Louviot had instructed him to go for the win. That, of course, was possible: the team was French and despite his popularity in his adopted country, Shay was, after all, still a foreigner.

Stablinski would say afterwards, 'In the last stage we passed by Verdun. I knew the roads here very well as I'd done my military service here. The roads were narrow and favourable to the escapees. It was difficult to organize a chase on this terrain. Elliott was at the back of the bunch and I brought him to the front. He said to me, "I have bad legs, I'm tired".'

The fact is that even if Shay had been struggling it was still not right for Stablinski to attack. Normally, the race leader's team would be obliged to control any dangerous breakaways and ensure they did not get too much of a lead. Ford-France had a team that was eminently capable of such tactics. But they didn't employ them and the result was that Ed Sels won that final stage with 'Stab' third as expected. Overall victory went to Stablinski, while Shay dropped to fourth overall. The 'team' prize was won ironically by Ford-France.

At the finish line Shay kept cycling, so angry that he felt he would come to blows with Stablinski if he had confronted him. He rode straight to the dressing rooms. He later revealed that he broke down in the showers: not only had he been betrayed by his friend, he knew he would now struggle to retain a contract with the Ford-France team. So distraught was he over what had happened he refused to join his team- mates at the post-race reception.

After the race, while Stablinski was claiming that Shay had been suffering from the start in Charleville, Shay was saying: 'Jean is telling us stories. Yesterday I had one moment of weakness, due to the intense efforts of the previous day. Today I was good again.' Tellingly, he added, 'Jean came to speak to me in the peloton shortly after the start, and he said, "You see Séamus, yesterday you held on to first place. Today you have recovered, but you will lose Paris–Luxembourg".'

For days afterwards commentators on the radio and press journalists discussed the affair, with the majority claiming that Shay had been badly let down by the Frenchman. The controversy was exacerbated due to the closeness of the pair: when Stablinski came to Paris he stayed at Shay's house, and Shay, similarly, would stay with Stablinski when he was racing in the North. Stablinski was even the godfather of Shay's son Pascal. This was not the normal disagreement between two riders. Shay even went as far as to say that he would never give Stablinski a moment of freedom in a race, and he would make the Frenchman pay. It was a very difficult time for Shay and it would haunt him for the rest of his life.

When questioned by French reporters about events on the last stage Anquetil took Shay's side: he claimed that Stab's treatment of the Irishman was not what was to be expected of a team-mate, and that this was the type of behaviour that could cause a team to fall apart. It was particularly abhorrent, he felt, given the loyalty Shay had shown and the service he'd given, not only to Stablinski, but also to the rest of the team, and that Stablinski could have no excuse. 'Stab should never have done this,' Anquetil said to the reporters. Others in the team – French riders Thielin and Wuillemin – were equally critical of Stablinski's behaviour.

So too was another Frenchman in the Ford-France team, André Darrigade, only he was having none of Anquetil's disingenuousness. Even on the finishing line he had caught the eye of race organiser Bobet and said, 'it's a shame and a pity to do a thing like that.' Anquetil, he later argued, had been weak and not shown any strong leadership. 'If Anquetil had been a real leader he would have intervened and would have given orders to Stablinski to stop his effort. Anquetil did not make the decision, so is therefore an accessory.'

Throughout all this Stablinski remained defiant. 'I played the role of the *domestique* for the first three days of the race, and for the first eighty kilometers of the last stage,' he argued. 'I then felt good and took my chance. There is nothing to indicate that Elliott would have saved the jersey, whereas I had wings. I had extraordinary form.'

It was days before Shay could speak to Stablinski again, and even then it was only to tell the Frenchman never to set foot in his house again. This was typical of Shay's temperament claims Bobet: 'In the evening at the hotel he didn't shout or display anger, nothing. Only one month later he left Anquetil's team to join Poulidor. I think he was not someone given to showing his emotions easily, but took his time to answer a traitor with coldness.'

Years later Stablinski put forward another version of the events. In the weeks prior to the race, he said, Shay had had a disagreement with Raphaël Géminiani. Shay was seemingly going to change teams for next season, but he needed to ride Paris–Luxembourg as preparation for the forthcoming World Championships. Géminiani hadn't wanted to include Shay in the team, and had only done so after he, Stablinski, had pleaded his friend's case, and invited him to train with him at his home in Northern France. Géminiani eventually relented. 'For you Jean, I cannot say no, but this goes against what is in my heart.' If that was true it was surely a shabby way for Shay to have been treated after so my years of loyal service to Géminiani's cause and now nearing the end of his career.

The race was also a turning point in the relationship between Anquetil and Stablinski: their friendship was never the same again. It would later be damaged further when Lucien Aimar, in the company of Stablinski, crashed Anquetil's Ford Mustang into a tree while bringing the car back to Anquetil in Rouen. Since Anquetil had not insured the car, he asked the pair of them to pay for the damage. However, their final real breaking point came nearly two years later on the final night of the 1967 Tour, which had been raced that year on the National team formula. Anquetil had chosen not to ride, and Raymond Poulidor had been been nominated as the French team leader. To Anquetil's relief, Poulidor didn't win and after a catalogue of accidents could only finish in ninth place, but that didn't prevent Anquetil from accusing Stablinski of betrayal for riding on the French National team and, thereby, for Poulidor. He even contrived to hold Stablinski responsible for Poulidor winning the final time trial – such was his obsession. But for Géminiani's intervention the two might well have settled their differences in a street brawl. At the end of that season they parted company, Stablinski, ironically, joining Poulidor's Mercier team, as Shay had done two years before. However, by that time Shay had retired.

After Paris–Luxembourg the next major event was the World Championships, the most important single-day race on the calendar and which, in 1965, were being held on a difficult 19-kilometre circuit near San Sebastian, in the Basque region of Spain. Two thirds of the way through the race, which was run off in very wet conditions, Tom Simpson and Rudi Altig bridged across to a group of riders who had broken away earlier. This would turn out to be the winning break as many of the other favourites, including Shay, Anquetil, Poulidor, Merckx and Stablinski, remained in the bunch, believing it was too early for this to be a significant move. At one stage in the race Stablinski did make a serious effort to close the gap, but Shay chased after him and did little to help the Frenchman get across to the leaders, although he knew he was ruining his own chances by using up a lot of his reserves. However, Shay did ride very strongly with the chasers while trying to catch the leading break, but it wasn't to be Elliott's day: he was held up on a couple of occasions with mechanical problems, then a puncture at a crucial time. He had no alternative but to retire from the event, and his retirement took much of the steam out of the pursuing group, which made little if any progress from that point on. At the finish Simpson easily outsprinted Altig for the title, and Stablinski was the only member of the French team to finish, in 10th place.

Shay bounced back from his disappointing Worlds, which had been one of his aims for the season, to win the Grand Prix d'Esperaza shortly afterwards. He and Stablinski met up again in the prestigious Criterium des As, a Derny-paced criterium held in Paris towards the end of the season. Entry was by invitation only, the organisers issuing invitations to the leading riders of the season. With Stablinski and Anquetil, the darlings of the Parisian crowd, both riding Shay probably found it too difficult to raise his morale, and didn't finish the race. Anquetil won, with Stablinski finishing nearly five minutes behind. At least Shay had been offered a good contract and so took home a few thousand francs from the race.

A few days afterwards Shay did manage another good win, in the Grand Prix d'Orchies, near Lille. Here the podium would be filled by English speakers: a group of seven riders, which included Shay and the two Englishmen, Barry Hoban and Vin Denson went clear, and Shay easily won the sprint from Hoban, with Denson third, 30 seconds behind these two.

Hoban revealed later something of the tactics that brought about this result. Four of the seven escapees were from the Ford-France team, and Hoban reasoned that the odds were stacked in their favour; indeed, his chances of a win were extremely slim. He decided, therefore, to put it to a couple of the Ford riders that he would not contest the sprint, if they would allow him to take second place. The young Englishman was a relative novice, albeit full of ambition, but he knew enough to know that if he was to renege on his word and try for the win at the end, then his life could be made hell by the Ford-France team. They would try to prevent him winning any future races and would chase down whatever attempt he made to break clear.

A few years later in the Four Days of Dunkirk, Hoban would experience what could happen to a cyclist who went against his word. Roger de Vlaeminck, who was leading the race, negotiated a price with Hoban's team for their services in helping him to defend his lead. De Vlaeminck duly won, but after the race refused to pay up. Hoban and his team-mates made de Vlaeminck's life very difficult afterwards, always chasing him down whenever he attempted to get clear. A frustrated de Vlaeminck finally turned to Hoban one day and asked him, 'How much is it that I owe you, again?'

Shay achieved his last win of the season in the very popular Grand Prix Puteaux, a race that attracted big crowds and was considered the Queen of the Criteriums. Despite a strong line-up he finished alone, over a minute and a half up on Hoban and future Tour winner, Dutchman Jan Janssen. An article appeared in *Miroir Sprint* shortly afterwards declaring Shay to have been fully deserving of not only his win in Puteaux, but also those in Orchies and Esperaza. The article went on to say that 'Shay showed great spirit and bravery after the treachery displayed by Anquetil and Stablinski in the recent Paris-Luxembourg to a model team-mate. The only aspect of the win which Shay could regret was the absence of Stablinski'. They had still not resolved their differences three months after the Paris–Luxembourg race, even though they'd met on a number of occasions. They would be civil to each other, but they were both resolute in their positions regarding the incident.

Shay was now 31 and once again started thinking of life beyond his cycling career. Towards the end of the season he made the decision to buy an hotel in Loctudy in Western Brittany. He used the collateral on his house in Paris, which was valued at £18,000, and also invested another £29,000, which he had borrowed on two loans. He also used another £2,000 cash for stocking the hotel. Because he was Irish the hotel had to be registered in Marguerite's name. When they learned of the idea Nell and Jim expressed their anxiety to Shay: apart from the size of the investment, they pointed out the obvious fact that Shay had no experience of running a hotel. But Shay was adamant; his intention was that it would be established as a going concern by the time he retired. He decided to rename the place, the 'Hotel d'Irlande'. It was to be a venture that would drastically change his life.

13

Big changes; life without Jacques

The Mercier-BP team that Shay had moved to was a team that was often run on a relatively shoestring budget. After paying Poulidor's salary there wasn't an awful lot of cash left to fund the rest of the team. Therefore, they could be quite frugal with paying for other expenses. It was a big change for Shay moving to Mercier after so many years with the world's best – and richest – team. 'Being popular did not always work in my favour,' Poulidor was candid enough to confess. 'Monsieur Mercier got sufficient advertising from "Poupou" so there wasn't the need for him to secure the best and most expensive riders for the team. Even if I didn't win races he got plenty of publicity for the team.'

The *Directeur Sportif* and manager was Antonin Magne. Magne himself had been a great cyclist, winning the Tour de France in 1931 and 1934, and the World Championships in 1936, amongst many other illustrious wins, but a lot of riders on the team felt that he was out of touch with current ideas in cycling and his guidance (banning his riders from eating spinach without explaining why, for instance) was not particularly useful. This was certainly a view shared by Barry Hoban, who spent his early years at Mercier. As for Shay, at this stage in his career he knew exactly what type of training and preparation worked for him, and he tended to disregard any advice from Magne.

At the start of the year Shay departed for a pre-season training camp on the Riviera, where he was introduced to new team-mates, many of whom he was familiar with, for the forthcoming season. Shay showed good form at the camp and returned to Brittany in high spirits, only to find the hotel in chaos. He'd only been away from Loctudy for a couple of weeks, but in that time Marguerite had fallen out with the staff, who told Shay, on his return, that they would walk out if she came near them again. Shay also discovered the hotel finances in a mess, with many unpaid bills and the account used by the hotel for running expenses overdrawn. Shay decided he had no option but to take two weeks off the bike and to try and get the business back on track. He started by sacking the manager.

Meanwhile Shay and Marguerite were arguing about who was to blame for the problems. He accused her of not managing the hotel properly and she blamed him for buying the hotel in the first place. His cycling commitments had already put a strain on the marriage, with Shay so often away from home racing around Europe.

Despite all these distractions, Shay somehow managed to retain his good form on the bike, and it didn't take him long to claim his first win of the year in the 167-kilometre Grand Prix Tregor, where he beat France's new climbing star, Raymond Delisle. It was not an important race, but all the same, it was an event that many big champions before him had won. After this came a couple of podium places in smaller races while he sought to earn as much money as he could to meet the debts incurred with the hotel. His campaign of riding criteruims though the season was, in fact, to earn him some reasonable income and some good wins. But what he was still hoping for was a major classic win if he got the rides.

He came close in the Belgian classic Ghent-Wevelgem, when he finished in fifth place, despite a run-in with the police, which Shay would later recount. In a scrappy race Belgium's future star, Herman van Springel, took one of his first major wins, escaping from three others to win alone by 50 seconds. Shay led the bunch home, proving himself faster than most of the world's best sprinters – men of the calibre of Walter Godefroot, Jan Janssen and a very young Eddy Merckx.

On the strength of this ride Shay was selected for Mercier's team in the four-day, six-stage Tour of Belgium, and buoyed by his fine fifth place in Ghent-Wevelgem, he decided to use the Belgian tour as preparation for the remaining classics. But that year's 50th edition of the race was to prove to be one of the hardest on record. The organisers had attracted most of the World's best riders; it was a line-up worthy of any classic, including Felice Gimondi and Eddy Merckx. The weather was also to play a major part throughout the race.

On the first 166-km stage, from Brussels to Namur, seven riders, including Shay's team-mates Victor Van Schil, who'd finished third in the previous year's World Championships, and the German star Rolf Wolfshohl, went clear and built up a substantial lead. Van Schil won the stage from the Italian Vittorio Adorni and with it the race leadership. The chasing riders finishing nearly six minutes behind. Having finished well down after working hard to ensure his two team-mates stayed clear, Shay had no incentive to produce a good time trial in the very short uphill climb to the Citadelle of Namur, which comprised the day's stage B, but Van Schil performed well enough to hold on to his overall lead.

Next day a hilly opening to another double stage of 164 kilometres saw a final break of six, with Shay amongst them, defending Van Schil's position. He finished a good fourth and took a little time back overall. In the day's stage B, a 10-kilometre team time trial, Shay tasted victory when his Mercier team won easily. So Van Schil was still in the leader's jersey and Shay had moved up to twelfth overall.

The third day was a long 256 kilometres around Ostend. The stage was won by the fast finishing Walter Godefroot in a big sprint, with both Shay and Van Schil securing their overall positions. So, it came down to the final 187-kilometre stage. This was going to be decisive and it was run off in some of the worst weather of the professional season.

On that final stage, which took the riders into the suburbs of Brussels, snow fell continuously driven by a freezing wind. Only 27 riders finished the race. Shay was the last man to cross the line, to finish in 17th position overall. So atrocious were the conditions that Van Schil, the overall leader going into the stage, retired from the race a mere 300 metres before the finishing line, in a state of severe exhaustion. By contrast, Rolf Wolfshohl, Shay's multi Cyclo-cross World Champion team-mate, thrived in the conditions: he finished second on the day and second overall to the future World Champion Vittorio Adorni. Shay and his team had ridden so strongly but their efforts had taken their toll. In spite of it all, the brave Irishman still felt optimistic after he'd recovered, and was still looking forward to the remaining spring.classics.

Before this year's edition of Paris-Roubaix the local council had, in its wisdom, decided to resurface many of the remaining historic cobbled roads that had been used in the race over the years. For the fans of the 'Hell of the North', however, smooth tarmac roads were sacrilegious, so the race organizers realized they needed to search for a new route. They asked Jean Stablinski, who had lived in the area for a long time, for his advice in planning the route and his suggestions for some new sections of *pavé*. The start of the route was also moved north to Chantilly. The race was won in fine style by over four minutes by the new Italian star Felice Gimondi, who'd been the surprise Tour de France winner the previous year and then gone on to win what was then a major classic – the Paris-Brussels. Shay was beset with a series of punctures and mechanical problems which left him struggling and he didn't finish the race. Nor would he get any decent results in any of the other spring classics that season, nor in the Autumn classics for that matter. Stablinski would go on for many years to work with the organisers in creating and advising on new race routes for the famous classic.

Shay's next target was meant to be the 557-kilometre Bordeaux-Paris. It was a race which had captured his imagination since his first years on the continent and so, despite everything that was going on in his life, he made great efforts to put in long hours in preparation. But with his mounting business problems his form started to slip. Not long before the marathon race, during the Four Days of Dunkirk, his *directeur sportif* told him that if he didn't start improving he wouldn't be selected for the race, even though he had just helped his Mercier team to a near win in the Dunkirk team time trial – they finished only a second behind the winning Peugeot team. Towards the end of that day's racing Shay gave up his bike to a team-mate who had mechanical trouble, and then told Magne that he wouldn't have to make up his mind about dropping him from the forthcoming classic, as he, Shay, was making the decision for him: he wouldn't ride the race that was often referred to as the 'Derby of the Road'. According to many of his contempories, Bordeaux-Paris would have been an ideal race for Shay and one that really suited his qualities. By 1966 the famous marathon event was slowly but surely in decline and would die out completely in the eighties. It was the last monument of a bygone age.

After this disappointment, Shay decided to visit his GP in the hope of finding some explantion for his disappearing form. He confided in the doctor and told him of all his troubles – both on and off the bike. To the doctor it was obvious: he was mentally exhausted, and that was not something medicine could cure. He would need to rest. Rest, however, was not going to sort out his financial worries.

Up to a point Shay followed some of his doctor's advice and took a short rest, but the truth was that he really couldn't afford not to race. His form did start to improve somewhat, but he was only riding criteriums, mostly between 100 and 140 kilometres. He came second in one at Poire-sur-Vie behind Lucien Aimar, after the duo had broken clear towards the end. That was no mean achievement since within two months Aimar would go on to win the Tour. The following weekend Shay won the 110-kilometre Tredion criterium, finishing over a minute clear of Hubert Ferrer, and Tom Simpson. The next day Shay won again in Ploudalmezeau, beating the French rider Christian Raymond in a two-man sprint after 140 kilometres, and the weekend after that he finished second behind Eddy Merckx in a criterium in Rousies.

The Tour, however, was another matter, and for the second year running Shay didn't ride; not that he had really expected he would. Instead, he continued to take part in as many criteriums in Brittany as possible. It was easy money and enabled him to keep the family's heads above water. On one particular day, for example, he won a 90-kilometre race in Lorient, and later that same day claimed second place in another criterium in Saint-Clet. The following weekend he won another criterium in Brittany, at Pluvigner, not far from his home in Loctudy. He was not to know that this would be the last win of his illustrious career, more than ten years after his first win. Shay, despite his domestic difficulties, was keeping his engine running. He may not have been riding in any important races, but he hadn't given up totally: he was still determined to have a crack at a couple of major races, including the World Road Race Championship. His dreams hadn't completely deserted him, if he could put at least some of his problems aside to train hard enough.

It was in some criteriums during this troubled summer, as Shay later admitted, that he took prohibited substances.. In a series of articles published in *The People* newspaper, after his return to Ireland, he told of having taken amphetamines as his personal woes mounted. After he had been diagnosed as being mentally exhausted due to his troubles, Shay came to the difficult decision that drugs might help him to win, and winning meant money, and money was what he desperately needed. He admitted that he had seen plenty of drugs during his decade on the continent, but he maintained that he had always steered clear of them. He had won many races without taking anything, so didn't feel that he needed them – although he must have known he was often beaten by riders who had been 'charged' as it was referred to at that time.

Having come to the decision that he would use amphetamines in a series of six criteriums in the Brittany area, Shay contacted a man who supplied them to cyclists and bought twenty Benzedrine tablets from him. He paid £1 for the drugs. Although Shay would be given good start money, the prize money for winning each of the races was at least £70 and sometimes more. The extra revenue could, therefore, be quite substantial. Benzedrine was an amphetamine that had originally been developed to help relieve hay fever and catarrh. After World War Two Europe was awash with millions of Benzedrine tablets, which had been produced to keep Allied troops awake during combat. Eventually they found their way on to the black market and soon began to be used by cyclists as a stimulant. They tended to be used by poorer riders, as the better paid could afford to buy other, more sophisticated, drugs.

This could prove very effective while racing but, along with many other long term effects (such as paranoia and depression), would affect recovery time, as more often than not they prevent you from getting a decent night's rest. Also, as the effects of the drug would be with you for many hours and take your appetite away, it could prove a debilitating habit for any athlete, such as a professional cyclist, who had to perform frequently.

Shay said that at first he felt exhilarated at the start of each race and felt he was unbeatable. But, as his first race progressed, he developed cramp and could only finish in third place. He thought it was due to the drug having allowed him to push his body more than he normally would, and that this was how he came to be tortured by cramp. It is also possible – and likely – that he wasn't eating properly or drinking enough.

At the end of the six races Shay had won only once, which was a poor return for him since the men he was been riding against would not have been nearly as strong as those he usually had to compete against. After this he decided that the use of drugs was not for him. He openly admitted that it wasn't ethical reasons or guilt which had stopped him, simply that they didn't seem to work for him. The only race he had won after taking Benzedrine was the criterium at Huelgoat. In the newspaper article Shay also recalled witnessing one young rider during an edition of Ghent-Wevelgem taking a hypodermic needle out of his back pocket, and jabbing himself with it mid-race. That particular rider didn't even finish the event. Although Shay recalled this one particular incident it is scarcely believable that this was the only time he witnessed such blatant behaviour. But, as nowadays, you never 'spat in the soup' and if you did, you did it in such a way that it wouldn't tarnish the reputation of the sport as a whole. But unfortunately this kind of drug use was very common practice at the time, even among amateurs, and with no official testing the sport was rife with this abuse.

He also talked of his arrest by the Belgian police on suspicion of smuggling drugs before that year's Ghent-Wevelgem. He'd been driving from Paris to Ghent for the start of the race in one of the team cars, loaded with bikes, equipment, as well as a few team-mates, when he was pulled over by armed police, who had been waiting just over the Belgian border. Shay stopped, as instructed, and was informed by the police that they had received information from Interpol that the vehicle was carrying drugs.

Shay told them that they were welcome to search the car, but they weren't asking for permission: they had already started pulling equipment and riders out of the station wagon. The police searched everywhere, including inside handlebars, through clothing, and even inside the riders' food. Shay, thinking that they had finished their search, asked the police if they could now go. He was curtly told that they could go when they'd finished searching the car. Then there was a shout as one of the policemen pulled a small packet from under the driver's seat. The packet contained Benzedrine. Shay told them that they were not his, but even so he was arrested for possession of and smuggling drugs.

He was then taken to the police station where he was charged, and subsequently released. He only just made it to Ghent on time, and because he finished fifth in the race, he had to provide a urine sample for the drug testers. His urine test from the race was negative, and this helped to persuade the magistrate that the Benzedrine tablets were not his. The solicitor he'd engaged argued that they must have been planted by somebody else from the team. The case was then adjourned and Shay never heard anything about the charges again. The irony of all this was that anyone could buy amphetamines (only slightly weaker in strength) without a prescription from any chemist shop in Belgium, or Benzedrine inhalers off the shelf in the UK.

Later that year there would be a halfhearted attempt by the Tour de France organisers to introduce drug tests into the Tour, which resulted in the riders going on strike, complaining that 'they felt degraded' by these tests. Shay's story has some similarities to that of Willy Voet, the *soigneur* of the Festina team, who was arrested while crossing the border from Belgium to France with a car load of drugs, prior to the 1998 Tour de France. His arrest would provoke one of the biggest scandals to hit the sport. Cyclists taking drugs was old news, but even seasoned fans of the sport were shocked to realise that entire teams were involved, with their team personnel complicit in systematically organising it.

At the end of August that year Shay was to take part in what would turn out to be his final World Professional Road Race Championship, an event he had usually ridden so well in over the years and had come so close to winning in 1962, before Jean Stablinski betrayed him. A victory in that race would certainly have changed his life totally.

The route for the 1966 Championship, on the famous Nurburgring motor racing circuit near Adenau in West Germany, was extra tough. In the period leading up to the race Rudi Altig and Lucien Aimar travelled to Brittany to stay with Shay in the Hotel d'Irlande, and the three of them trained intensely together. Peter Crinnion had decided not to race; instead he would be staying behind in Brittany to look after the hotel. Shay did have company for the journey to the race, however, giving a lift to John McCarthy and Liam Horner, two very promising Irish amateurs who were then living and racing in Brittany.

As the circuit at the Nurburgring was very hilly Shay fitted a triple chain-ring, determined to have every advantage he could muster to help him get over the steep climbs on the circuit. On the day the Irishman was on great form. Riding very strongly from the start, he escaped with a dangerous group that included Anquetil, Aimar and that year's classic star Felice Gimondi. However, not surprisingly, the peloton rode particularly hard to ensure the break was recaptured.

Unfortunately for Shay, on the penultimate time up the hardest climb, his chain was derailed. Unable to get his feet out of his toe clips quickly enough, he fell sideways towards the crowd on the narrow climb. 'Poussez', (push me) he shouted at the crowd, forgetting that he was in Germany, as he tried to get himself back upright as quickly as possible. The spectators didn't understand, or maybe pretended not to. Eventually he managed to get going again and caught up with Altig. Although just a little behind the leaders, he had given up hope and promptly said to Shay: 'It's all over now'. Shay urged the German to think positively; he knew that after his very difficult chase his own race was over, but his German friend was flying. Furthermore, he reminded Altig that Poulidor and Anquetil would be watching each other so anxiously that it would give him a fair chance of getting back on. The relationship between the French pair had deteriorated to such an extent that they were only communicating to each other through their wives.

On the last time up the hill Shay gave his all to try and ensure that Altig made it across to the break. Altig then started to haul them back, with the help of another ally, that year's surprise Tour winner Lucien Aimar. This might seem to go against the grain, but the Frenchman perhaps wanted to be there to help Anquetil. Finally, the now flying Altig caught the leaders by surprise, and with his sprint won easily from Anquetil, with Poulidor in bronze medal position. For the record, Jean Stablinski finished fifth at 10 seconds. After crossing the line in 15th position, only one minute and a second behind, Shay went over to Altig to congratulate him. Altig thanked Shay for his help and for giving him the belief that he could do it. Shortly afterwards, Altig returned to Loctudy to make an appearance at Shay's hotel in a show of gratitude. The cycling mad people of Brittany turned up in their droves to see the new World Champion, and the hotel received some great publicity from the visit.

At the end of the race Anquetil had refused to step up onto the podium at the medal presentation ceremony, as a protest at having to undergo a drug test, which had been introduced to the World Championships for the first time. Many of the other top riders had also refused to take a test, including Altig and Stablinski. Raymond Poulidor was the only medalist who obliged, but due to dehydration he had trouble providing a sample to the doctor. Altig and Anquetil were initially suspended, but these bans were quickly overturned.

The week after the Worlds Shay returned to Paris-Luxembourg, which had been the scene of so much drama the previous year, and finished the race in sixth place overall. He may have taken some consolation from the fact that Stablinski had to pull out prior to the second stage. Shortly afterwards, the British journalist, Jock Wadley, who had stayed with Shay on the Côte d'Azur all those years ago, wrote of visiting Hotel d'Irlande during a cycling trip around Brittany. Shay was not there when Wadley first called, but Peter Crinnion and his wife Mary were there to greet him. The Crinnions had moved to Loctudy to help Shay renovate the hotel. Then, when Shay found himself in real difficulties, Crinnion agreed to sacrifice his season to allow him to concentrate on racing and earning as much money as he could. He felt he owed his compatriot a favour for all the help Shay had given him earlier in his career. They were offered accommodation in the hotel, but declined due to all the continuing work going on in the hotel, and decided instead to live nearby. They helped around the hotel, working in the bar and doing various other jobs as required.

One idea that Shay had at this stage to increase income was running training camps for cyclists at the hotel; they could then go on to race in local events in Brittany. It could have been an attractive environment for any keen amateur: Shay had adorned his hotel with dozens of photographs from his career, leader's jerseys from the Tour and Vuelta and a green Irish jersey, in addition to numerous trophies and sashes he had won over the years. But the idea never came to fruition.

Instead, the situation at the hotel went from bad to worse. Crinnion arrived back one afternoon from a training spin to find more problems. While quenching his thirst in the bar he overheard a commotion next door in the restaurant. Some English tourists were complaining that they were being overcharged, which surprised him, as the Hotel d'Irlande was one of the cheapest places to get a meal in Loctudy. He spoke to the tourists, and quickly realised that what they were being charged did not tally with the price he had written up himself on the blackboard menu. It turned out that the waiter and the chef had been overcharging many of their customers, especially tourists, and pocketing the difference. Foreign tourists would be given the 'special' menus with increased prices. In a scene more likely to be found in Fawlty Towers, the chef later attempted to attack the waiter with a knife, as he thought that he had informed on him to Crinnion.

In despair, Shay decided to employ an old aquaintance from his ACBB days, Augustin Corteggiani, to manage the hotel, but Corteggiani was also to take advantage of Shay's regular absences from the Hotel d'Irlande. He would buy new wines from visiting salesmen which did not appeal to the tastebuds of the Parisians, who made up the majority of customers at the hotel. As the hotel's cellar grew, with cases of unused wine, Corteggiani's personal wine collection was also expanding. At one time, when Corteggiani was away, his wife was having trouble with the plumbing in the house and asked Peter to have a look at it. Peter obliged, and upon visiting the house happened upon the stack of wine with the same labels as those in the hotel. Corteggiani had been helping himself to wine from the hotel. Despite the fact that they were selling forty dinners per night, the hotel was continuing to lose money. Peter had to break the news to Shay that he had been ripped off by his old mate from ACBB. Shay sacked him immediately.

To add to his troubles, Shay's friends who had lent him the money for his investment in the hotel were now looking for their money to be returned. He had to sell his house in Paris, which overlooked the Seine, to pay back his investors. It was a fine house which should have garnered a handsome sum. However, a large road works project had been started around the house, blocking the view from the house and putting off any potential buyers. Eventually an offer for the house was put in – well below the asking price. Shay, under increasing pressure from his friends who had lent him the money, had no choice but to accept the offer. It later transpired that his 'friends' were the very same people who had bought the house at the lower price.

Life at the Hotel d'Irlande was becoming difficult for the Crinnions as well. An employee at the hotel took exception to the pair working there, and informed on them to the authorities for not having work permits. At this time Mary was expecting their first child, and she was going to fly back to Ireland as they wanted to have the baby in Ireland. Peter decided he would take the ferry back home to cut their costs, and told Shay he would be leaving the following Friday. Shay informed him that he would be going home with him. He had had enough and just wanted to leave his problems behind.

Peter stayed up all night trying to dissuade Shay from returning home and abandoning his business, but he was adamant. On top of his waning cycling career and his business problems, the staff who systematically fleeced him and the friends who took advantage of him, his wife, Marguerite, was asking for a separation. In reality they had separated: she had not been living at the hotel for some time, but now she wanted to make the separation legal, and under French law this would have made her entitled to half of everything. Shay did not want to have to slave away to save his business, only for half of whatever earnings he did make going to Marguerite.

Having reached the decision to abandon his business and to leave France, Shay sought to save something from the wreckage. One disposable asset he had was his stock of wine and he found somebody in Quimper, 20 kilometres from Loctudy, willing to buy it. But he had to off-load the stock clandestinely; he didn't want the staff realising what he was up to.

So Shay and Peter hatched a plan whereby they would move the wine from the cellar at night, while Mary distracted the staff upstairs. Peter went down to the cellar and handed each bottle through the basement window (which could just be reached from ground level) to Shay who then placed them into Peter's car. The bottles at the front of each rack they left alone, so that it would appear that the stock had not been touched.

However, there was another problem: legally they were not permitted to move or sell the stock at night, and this was very nearly their downfall. When they'd loaded up Peter's car the pair set off in the direction of Quimper, but on the way they came across a traffic accident. They were halted by a policeman who asked them for a lift into Quimper. Both the boot and the back seat of the car were full with bottles which they'd not had time to wrap. If the policeman got in the back seat he could not have failed to notice their cargo. Just as Peter feared that they were about to be rumbled, a call came over the police radio. As the policeman went to answer it Peter slipped the car into gear, and drove off.

After a few kilometres at top speed he pulled off the road into a forest. There they waited, fearing that they might have been followed by the police car. When they felt the danger had passed they resumed their journey and sold the wine in Quimper. It might have been like a scene from the Keystone Cops, but Shay had lost enough of his savings without losing more through having his drink confiscated.

There was just one final issue that he wanted to resolve before he left France for Ireland – his son, Pascal, who was currently living with his mother. Shay wanted to take him out of the country; he felt he would take better care of him than Marguerite could. Pascal suffered from rickets, and it had often been left to Mary, rather than Marguerite, to tend to him by bandaging his legs at night. So, before they finally left, Shay and Peter went looking for Pascal, who they thought might have been living with Marguerite's family somewhere in the Mulhouse area. They were unable to locate him, however, and Shay had to return without his son. He vowed to continue to try to get custody, but his chances were slim.

The only person other than the Crinnions who knew of Shay's intentions to abandon everything was the hotel receptionist. After Shay left she kept the hotel open for the rest of the week, without revealing his whereabouts to anybody. Shay had been living in France for twelve years, had raced and won all around Europe, but he returned home with only a fraction of what he had earned over the years. If it had not been for the hotel wine he would have been going back to Ireland with less money than he had gone to Paris with in 1955. As Pierre Chany wrote: 'He arrived at the ACBB with his little suitcase and after all those years he left with all his belongings again in one small suitcase.'

14

Home in Ireland

On the night that he returned to Dublin Shay met John Cleary in the International Hotel and told him about what had happened to cause his sudden return home. John was one of Shay's best friends and had been one of his training partners before he left for the continent. That night he indicated to John just how bitter he felt about how he'd been let down by those he trusted and about how his wife had run his business into the ground.

Shay now had to consider his future. He told John that he wanted to return to panel beating. John reckoned he would be able to help him. One of his friends, Willie Madden, had his own panel beating business on Usher's Quay and, with John's intervention, Willie took Shay on for a month to show him the ropes.

It wasn't long before Shay found his own business premises on South Prince's Street, near the Quay's. The garage was in quite a dilapidated state when he took it over, but his friends rallied around and helped with bricklaying, painting and general cleaning. Before long it was in a much better state. Shay even built a flat for himself on the top floor. He had been living with his parents in Kilmacanogue when he first moved home, but he needed to be closer to work.

To help fund his new venture Shay sold his story to one of the British tabloid newspapers, *The People*, the same paper to which Tom Simpson had sold his story in the year he became World Champion. In the serialised articles Shay spoke of various different aspects of professional cycling, a sport about which many of the British and Irish public would not have had much knowledge. He spoke of how much could be earned, and how he considered it to be a poor year if he earned less than £100 a week. During his best years he was earning as much as £9,000. Somewhat surprisingly to many people, he also spoke of how he never felt fully at home in France, and revealed that, although he was French-speaking and married to a French woman, with hindsight, he felt he had always been an outsider. Shay earned £500 for the series of ghostwritten articles.

He also spoke of drugs, a subject that riders never normally spoke of beyond the confines of the peloton or with close friends. He revealed different methods by which riders administered drugs during races. Apart from tablet form, which was the type he had tried, he also spoke of hypodermic needles being used, which riders would have in their jersey pockets, and he claimed that some riders were also using inhalers. Some have written of Shay being ostracised by the peloton for writing these articles, but his own view was that he had already left professional cycling. However, it did mean that if ever he considered a return he had made it much more difficult for himself through their publication. He had, as they say, 'spat in the soup'.

He also spoke of a method of drug taking unbeknownst to the cyclist. A *soigneur* under the direction of the manager would place stimulants in his bidon. He told of times when he would be swigging from his bottle unaware that his drink had been spiked. He would then feel light-headed and reckless. Instead of sitting comfortably in the bunch he would then start initiating breakaways or putting his team leader's rivals under pressure by setting a fearsome pace. Normally the effects of the drugs would wear off well before the end, when the work for his team was done. There were times though when he could still feel the amphetamines in his system at the finish. With that in his system he would never win, as apart from feeling over-confident, he was not able to judge distances accurately. He would start his sprint too early – 500 metres from the end, a distance that he could not sustain in a full-on sprint – and he would fade well before the finish. For the brief period of time in which Shay knowingly doped, and also for the races in which his drinks were spiked, he never failed a test. This was because it would only be the first five riders who would be tested, and in the smaller criteriums there were no tests. He spoke of situations whereby cyclists had taken banned substances but would still pass the drugs tests. He revealed that they would carry sachets with clean urine, and when asked for a sample at the end they would claim that they were embarrassed and would request some privacy in a cubicle. Once there they would empty the sachet into the test tube and therefore pass the test.

Twelve years after Shay's revelations the yellow jersey wearer in the 1978 Tour de France was caught in nearly the exact situation he had described. Michel Pollentier, one of Belgium's top riders, when asked to provide a sample, emptied a clean sample of urine from a condom strapped to his body, to give the impression of urinating into the test tube. An observant official spotted him and he was thrown out of the Tour. The Dutch cyclist, Eef Dolman, was also caught cheating in this same manner. Dolman, who had become the World Amateur Champion in 1966 at Nurburgring, was caught the following year after finishing first in the Dutch professional championships with rubber tubes linked to a supply of clean urine. Dolman would go on to suffer various health problems and would subsequently spend time in hospital with mental illness. Pollentier would also suffer from mental illness after his retirement, having lost much of his savings through bad investments – a common enough occurrence in those days. A decade previously Fausto Coppi had also been candid in speaking of drug use. He'd been asked on a live TV interview if he had ever taken drugs, to which he admitted, 'Only when necessary'. Asked how often that was he replied: 'Almost always.'

Throughout cycling history riders had always used stimulants. In the 1896 Bordeaux-Paris, a British cyclist, Arthur Linton, had died after overdosing on morphine, and another team in that same race had been given wine, port and champagne to help dull the pain during the marathon race. Shay's own team leader during most of his years in the professional peloton, Jacques Anquetil, also spoke to the media about drug use. He told a French newspaper, 'You'd have to be an imbecile or a hypocrite to imagine that a professional cyclist who rides 235 days a year can hold himself together without stimulants.'

After he returned to Ireland Shay also sold most of his jerseys to earn extra cash to fund the business. Work soon started to pick up, with numerous customers wanting to have their car fixed by the great Shay Elliott. He had to take on extra staff. Shay didn't touch a bike for many months after his return from France, but eventually, friends of his from Bray Wheelers persuaded him to start riding again. Early the following year Shay and a number of members of the club were invited to attend a club dinner organised by an NCA club in Tipperary. So, on a Saturday morning in February, Shay once more threw his leg over the saddle of a bicycle and set off on the long road, along with Peter Crinnion, Phil O'Brien, Peter Doyle and Tommy Campbell. Despite not having ridden for months Shay was able to keep up with the others, who had put in a good winter's training. However, eventually fatigue set in, and the group started to disintegrate. It was later than expected when they arrived in Clonmel. Peter Doyle had punctured in the later stages and had to cycle the last few miles in the dark of night.

When they gathered in the hotel in Clonmel there was still no sign of Shay. It turned out that he had given up in Graiguenamanagh, and climbed off his bike at a hotel in the town (it would be six months before he collected it). He then hitched a lift to Clonmel to meet up with his friends. They still weren't too late for the club dinner, where they relaxed and recounted their tales from the journey that day. They had a good laugh with Shay about him giving up. The next day, despite his fatigue, he was up bright and early to indulge in his first love and go hunting with some members of the Clonmel club.

Although his business was going well and he'd found some sort of renewed interest in cycling, Shay was noticeably more disconsolate than he had been before he first left for France. John Cleary noticed how he had changed considerably in the way he related to people over the intervening years. One of his employees, Pat Norton, recounted how Shay's GP made the harsh comment that he was 'maybe a better cyclist than he was a human being'. However, after all that had happened to him during the previous few years, his distrust of others is perhaps understandable.

Later that year there was more tragedy for the sport of cycling during the Tour de France when Tom Simpson collapsed and died while climbing the vicious, exposed climb of Mont Ventoux. Despite receiving medical assistance he could not be revived. On the same climb, some years earlier, Frenchman Jean Mallejac had collapsed and then had a fit in the ambulance on the way to hospital. The postmortem on Simpson revealed traces of alcohol and amphetamines in his bloodstream, and the doctors concluded that drugs had contributed to his death. The following year the Tour organisers marketed the Tour as the '*Tour de Sante*' (Health Tour), as drug tests were brought in, and two riders tested positive.

Shay took the death of Tom Simpson hard, as they had got on very well during their years racing together. Later he spoke of Tom's determination to win: 'Tom wanted to win anything, no matter what it was, even if it was just a small criterium. This was Tommy's ambition all the time, he never wanted to play second fiddle. Tommy gave everything. The day that Tommy died, Lord rest him, was the day that he could have won the Tour. Had he got through this stage in a good position, the Tour win was in his grasp.' It was Tonedrin which had been found in Tom Simpson's blood stream after his death. Simpson had said before that if it took ten pills to kill him, he was willing to take nine to win.

Shay also kept in touch with his son, Pascal, in Mulhouse. He used to phone him regularly, and still harboured ambitions of becoming reunited with him. Slowly he was picking up the pieces of his life, and his interest in cycling was returning. He even ran for election as Vice-President of the Irish Cycling Federation (as the CRE was now known). However, he was beaten in the vote 21-12 by Paddy McQuaid.The following year Bray Wheelers set out again on a trip south, as part of their preparation for their forthcoming season. This time, there would be no repetition of the previous year, and Shay was able to complete the journey to Kilkenny. He had also started to become more involved in Irish racing and used to turn up to see the finish of many of the bigger races in Dublin, where he would usually end up becoming the centre of attention. He was also in the spotlight at a shooting competition in Bray in the summer, where he scored well, despite missing out on the prizes.

Towards the end of 1969 he made the decision to attempt a comeback. He contacted Jock Wadley, the journalist who'd been so helpful to him at the start of his career on the continent, to ask him what he thought of the possibility of this and about racing in England. He also asked him if there was any chance that somebody might sponsor him and provide him with a bike and equipment. Shay was hoping to use the London-Holyhead race as the springboard for the 1970 season, where he wanted to compete at the World Championships Road Race; it was being held as close to home as it had ever been, in Leicester. The only stumbling block in his quest to compete would be the lack of a sponsorship deal he explained to Brendan O'Reilly in an RTE interview, which was as much a plea for sponsorship, as it was an insight into professional cycling. One consequence was that his old mentor at ACBB, Mickey Wiegant, promised to provide him with racing jerseys and shorts.

Wadley, meanwhile, discussed Shay's return with Ernie Clements, head of Falcon, the bicycle manufacturers, who agreed to sponsor him for the forthcoming season.When Shay had told Mick Byrne of his intention to make a comeback, Mick asked him if he intended racing in some of the bigger Irish events. Shay said no, because he felt he would be a watched man in Ireland and marked out of the race by the others. He thought he'd be better off (wrongly as it turned out) in England. Furthermore, he decided his best chances would be in an event that was more of a test of strength and stamina than the Irish races. That was why he was keen to take part in the 430-kilometre London-Holyhead race, and with that decision made, Shay started going on massive training spins from Dublin to Longford and back in preparation for the event. When he originally quit in 1966 Shay had still been winning races and at 32 years of age could not by any means have been considered over the hill. It's not unknown for riders to race professionally into their late 30s or even early 40s. He therefore felt he had some unfinished business in the sport, and that he had not retired from the peloton in the way he'd wanted to.

In his RTE interview Shay was asked what his expectations were for his comeback. He told O'Reilly that he felt that he could be as successful as he had ever been during his continental career. The rest from the bike would have done him the world of good, he claimed, and despite his age (he was 35 at the time), his enthusiasm would help him in his return.Shay explained that he had started training behind a Honda 50 motorbike, and he would set off after work on a Saturday afternoon and would cover up to 400 kilometres over the weekend. O'Reilly finished the interview by asking Shay how he had lost everything after earning so much. Shay simply replied that it was due to unfortunate circumstances at the time. 'Just one of those things that happens in somebody's life,' he said. He knew it would take an awful lot to regain what he had lost in monetary terms, but from a personal point of view he thought he could gain a lot through his comeback.

London-Holyhead started in the centre of Britain's capital, and the riders were waved off from the start by Northern Irish football star, Danny Blanchflower. At the early hour of 5am only a few hardened cyclists had turned up to spectate, along with some other curious onlookers returning home from nightclubs. Shay wasn't giving much away to those who spoke to him at the race start, but nobody was very talkative, nervous no doubt at the prospect of the 265 miles which lay ahead. There was a long neutralised section up the Edgware Road, which gave the riders a chance to digest their breakfasts, and for Shay to have his bike sorted out! Falcon had only delivered it to him the evening before, and he discovered the mechanic had fitted a bottle cage over the gear cables, which made changing impossible.

An early break went in the race, but this didn't cause any panic because there was so far still to go. This break would tire soon enough, or so they thought. However, their lead grew ever bigger as the race progressed, until finally Shay decided that enough was enough, and started to chase. But the rest of the pursuing group wouldn't contribute; they were content to sit on his wheel. They closed the gap considerably, but did not regain contact.

The British riders all knew each other and chatted constantly among themselves, but Shay rode in silence. 'He never seemed confortable within himself and the British cyclists were not the slightest bit welcoming,' said Brian Tadman, who finished the day in 13th place. 'Coming through the last feed off the main A5 Pete Smith, the National 50-mile time trial champion, attacked, much to every body's consternation, and riders were engaged in an individual pursuit at the same time trying to get food and drinks into pockets. Shay uttered his only word throughout the whole race when Smith was finally caught, and it wasn't a kind one.'

It is difficult to imagine what a miserable, lonely day that must have been for Shay, and in North Wales the race started to take its toll on him. Mick Byrne, who was a member of his support team, went ahead at Bangor to perform some minor work on the van. When they left Shay he was still riding strongly. With the repairs completed they waited for him after Bangor. A couple of riders appeared but Shay wasn't with them. Other riders then passed, in ones and twos, but still no sign of Shay. Eventually he appeared on the horizon, pedalling slowly, as white as a ghost. He had hunger knock, and was totally devoid of energy.

Shay did finish, 21st, with only one other rider behind him, and over half an hour behind the winner Sid Barras. Some of the other riders realised that they hadn't been fair to Shay, having sat on his wheel during the chase, and tried to make amends by apologising to him. For Shay this just added insult to injury. This was the very reason he'd chosen to race in England rather than in Ireland, but had it had happened to him anyway. He had planned to take part in the London to York race, but after his experience in London-Holyhead he pulled out.

That same year, his brother Paul – he, too, not having raced for a number of years – also decided to make a comeback. He won both the National Championships and the Tour of Ireland, using the same Falcon bike which Shay had been given for London-Holyhead. The Tour was won on the Buncrana stage, which Pat McQuaid remembers well: 'Going into the Buncrana stage I was well up and in a good position to take the lead - however I was heavily marked and as soon as the break with Paul Elliott got away the Bray Wheelers (Doyle and Dawson) stuck to my wheel and I couldnt make it into the break. It went on to gain several minutes.' The Tour of Ireland ended in Phoenix Park, where it was Shay who presented his younger brother with the winner's trophy.

At the third annual convention of the I.C.F. in November of that year, John Lackey read an application from Shay for reinstatement as an amateur. There was some debate amongst the delegates as to the length of time he would have to wait to compete again in amateur races. But Shay had also mentioned in his letter that he wanted to make himself available for coaching. This was an offer that couldn't be turned down, and so there was unanimous agreement that he could compete again as an amateur. But, in fact, Shay would not get an opportunity to compete again. London-Holyhead would turn out to be his last race.

15

The end

Following his demoralising return to the peloton, Shay decided he would like to use his experience and the vast store of knowledge he had acquired to help the future of Irish cycling, and prepare the team for the next Olympics in Munich in 1972. Together with John Lackey he set up a training weekend in Longford. Shay led a group of eleven promising cyclists on a 120-kilometre run to Edgeworthstown, then, in the evening, he lectured them on various aspects of training and racing.

As it turned out the Munich Olympics would see a repeat of the incident at the World Championship in Frascati back in 1955. The two Irish cycling bodies were still at loggerheads, and the nationalist NCA once again decided to stage a protest at their exclusion from international competition by sending a rival team to the Games. Their demonstration delayed the start of the Olympic road race and they caused further confusion when a number of their 'team', wearing false race numbers, managed to infiltrate the race. Shay, however, would not be around to see any of that.

His world turned upside down in April of 1971. At home one evening in Kilmacanogue his father heard the noise of a pheasant just outside the house. He grabbed his shotgun and summoned his Weimaraner hunting dog. The dog ran into some bushes and scared the pheasant into flight, but then ran into the line of fire. Jim was an excellent shot, but he accidentally shot the dog. He quickly ran towards his beloved pet, which, although alive, had his head stuck in some bushes. In his anxiety and hurry to free the dog Jim jerked his own head back, causing himself considerable pain. But he was more concerned with the fate of his dog and thought he had done nothing more than pull a muscle.

Visiting his local doctor he expected simply to be given some painkillers and sent on his way, but instead the doctor noticed something else wrong with Jim and he was hospitalised immediately. It was much more serious than he thought. Shay went to see his father in St. Vincent's

Hospital as often as possible, but prior to one visit he hit a pothole and fell off his bike, coming down the descent of the Embankment outside the city. He tried to clean up the blood from his face as best he could, as he didn't want his father to see him in such a state. Jim might perhaps not have noticed, because when Shay went in he saw that his father was looking much worse than he had previously. Jim told his son that he would not be coming home, and Shay was left reeling. The doctors could do nothing more for Jim and he died shortly afterwards.

Marguerite travelled from France for the funeral, and some thought that might signal the start of a reconciliation between her and Shay, but it was not to be. Too much had happened in the past, and Shay didn't show any desire to try and salvage the relationship. They were civil to each other but no more than that. It was as if he had put France behind him and rebuilt his life. Shay went back to work shortly afterwards, while Marguerite returned to France.

One of Shay's employees, Pat Norton, noticed a profound change in Shay when he returned to work, as did Eddie, the eldest of the Elliott brothers. 'He wasn't the same Shay Elliott after that. He used to lean on father: "Da, what do you think I should do?"'

A few weeks after his father's funeral, on the afternoon of the 3rd of May, Shay's lifelong friend Noel O'Brien was involved in a minor car crash. There was some damage to the car, so he dropped it off at Shay's garage in South Prince's Street. Noel had a long conversation with Shay at the garage and didn't notice anything unusual in Shay's behaviour. He was in his usual good spirits, Noel later commented. Jack Blake also visited the garage that evening around 6.15pm. He gave Shay a hand in pulling the chassis off a car, and when the job was finished left the garage at around 7.45 pm. In his statement to the *Gardaí* Jack said, 'Elliott seemed quite normal and did not complain of any illness.' Jack was the last person to see Shay alive.

Pat Norton had started work for Shay the previous year. His father knew Shay through the motor trade, and Pat had been taken on as an apprentice panel beater. He lived in Drumcondra on the opposite side of the city. Each morning he cycled across to the garage, usually arriving around 9 o'clock. On the morning of the 4th of May Pat turned up at work to find the garage door locked. This was unusual as he would normally find Shay already there and working. On the other hand, Shay sometimes had to be away from the garage on business, so Pat didn't think too much of the fact that there was no sign of his boss. He didn't have a key but managed to prise the door open using a piece of wood. By now Shay's other employees, Tommy Doyle and Patrick Hesnan, had arrived for work.

Later that morning Pat went upstairs to the kitchen where they used to make themselves a cup of tea, and there, in a cupboard adjacent to the kitchen, he saw the body of Shay lying on top of a shotgun in a pool of blood. Immediately he ran downstairs and told Joseph Cooke, a friend of Shay's, who had just come into the garage, and it was Cooke who phoned the *Gardaí*.

Sergeant James Hoare from the nearby Pearse Street station, accompanied by other members of the *Gardaí,* arrived shortly afterwards. They didn't find any indication of a forcible entry to the flat. The following is taken from Sergeant Hoare's report:

The legs were at right angles to the body and slightly bent at the knees. The forearms were bent up towards the head. The deceased was dressed in his underwear and wearing slippers. There was a spent cartridge case on the floor close by the deceased's left knee joint. The stock and bolt of the shotgun were protruding from under the deceased's left thigh. I was informed by Patrick Norton, who was present on my arrival, that the body was that of Shay Elliott, his employer. The cloakroom where the body was found measures approximately 6ft by 4ft. The contents of the flat were not disarranged and appeared quite normal. Having a shotgun to protect himself would not be unusual. I couldn't say if it was an accident or not.

Pat Norton concurred with Jack Blake and Noel O'Brien about Shay's mood: in his statement to the *Gardaí* he said that when he'd left work the previous evening, Shay appeared to be in his normal good physical health. The *Gardaí* had immediately closed the garage after the body had been discovered, and they were later joined there by members of the Technical Bureau from Dublin Castle. Shay's body was not moved until a doctor had arrived to carry out an examination and to assess the extent of the wounds. People interviewed in various premises adjoining said they had not heard any shots. When Shay's brother Paul received the news he rushed up to the city from Kilmacanogue. Father Kieran Mulcahy, curate at City Quay Parish, said that he got a call just after 12.45 pm Mass and went immediately to anoint the dead cyclist.

A post-mortem to be conducted by the State Pathologist was arranged for the following morning. His report read as follows:

There is a gunshot wound on the front of the chest. There is a second burn of similar nature (to that of the chest) on the inside of the right wrist. Internal Findings – Cardio Vascular System – Heart – The heart otherwise shows no disease process, however, the myocardium of the left ventricle measures 15mm which represents a degree of muscle hypertrophy of this chamber. Cause of Death – Shock and Haemorrhage due to traumatic rupture of the heart and liver by gun shot.

For the second time in as many months Marguerite found herself back in Ireland for a funeral, and along with Nell, Paul, Eddy and John Flanagan, she made the sad journey to Dublin City Mortuary on Usher's Island, where Shay's body was laid out. Despite their differences in the past and their eventual parting, Marguerite was grief stricken, and she cried as she tenderly caressed Shay's forehead. Her anguish might well have been increased by the fact that, even before the funeral, rumours had started to spread in Dublin that Shay had taken his own life. The timing of his death – so soon after that of his father – perhaps gave credence to this view. At the inquest in Dublin, however, an open verdict was returned. What was certain was that Shay had killed himself; what was not certain was whether his death had been accidental or deliberate.

All the people I have spoken to are more or less of the belief that what happened was a tragic accident. His brothers and his mother, too, did not or could not believe that Shay would have taken his own life. Those who had spoken to him in the days previous to his death had not noticed anything particularly strange in his behaviour. Noel O'Brien, for instance, who had been speaking to him the night before, has never believed that Shay committed suicide. His theory was that Shay may have heard a burglar in the garage below and while grabbing his gun to go downstairs and investigate, accidentally discharged it. Shay always slept with a loaded shotgun beside his bed; it was a habit he'd picked up from his father, who'd forever been worried about the house being burgled.

Another theory in circulation concerned the shotgun itself, which, according to John Flanagan, another of Shay's friends who believed his death to have been an accident, had developed a fault. It was the Luigi Franchi shotgun which Shay had won as his stage-winning prize in the

1963 Vuelta, and was designed primarily for hunting smaller game, such as snipe, or for clay pigeon shooting. Shay, however, used it for hunting geese and ducks which required a heavier duty cartridge. Continuously using this more powerful shot had taken its toll on the gun and the cartridge ejector wasn't working correctly. Shay was advised by various people, John Flanagan and his brother Paul among them, to get the gun repaired or to dispose of it, but Shay never did. According to Flanagan, the fault meant that when the safety catch was disengaged the firing pin would click forward if the gun were subjected to a sudden impact. In other words, the shotgun could discharge without the trigger being pulled. It is Flanagan's belief that Shay may have fallen over the shotgun in the middle of the night, perhaps believing he had heard an intruder.

Both of these are plausible explanations, but either, if true, would represent a particularly sad irony because Shay had not only been expert at handling guns, but was also known to have been generally very safety-conscious with regard to them. Peter Crinnion recalls one particular occasion when he, along with Shay and his brother Paul, were hunting in Wicklow. A pheasant rose from the long grass and Paul tracked the path of the pheasant with his gun and shot over the heads of Shay and Peter. Shay severely rebuked Paul for what he had done, and the two briefly came to blows.

Fuelling the view that suicide was the more likely explanation was the fact which emerged after his death that he had attended two doctors in the previous few months, for what was termed 'mental stress'. At that time depressive conditions were not as well understood as they are now, and often not treated by the medical profession as an actual clinical condition. We know Shay was in good physical shape, but his mental state in the period leading up to his death is something we can only guess at. What we do know, however, is that 'acute clinical depression', the likely condition he was being treated for, might well not have been apparent to his family and even very close friends.

Pat Norton later disclosed that in Shay's garage he'd found a quantity of Roche 5, also known as Diazepam. Diazepam, first marketed as Valium, is a benzodiazepine derivative drug which is commonly used for treating anxiety, insomnia and depression, amongst other medical conditions. However, Diazepam is known to have a range of side effects which are common to most benzodiazepines; these include addiction and the potential to make the depression even worse. It is also recommended that the prescription of Diazepam should be avoided, whenever possible, for individuals suffering from severe depression, particularly when accompanied by suicidal tendencies. If Shay's death had been a suicide, is it conceivable that the Diazepam might have been a contributing factor?

In any professional sport the end of a successful career can mark a difficult transition in life. Most sports can probably list a number of suicides among its participants, but ex-cyclists do seem particularly prone to depression and self-destruction. In recent decades one can think of men like Hugo Koblet, Luis Ocaña, Thierry Claveyrolat, Marco Pantani and José María Jiménez – all of whom had stood on the podium of the grand tours. Cyclists in Shay's era, when they retired, usually opened a café, a bicycle shop, or a hotel, financed with whatever they had saved from their days in the saddle. Its walls would be bedecked with their emblematic racing jerseys and evocative photographs of them in their pomp. Their customers would have known them in their racing days, and would be a constant reminder of what they had achieved. But Shay retired into obscurity. Any Frenchman who had once worn the *maillot jaune* would forever be remembered and revered in his locality, but what did a yellow jersey signify in the back streets of Dublin?

For all his impressive *palmarès* of racing victories, Shay was the quintessential team rider. In part this came from his strength and from his racing intelligence. As Bobet remarked: 'He didn't need someone saying, "Now go to the front, do this, do that." He could read the situation and he did what was required without being told. He was a team rider with capital letters.' In equal part this came from a moral sense of what he was there for: for Shay loyalty trumped everything, including personal ambition. In his amateur days with the Dublin Wheelers there were people, jealous perhaps of his precocious talent, who called him selfish and interested only in winning for himself. In his professional years on the continent there was nobody who ever said anything of that sort about him. Quite the contrary, Shay was sometimes criticised for his generosity and willingness to sacrifice his own chances for the sake of his team, or its leader. The hard fact is that in a ruthless world honour has little place, and any act of kindness can be seen as naïveté, a weakness to be exploited. And how Shay was exploited, in his professional career and in his business dealings, and – worst of all – by those who called themselves his 'friend'. However ingenuous he might have been when he left Ireland for the continent, when he returned he knew he had been repeatedly let down by people he had trusted.

Perhaps the worst thing for Shay was that he suffered so much in silence. There were races he could have won, should have won, but didn't. Fate intervened in the form of a puncture or a mechanical failure; or he was not given the support his talent warranted. But rarely would he express his disappointment. Even in that dreadful betrayal in Luxembourg he maintained a stone cold silence and moved to another team. Others would have roared 'Injustice' from the rooftops and the whole world would have known, but that was not Shay's way. He kept it bottled up inside himself. That kind of stoicism has a dignity to it, but if the therapists are right, it may do us no psychological good in the long run. Far better, they say, to talk, to give expression to our feelings, rather than keep them contained. All of that gives some weight to the suicide theory, but that is all it does. The simple fact remains that how Shay actually came to kill himself is something that will never truly be known.

After Shay's death a member of Bray Wheelers, Denis Kearns, took upon himself the task of having a memorial erected in memory of Shay. After a lot of hard work an engraved stone was unveiled by Nell Elliott at the top of the Glenmalure climb, which he had passed so many times on his youthful training rides. This climb is now used in the Shay Elliott Memorial Race.

Sadly, Shay's death was but the first of a sequence of tragic events that would befall the Elliott family. In 1978, aged just 16, Shay's son Pascal had decided that he wanted to grow up in Ireland. He'd written to his grandmother Nell about this and the plan was that he would live with his uncle, Paul. However, shortly before he was due to leave France he was killed in a traffic accident. He had skidded in the rain on his moped and crashed into the back of a van. It was one of the rare occasions when he was not wearing his helmet. He is buried in Mulhouse, but he is remembered on the Elliott family gravestone in Kilmacanogue cemetery. Shay's brother Paul died in 1988 during a hunting trip on the River Shannon. He had been duck shooting when he fell in the water and, impeded by his shotgun, drowned. Ellen Elliott died one year after Paul, broken hearted. After two of her children and one of her grandchildren had died tragically it seems she lost the will to live.

In looking back on Shay's life what immediately stands out is that he was a true pioneer. He and Brian Robinson were the first from outside the traditional cycling nations of western Europe to make an impact in professional road racing. In so doing he was hugely significant in helping to globalise the sport. A simple comparison makes the point: in the 1963 Tour de France riders from 11 different countries lined up at the start, whereas in 2010 there were 31 countries that had riders at the start, with every inhabited continent represented. Shay also opened the doors to the ACBB club which so many English speakers, including Robert Millar, Stephen Roche, Phil Anderson and Sean Yates, would pass through. Its director, Mickey Weigant, must surely have thought back to the young Irishman that he'd taken under his wing decades previously and understood that there was talent to be found beyond cycling's traditional borders. Shay had shown that if you had the determination to make it as a professional, you could. Nationality need not be an excuse.

Cycle racing is not a sport that responds kindly to talk of 'if only' and 'what might have been'. Team results count for nearly everything, whether it's winning races or successfully carrying out a job as a *domestique*, and a rider's excuses are soon forgotten when his performance is evaluated at the end of the season. Except perhaps, within the professional peloton itself, where they understand more completely what lies behind the performances, whatever results are yielded, and they know that things are rarely ever black and white. Shay was among that small handful of riders who won stages in all three grand tours; to the general public that may have counted for little – it hardly stood comparison with, say, winning one of the major Classics – but his fellow professionals knew just what that unsung achievement demanded. The record book indicates that he was only second in the World Championship, but in the peloton they knew better. His fellow professionals were very well aware of the qualities he repeatedly demonstrated over the seasons, both as a race winner, and as one of the strongest and most scrupulously honest team riders of the time. Perhaps it was because Shay was from Ireland that many of his achievements were not fully appreciated by continental cycling fans. His *palmarès* is impressively long, but Shay could rightly have felt disappointed that it didn't include more of the top races and at least one major classic, and few would argue against that. He certainly never had his share of 'the luck of the Irish', but certainly he was never lacking in their courage.

Shay Elliott should be remembered not for the tragic circumstances in which his life ended, but for putting Irish cycling on the map. He was the first Irish rider to be known on the continent. Others followed him, some more famous with a richer haul of victories to their name, but Shay will always remain the first.

Shay Elliott's Palmarès

1952 (amateur – Dublin Wheelers)
1st Mannin Veg
1st Dublin-Galway-Dublin
1st Grand Prix of Ireland

1953 (amateur – Dublin Wheelers)
1st Irish Road Race Championships
4th Manx International
10th Tour of Ireland

1954 (amateur – Dublin Wheelers)
1st Irish Road Race Championships
1st stage 4 Tour of Ireland
1st stage 9 Route de France
1st King of the Mountains Tour of Ireland
1st Dublin-Waterford-Dublin
4th Route de France
7th Manx International

1955 (amateur – A.C.B.B.)
1st Paris-Evreux
1st Paris-Vailly
1st Grand Prix de Boulogne-Billancourt
1st Grand Prix de l'A.P.S.A.P
1st Grand Prix de ACBB
1st Grand Prix de Boulogne
1st Prix de Breuil
1st Circuit de Boulogne
1st stage 1 Route de France
1st stage 3 Route de France (Team Time Trial)
1st Vél d'Hiv Omnium (Tour de France support race)

2nd Grand Prix Champignomistes
2nd Courbevoie (12 May)
2nd Criterium des Vainqueurs
2nd Paris-Reims
2nd Courbevoie (3 July)
2nd Paris-Noyon
2nd Grand Prix de Senonches
3rd Grand Prix de *l'Equipe*
2nd Mantes
2nd Paris–Noyon
5th World Road Race
    Championship
6th Paris-Mantes
World Record – 1000m flying start
World Record – 5km : 6'34"
World Record – 10km : 13'36"
"Meilleur Amateur de France 1955"
– Best Amateur in France

1956 (Professional – Helyett-Potin)
1st Grand Prix d'Isbergues
1st Grand Prix Catox
1st Grand Prix de l'Echo d'Alger
1st 3rd stage of the Tour du Sud-Est
1st Prix de Montignies
1st Prix d'Hennebont
1st Grand Prix de Montsauche
2nd Grand Prix de Saint-Raphaël
2nd Points Competition Tour de l'Ouest
2nd Prix de Boussac
2nd Prix de Plougasnou
5th Tour de l'Ouest
    2nd Stage 2
    2nd Stage 6

7th Circuit de l'Indre
7th Paris-Bourges
11th Circuit de la Vienne
12th Paris-Tours
13th Tour du Sud-Est
  2nd Stage 7b
14th World Road Race
  Championships
17th Paris-Camembert
19th 3-Days of Antwerp
  3rd Stage 2a
  8th Stage 3b
26th Paris-Nice
  3rd Stage 2
  3rd Stage 4a
  3rd Stage 4b
  7th Stage 3
44th Milan–San Remo
Abandoned Tour de France Stage 4b

1957 (Helyett-Potin)

1st Semaine Bretonne
1st Circuit de la Vienne
1st Prix de Langon
1st Prix de Boussac
1st Prix de Boucau
2nd Prix de La Châtre
2nd Prix de Quimperlé
3rd Grand Prix de Monaco
3rd Paris-Bourges
3rd Ploneour-Lanvern
4th Grand Prix de Nice
7th Tour of Flanders
7th Ghent-Wevelgem
7th Paris-Limoges
7th Het Volk
18th Paris-Roubaix
28th Paris-Nice
  1st Points competition
  2nd Stage 3
  2nd Stage 5b

1958 (Helyett-Potin)

1st Grand Prix Sigrand
1st Prix de Zingem
1st Londerzeel (Omnium with Peter
Post)
1st Stage 2a Team Time Trial Grand
Prix Marvan
2nd Grand Prix de Nice
2nd Stage 1 Tour de Picardie
2nd Tour de Picardie
  2nd Stage 1
2nd Prix de Rouen
2nd Prix d'Amiens
2nd Prix de Macon
2nd Prix de Chateau-Chinon
2nd Pont l'Abbe
3rd Grand Prix de Saint-Raphaël
3rd Grand Prix de Copenhagen
3rd Stage 3a Team Time Trial
Circuit d'Aquitaine
3rd Stage 3b Circuit d 'Aquitaine
3rd Londerzeel Criterium
4th Four-Days of Dunkirk
  1st Stage 2
  1st Stage 3
  1st Points competition
5th G.P. Midi-Libre
  2nd Stage 1
5th Stage 2 Circuit d'Aquitaine
5th Paris-Valenciennes
6th Four Days of Dunkirk
6th Trophee des Flanders
7th Ghent-Wevelgem
7th Stage 1 Tour de France
7th Stage 2 Tour de Picardie
9th Paris-Nice
  1st Points classification
  2nd Stage 5b
  2nd Stage 6
  5th Stage 2

10th Milan-San-Remo
12th Het Volk
15th Liège-Bastogne-Liège
20th Paris-Roubaix
27th Tour of Lombardy
28th Paris-Brussels
40th Paris-Tours
48th Tour de France
    2nd Stage 6
    3rd Stage 2
    4th Stage 10
    7th Stage 1
    7th Stage 9

1959 (Helyett-Leroux-Hutchinson)
1st Het Volk
1st Grand Prix de Denain
1st Grand Prix de Nice
1st Manx Trophy
1st Prix d'Algiers
1st Trophée Longines (TTT with Anquetil, Darrigade, Graczyk and Vermeulin)
2nd Prix de Charleroi
3rd Plaugasnou
5th Circuit de l'Aulne
9th Tour of Flanders
12th Paris-Roubaix.
22nd World Road Race Championships
30th Tour de l'Ouest
    4th Stage 1
    5th Stage 3
32nd Milan-San Remo
34th Paris-Brussels
37th Paris-Tours
40th Giro d'Italia
    6th Stage 4
    10th Stage 6

DNF Tour de France (eliminated Stage 14)
    3rd Stage 8
    3rd Stage 12
    10th Stage 2
DNF Paris-Nice-Rome
    5th Stage 2
    10th Stage 3

1960 (ACBB-Helyett-Leroux)
1st stage 18 Giro d'Italia
1st Trophée Peugeot / Grand Prix Stan Ockers (Rennes-Brest)
1st Stage 3a Grand Prix Ciclomotoristico
1st Prix *l'Echo* d'Oran.
1st Prix de Gouesnou
1st Prix de Plougasnou
1st Circuit du Tregor
2nd Circuit de l'Indre
2nd Nice-Genoa
2nd Prix d'Argentan
2nd Prix de La Clayette
2nd Prix de Solesmes
3rd Trophée Longines (TTT with Anquetil, Darrigade, Graczyk and Stablinski)
4th Four Days of Dunkirk
    4th Stage 1
7th Trophée Baracchi (with Tom Simpson)
11th Paris-Roubaix
12th Paris -Tours
15th Tour of Flanders
17th World Road Race Championships
26th Paris-Nice
    7th Stage 8b
31st Tour of Lombardy
68th Giro d'Italia

1961 (Fynsec)
1st stage 2 Four Days of Dunkirk
1st Prix de Mâcon
1st Prix de Gouesnou
2nd Prix de Vergt
2nd Prix de Gueret
24th Het Volk
27th Paris-Nice
36th Paris-Brussels
40th Flèche Wallonne
47th Tour de France
   5th Stage 1a
64th Paris-Tours
DNF Giro d'Italia
   3rd Stage 11
   6th Stage 1

1962 (ACBB-St-Raphaël-Geminiani)
1st Prix de Villiers
1st Prix de Felletin
1st Prix de Ploneour-Lanvern
1st Prix de Labastide-d'Armagnac
1st Prix d'Aubusson
1st Prix de Châteaugiron
2nd World Road Race
   Championships
2nd Circuit de la Vienne
2nd Paris-Camembert
2nd Grand Prix du Vercors
2nd Prix d'Armentieres
2nd Prix d'Arras
2nd Prix de Dijon
3rd Vuelta a España
   1st Stage 4
   2nd Stage 1
   2nd Points classification
   4th Stage 9
   7th Stage 2
   9th Stage 17
3rd Circuit Mandel-Lys-Escaut
3rd Grand Prix d'Orchies

8th Trophée Baracchi (with Jean
   Stablinski)
10th G.P. Midi-Libre
46th Ghent-Wevekgem
49th Paris-Tours
8th Super Prestige Pernod.

1963 (Saint-Raphaël-Geminiani)
1st stage 3 Tour de France (and
   wore the yellow jersey) 61st overall
1st stage 13 Vuelta a España
   2nd Stage 3
   41st overall
1st Grand Prix de Vayrac
1st Prix de la Trinite a Guérêt
2nd Paris-Camembert
2nd Tour de l'Oise
2nd Grand Prix de Miniac-Morvan
2nd Grand Prix de Gouesnou
3rd Issoire
3rd Boucles Roquevairoises.
3rd Circuit d'Auvergne.
3rd Grand Prix de Riom
3rd Grand Prix de Luxembourg
3rd Grand Prix du Parisien (TTT)
6th Grand Prix d'Eibar
   3rd Stage 3
   9th Stage 2
7th Grand Prix of Frankfurt
15th Paris-Tours
22nd Tour of Luxembourg
23rd Ghent-Wevelgem
24th Paris Luxembourg
   2nd Stage 2
26th World Road Race
   Championship
38th Paris-Nice
39th Paris-Brussels
61st Tour de France

1964 (Saint-Raphaël-Geminiani)
1st Manx Trophy
1st Tour du Morbihan
2nd Prix de Felletin
2nd Prix d'Alençon
3rd Ronde de Seignelay
15th Paris-Luxembourg
34th Paris-Brussels
35th Milan-San Remo
55th Tour of Belgium
58th Criterium du Dauphiné Libéré
  5th Stage 1
  5th Stage 9
DNF Tour de France

1965 (Ford-France)
1st Tour de l'Oise
  1st Stage 1
1st Grand Prix de Saint-Raphaël
1st Grand Prix d'Espéraza
1st Grand Prix d'Orchies
1st Prix d'Alençon
1st Prix de Puteaux
2nd Grand Prix de Monaco
2nd Prix de Poire-sur-Vie
2nd London-Holyhead
2nd Prix du Trelissac
2nd Circuit du Morbihan
3rd Prix d'Oradour-sur-Glane
3rd Prix de Tredion
3rd Prix de Ploerdut
3rd Prix de Cajarc
3rd Chef-Boutonne
3rd Champs-sur-Tarentaine
4th Ghent-Wevelgem
4th Paris-Luxembourg
  4th Stage 2
  8th Stage 1
11th Tour of Luxembourg
  7th Stage 1

  9th Stage 3
14th Grand Prix of Frankfurt
28th Four-Days of Dunkirk
30th Tour of Holland
  3rd Stage 2
50th Paris-Tours

1966 (Mercier-BP-Hutchinson)
1st Grand Prix du Trégor
1st Prix de Tredion
1st Prix de Plancoët
1st Prix de Lorient
1st Prix de Pluvigner
1st Prix de Ploudalmezeau
1st Prix de Huelgoat
2nd la Meaugon
2nd Sevignac
2nd Poire-sur-Vie
2nd Grand Prix de Rousies
2nd Saint-Clet
3rd Bourbriac
3rd Plemet
3rd Prix de Camors
5th Ghent-Wevelgem
6th Paris-Luxembourg
  8th Stage 3
15th World Road Race
  Championships
17th Tour of Belgium
  4th Stage 2a
46th Paris-Brussels

1967 (Mercier-BP-Hutchinson)

1968 and 1969 did not compete

1970 (Falcon)
21st London-Holyhead

Bibliography

Books
Anquetil, J., *Je Suis Comme Ça* (Voici, 1964)
Bobet, J., *Tomorrow, We Ride* (Mousehold Press and Sport & Publicity, 2008)
Daly, T., *The Rás – The Story of Ireland's Unique Bike Race* (Collins Press, 2003)
Denson, V., *The Full Cycle* (Mousehold Press and Sport & Publicity, 2008)
Fallon, L., & Bell, A., *Viva la Vuelta – The Story of Spain's Great Bike Race* (Mousehold Press and Sport & Publicity, 2005)
Fotheringham, W., *Put Me Back on My Bike* (Yellow Jersey Press, 2002)
Fotheringham, W., *Roule Brittania* (Yellow Jersey Press, 2005)
Geminiani, R., *Mes 50 Tours de France* (Rocher, 2003)
Guinness, R., *The Foreign Legion* (Springfield Books, 1993)
Howard, P., *Sex, Lies and Handlebar Tape* (Mainstream Publishing, 2008)
Loughman, J. *Trusty Steeds and Rain Like Stair Rods* (2001)
Novrup, S., *A Moustache, Poison and Blue Glasses* (Bromley Books, 1999)
Saunders, D., *Cycling in the Sixties* (Pelham Books, 1971)
Sidwells, C., *Mr Tom – The True Story of Tom Simpson* (Mousehold Press, 2000)
Simpson, T., *Cycling is my Life* (Yellow Jersey Press, 1966)
Stacey, S.A., *Essays on Heroism in Sport in Ireland and France* (Edwin Mellen Press, 2003)
Watiez, L., *Day of Glory or Day of Pain* (De Eecloonaar, 2000)
Woodland, L., *Cycling Heroes* (Springfield Books, 1994)
Woodland, L., *This Island Race* (Mousehold Press, 2005)
Yates, R., *Master Jacques – The Enigma of Jacques Anquetil* (Mousehold Press and Sport & Publicity, 2001)

Magazines
The following list includes various magazines, newspapers and other articles, which I have referred to during my research.

Cycle Sport
Cycling
Cycling Weekly
International Cycle Sport
Irish Cycling Review
L'Équipe
Miroir des Sports
Miroir du Cyclisme
Miroir-Sprint

Procycling
Shay Elliott – A Sporting Life – by John Flanagan
Sporting Cyclist
The Irish Times
The Irish Independent
The Irish Press
The People
The Times

Other books published by
Mousehold Press and Sport and Publicity

Mr Tom: the true story of Tom Simpson
Chris Sidwells

Master Jacques: the enigma of Jacques Anquetil
Richard Yates

Golden Stages of the Tour de France
edited by Richard Allchin and Adrian Bell

A Peiper's Tale
Allan Peiper with Chris Sidwells

Viva la Vuelta!
Lucy Fallon & Adrian Ball

In Pursuit of Stardom
Tony Hewson

This Island Race: inside 135 years of British bike-racing
Les Woodland

From the Pen of J. B. Wadley
selected and edited by Adrian Bell

The Sweat of the Gods
Benjo Maso (translated by Michiel Horn)

Induráin: A Tempered Passion
Javier García Sánchez, Jeremy Munday (Translator)

Wheels along the Waveney; a history of the Godric Cycling Club
Tim Hilton

The Eagle of the Canavese: Franco Balmamion and the Giro d'Italia
Herbie Sykes

Tomorrow, we ride…
Jean Bobet (translated by Adam Berry)

A Racing Cyclist's Worst Nightmare
Tony Hewson

Lapize: now there was an ace
Jean Bobet (translated by Adam Berry)

The Full Cycle
Vin Denson

Brian Robinson: Pioneer
Graeme Fife

Also available only from Sport and Publicity:

21 Years of Cycling Photography
Phil O'Connor

Ride and be Damned: the glory years of the British League of Racing Cyclists
Chas Messenger